Kilmainham Jail: The Entrance

LAST

WORDS

PIARAS F. MAC LOCHLAINN

A CHUIR IN EAGAR

LETTERS

AND

STATEMENTS

OF

THE

LEADERS

EXECUTED

AFTER

THE

RISING

AT

EASTER

1916

THE OFFICE OF PUBLIC WORKS

ISBN 0-7076-0101-0
© Government of Ireland 1990

DUBLIN

PUBLISHED BY THE STATIONERY OFFICE

————————

To be purchased through any Bookseller or directly from the

GOVERNMENT PUBLICATIONS SALE OFFICE, SUN ALLIANCE HOUSE,
MOLESWORTH STREET, DUBLIN 2.

CONTENTS

v

ILLUSTRATIONS

Buíochas

For permission to publish, or republish, letters, statements, poems, photographs, extracts from books, periodicals, newspapers; for statements oral or written; for assistance in research, etc.; and for help in any other way in the compilation of this book, I am deeply indebted to all of the following:

A Shoilse Éamon de Valera, Uachtarán na hÉireann; His Eminence Cardinal Michael Browne, O.P.; Bro. W. P. Allen; An tAth. Annraoi, O.F.M.Cap.; Ard-Mhusaem na hÉireann; The Army Records Centre, Hayes, Middlesex; Éamonn de Barra; Fr. Benedict, O.F.M.Cap.; Colum Breen; John Breen; "John Brennan" (Mrs. Sidney Czira); Maurice Brennan; James J. Brennan; Proinnsias de Búrca; Dr. Rónán Ceannt; Phillis Bean Uí Cheallaigh; John Daly Clarke; Dr. Kathleen (Mrs. Tom) Clarke; Lila Colbert; Comhar; The Commissioner of Police, New Scotland Yard; W. H. B. de Courcy-Wheeler; Seán Cullen; Madge Daly; Cearaí Ní Dhálaígh; Dr. Geraldine (Mrs. Thomas) Dillon; Maeve Donnelly; Éamon T. Dore (Éamonn T. de hÓir); Mrs. Éamon Dore; Seán Dowling; Séamus Doyle; G. A. Duncan Photo Service; C. J. Fallon Ltd.; Foilseacháin Náisiúnta Teoranta; Richard P. Gogan, T.D.; Julia Grenan; Bill Hammond; Mrs. Eileen Harbourne; Fr. John M. Heuston, O.P.; Theresa Heuston; The Imperial War Museum; Independent Newspapers; Inniu; The Irish Press; the Irish Transport and General Workers' Union; Rev. Thomas F. Kelleher; Helen Landreth; Séamus Layng; An Leabharlann Náisiúnta; Fr. Leonard, O.F.M.Cap.; Fr. J. P. Leonard, S.J.; Mrs. O'Donnell Loughrey; Dr. John Mackey; John Maher; Éamon Martin; The Ministry of Defence, London; General Richard Mulcahy; Mrs. Richard Mulcahy; John MacBride; Mrs. Seán MacBride; Ald. John McCann, T.C.; John MacDonald; Paddy McDonnell; An Ceannfort S. Mac Giolla Fhendein; Máiréad Mhac an tSaoi; An tOllamh Liam Ó Briain; Dr. Nora Connolly O'Brien; William O'Brien; Kevin O'Carroll; Pádraig Ó Ceallaigh; Major Florence O'Donoghue; Seán O'Duffy; The Officers' Association of the British Legion; Oifig na Stát-Pháipéar; Seán Ó Lúing; Séamus Ó Mealláin; Séamus Ó Murchadha; An tAth. Aodh Ó Neill, S.P.; Tomás Ó Néill; Mrs. Ely O'Hanrahan O'Reilly; Michael O'Riordan, Fermoy; Fred O'Rourke; Cathal Ó Seanáin; Senator Margaret Pearse; Christopher Power; The Public Record Office, London; Radio

Telefís Éireann; Mrs. Desmond Ryan; Dr. James Ryan; Sáirséal agus Dill; Dan Stephenson; The Surrey Constabulary; Right Rev. Monsignor Troy.

Go gcúití Dia a saothar leo uilig. If any name has been inadvertently omitted, I am sorry.

AN tEAGARTHÓIR.

BIBLIOGRAPHICAL NOTE

Unless otherwise indicated, citations from Le Roux, Diarmuid Lynch, Liam Ó Briain, Seán T. Ó Ceallaigh and Desmond Ryan are from the following works:

LE ROUX (Louis N.): Patrick H. Pearse: adapted from the French and revised by the author, translated into English by Desmond Ryan. Talbot Press, 1932.

LYNCH (Diarmuid): The IRB and the 1916 insurrection: a record of the preparations . . . and a report on operations . . . ed. . . . by Florence O'Donoghue, Mercier, 1957.

Ó BRIAIN (Liam): Cuimhní cinn . . . cuimhní an éirí amach. Sairséal agus Dill, 1951.

Ó CEALLAIGH (Seán T.): Seán T. Scéal a bheatha á insint ag Seán T. Ó Ceallaigh. Arna chur in eagar ag Proinsias Ó Conluain. Foillseacháin Náisiúnta, 1963.

RYAN (Desmond): The rising: the complete story of Easter week. Golden Eagle, 1949.

RÉAMHRÁ

Cnuasach an leabhar seo de na focail deiridh a scríobh na fir a básaíodh tar éis Éirí Amach na Cásca, 1916.

Tá ann chomh maith roinnt de na ráitis a d'eisigh na taoisigh agus de na tuairiscí a chuir siad amach i rith na Seachtaine, am an ghéillte, agus ina dhiaidh sin, maraon le corrthagairt dá ngníomhartha le linn an troda.

Ceapadh go mba cheart, freisin, cuntais a chur isteach, áit a raibh a leithéid le fáil, faoi nóiméid dheiridh na dtaoiseach, ó na gaolta nó na cairde 'bhí ar cuairt acu nó ó na sagairt a rinne friotháil orthu.

Tá cuid de na litreacha anseo á bhfoilsiú don chéad uair.

Ceapadh, tráth, nár cheart go gcuirfí litreacha na laochra dá ngar-ghaolta ar fáil don ghnáthléitheoir, go raibh siad róphríobháideach, ródhlúth, don phobal i gcoiteann, ach ó tá breis is leathchéad blian imithe thart ó scríobhadh iad, agus ó's cuid de stair ár dtíre anois na laochra a thug a n-anam ar son na hÉireann—agus, ar ndóigh, iadsiúd uilig a ghlac páirt san Éirí Amach—glacfar leis gur cóir go mbeadh áit do gach a ndearna siad, do gach a ndúirt siad, agus do gach a scríobh siad, in annálacha, agus i gcroíthe mhuintir na hÉireann.

This book is a compilation of the last written words of the men who were executed after the Rising of Easter Week, 1916.

It includes also some of the statements made and dispatches issued by the leaders during the Week, at the surrender, and after it, as well as some references to their activities while fighting was in progress.

It has been thought well, too, to include accounts, where it has been possible to come upon such, of the last moments of the leaders from the lips of the relatives or friends who visited them or the priests who attended them.

Some of the letters herein are being published for the first time.

Time was when it was felt that the letters of the leaders to their near relatives were too intimate for them to be read by the public in general, but it will be accepted now, more than half a century later, that, having given their lives for Ireland, the leaders of the Rising—as, indeed, all who took part in it—have become part of our history, so that everything they did, or said, or wrote, has a rightful place in the annals as well as in the hearts of the Irish people.

AN tEAGARTHÓIR.

Bhí foilsiú an leabhair seo ag druidim chun críche agus an t-ábhar fé láimh an chlódóra nuair a fuair an t-eagarthóir bás, 19 Nollaig, 1969. Cúis mór méala dá mhuintir agus dá cháirde a bhás in ard a intleachta agus a fhuinnimh.

Nuair a cuireadh cumann ar bun chun Priosún Chill Maighneann a athchóiriú mar iarsmalann staire bhí Piaras Mac Lochlainn orthu san ba dhioghrasaí a shaothraigh ar a shon. Níl insint fós ar an méid oibre a rinne sé mar rúnaí, mar chláraitheoir agus mar eagarthóir.

An dúthracht agus an daonnacht a bhí le sonnrú ina shaol phríomháideach, agus ina shaol phoiblí mar oifigeach stáit, dháil sé go fial iad ar Chill Maighneann.

AN RIALTAS SEALADACH
THE PROVISIONAL GOVERNMENT

Proclamation of the Republic, 24 April, 1916

POBLACHT NA h-EIREANN.
THE PROVISIONAL GOVERNMENT
OF THE
IRISH REPUBLIC
TO THE PEOPLE OF IRELAND.

IRISHMEN AND IRISIIWOMEN: In the name of God and of the dead generations from which she receives her old tradition of nationhood, Ireland, through us, summons her children to her flag and strikes for her freedom.

Having organised her manhood through her secret revolutionary organisation, the Irish Republican Brotherhood, and through her open military organisations, the Irish Volunteers and the Irish Citizen Army, having patiently perfected her discipline, having resolutely waited for the right moment to reveal itself, she now seizes that moment, and supported by her exiled children in America and by gallant allies in Europe, but relying in the first on her own strength, she strikes in full confidence of victory.

We declare the right of the people of Ireland to the ownership of Ireland and to the unfettered control of Irish destinies, to be sovereign and indefeasible. The long usurpation of that right by a foreign people and government has not extinguished the right, nor can it ever be extinguished except by the destruction of the Irish people. In every generation the Irish people have asserted their right to national freedom and sovereignty; six times during the past three hundred years they have asserted it in arms. Standing on that fundamental right and again asserting it in arms in the face of the world, we hereby proclaim the Irish Republic

I

as a Sovereign Independent State, and we pledge our lives and the lives of our comrades in arms to the cause of its freedom, of its welfare and of its exaltation among the nations.

The Irish Republic is entitled to, and hereby claims, the allegiance of every Irishman and Irishwoman. The Republic guarantees religious and civil liberty, equal rights and equal opportunities to all its citizens, and declares its resolve to pursue the happiness and prosperity of the whole nation and of all its parts, cherishing all the children of the nation equally, and oblivious of the differences carefully fostered by an alien Government, which have divided a minority from the majority in the past.

Until our arms have brought the opportune moment for the establishment of a permanent National Government, representative of the whole people of Ireland and elected by the suffrages of all her men and women, the Provisional Government, hereby constituted, will administer the civil and military affairs of the Republic in trust for the people.

We place the cause of the Irish Republic under the protection of the Most High God, Whose blessing we invoke upon our arms, and we pray that no one who serves that cause will dishonour it by cowardice, inhumanity, or rapine. In this supreme hour the Irish nation must, by its valour and discipline, and by the readiness of its children to sacrifice themselves for the common good, prove itself worthy of the august destiny to which it is called.

Signed on behalf of the Provisional Government :

THOMAS J. CLARKE,

SEÁN MAC DIARMADA,   THOMAS MACDONAGH,

P. H. PEARSE,   EAMONN CEANNT,

JAMES CONNOLLY,   JOSEPH PLUNKETT.

The Proclamation of the republic must be regarded as the collective work of the signatories, members of the Provisional Government, all of them among the sixteen leaders later executed. It was read in front of the G.P.O. by Pearse at 12.45 p.m. on

Easter Monday, and posted publicly throughout the centre of the city.

It had been printed on the previous day in Liberty Hall. Joseph Bouch, who has given a detailed account of the printing of the document,[1] wrote: "The actual literary composition of the document appears to have been the work of Patrick Pearse; but it also shows, in parts, the trace of change and amendment by James Connolly and perhaps by Thomas MacDonagh."

The handwriting of the manuscript handed to the printers has been tentatively identified by Bouch on the basis of the printers' recollection, many years later, of its appearance, as that of either Pearse or Ceannt. The manuscript is not known to have survived.

---

[1] *The Republican Proclamation of Easter Monday, 1916* (Bibliographical Society of Ireland, 1936).
And see bibliographical note p. x.

Pádraic Mac Piarais

P. H. Pearse

1879–1916

PÁDRAIC MAC PIARAIS   P. H. PEARSE

Statement, 25 April, 1916

The Irish Republic was proclaimed in Dublin on Easter Monday, 24th April, at 12 noon. Simultaneously with the issue of the proclamation of the Provisional Government the Dublin division of the Army of the Republic, including the Irish Volunteers, Citizen Army, Hibernian Rifles, and other bodies, occupied dominating points in the city. The G.P.O. was seized at 12 noon, the Castle was attacked at the same moment, and shortly afterwards the Four Courts were occupied. The Irish troops hold the City Hall and dominate the Castle. Attacks were immediately commenced by the British forces, and were everywhere repulsed. At the moment of writing this report (9.30 a.m. Tuesday) the Republican forces hold all their positions and the British forces have nowhere broken through. There has been heavy and continuous fighting for nearly 48 hours, the casualties of the enemy being much more numerous than those on the Republican side. The Republican forces everywhere are fighting with splendid gallantry. The populace of Dublin are plainly with the Republic, and the officers and men are everywhere cheered as they march through the street. The whole centre of the city is in the hands of the Republic, whose flag flies from the G.P.O.

Commandant General P. H. Pearse is Commanding in Chief of the Army of the Republic and is President of the Provisional Government. Commandant General James Connolly is commanding the Dublin districts.

Communication with the country is largely cut, but reports to hand show that the country is rising, and bodies of men from Kildare and Fingal have already reported in Dublin.

A "Stop Press" edition of *Irish War News*, Vol. 1. No. 1, Tuesday, April 25, 1916—it was the only edition issued—

announced the declaration of the Irish Republic and the appointment of the Provisional Government. Having given the names
of the members of the Provisional Government, it continued:

> At 9.30 a.m. this morning the following statement was
> made by Commandant-General P. H. Pearse:—

Then followed the statement as above.

Pearse's manuscript of this statement of 25 April (with his
manuscript of the manifesto of the Provisional Government to
the citizens of Dublin, see below) remained in the hands of the
printer. In 1951 the then owner allowed the National Museum
to make photocopies for the national collections.

Manifesto to the Citizens of Dublin, 25 April, 1916

THE PROVISIONAL GOVERNMENT
To The
CITIZENS OF DUBLIN

The Provisional Government of the Irish Republic
salutes the Citizens of Dublin on the momentous occasion
of the proclamation of a

SOVEREIGN INDEPENDENT IRISH STATE,

now in course of being established by Irishmen in arms.
The Republican forces hold the lines taken up at twelve
noon on Easter Monday, and nowhere, despite fierce and
almost continuous attacks of the British troops, have the
lines been broken through. The country is rising in answer
to Dublin's call, and the final achievement of Ireland's
freedom is now, with God's help, only a matter of days.
The valour, self-sacrifice and discipline of Irish men and
women are about to win for our country a glorious place
among the nations.

Ireland's honour has already been redeemed; it remains
to vindicate her wisdom and her self-control.

All citizens of Dublin who believe in the right of their
country to be free will give their allegiance and their loyal

help to the Irish Republic. There is work for everyone : for
the men in the fighting line, and for the women in the
provision of food and first aid. Every Irishman and Irishwoman worthy of the name will come forward to help their
common country in this her supreme hour. Able-bodied
citizens can help by building barricades in the streets to
oppose the advance of the British troops. The British troops
have been firing on our women and on our Red Cross.
On the other hand, Irish Regiments in the British Army
have refused to act against their fellow-countrymen.

The Provisional Government hopes that its supporters—
which means the vast bulk of the people of Dublin—will
preserve order and self-restraint. Such looting as has already
occurred has been done by hangers-on of the British Army.
Ireland must keep her new honour unsmirched.

We have lived to see an Irish Republic proclaimed.
May we live to establish it firmly, and may our children
and our children's children enjoy the happiness and prosperity which freedom will bring.
Signed on behalf of the Provisional Government,

    P. H. PEARSE,
        Commanding in Chief of the Forces of
        the Irish Republic,
        and President of the
        Provisional Government.

Diarmuid Lynch, a member of the G.P.O. Garrison, tells
that Pearse read this manifesto out on Tuesday afternoon. It
was printed as a small broadside.[1] Some, at least, of it bears the
stamp of "propaganda" though, rumours being rife, the Provisional Government, on whose behalf Pearse signed the manifesto, could well have believed that, for instance, Irish regiments
in the British Army had refused to act against their fellow-
countrymen. There is no evidence of this, but Diarmuid Lynch
states that when, on the following Friday night, prisoners in the
G.P.O. "were given the option of remaining or advancing freely
to the British lines all took their departure except three (members
of Irish Regiments in the British Army), two of whom whole-
heartedly threw in their lot with the Republican forces."

Message to his Mother from the General Post Office, 26 April, 1916

We are all safe here up to the present (6.30 Wednesday evg.). The St. Enda's boys have been on duty on the roof ever since we came in, but have been relieved this evening and will spend tonight on the ground floor with me. They are all in excellent spirits, though very sleepy. We have plenty of the best food, all our meals being as good as if served in a hotel. The dining room here is very comfortable. We sleep on mattresses and some of us have sheets, blankets, pillows and quilts. The men have fought with wonderful courage and gaiety, and, whatever happens to us, the name of Dublin will be splendid in history for ever. Willie and I hope you are not fretting, and send you all our love.

P.

Pearse's sister, Senator Margaret Pearse, recalled, in 1962,[2] that her mother did not receive this message "until some weeks after Easter, 1916, when Máire Nic Shiubhlaigh's[3] father brought it to us." The original manuscript of the message is now in the National Museum. William Pearse added a short note. (See below.)

War Bulletin, Thursday morning, 28 [27] April, 1916

Irish Republic
War Bulletin
Thursday Morning, 28th April, 1916.

The main positions taken up by the Republican Forces in Dublin at 12 noon on Easter Monday, 24th instant are all still held by us. Our lines are everywhere intact and our positions of great strength.

The Republican Forces have at every point resisted with extraordinary gallantry.

Commandant-General Pearse, Commander-in-Chief, and Commandant-General Connolly, commanding in Dublin, thank their brave soldiers.

Despite furious and almost continuous attacks from the British forces our casualties are few. The British casualties are heavy.

The British troops have repeatedly fired on our Red Cross and even on parties of Red Cross women nurses bearing stretchers. Commandant-General Pearse, commanding in chief for the Republic, has notified Major-General Friend, commanding in chief for the British, that British prisoners held by the Republican forces will be treated as hostages for the observance on the part of the British of the laws of warfare and humanity, especially as regards the Red Cross.

Commandant-General Pearse, as President of the Provisional Government, has issued a proclamation to the citizens of Dublin, in which he salutes them on the momentous occasion of the proclamation of an Irish Republic, and claims for the Republic the allegiance and support of every man and woman of Dublin who believes in Ireland's right to be free. Citizens can help the Republican Forces by building barricades in the streets to impede the advance of the British forces.

Up with the barricades!

The Republican Forces are in a position to supply bread to the civil population within the lines occupied by them.

A committee of citizens known as the Public Service Committee has been formed to assist in the maintenance of public order and in the supply of food to the civil population.

The Provisional Government strongly condemns looting and the wanton destruction of property. The looting that has taken place has been done by the hangers-on of the British forces.

Reports to hand from the country show that Dublin's call is being responded to, and that large areas in the West, South, and South-East are now in Arms for the Irish Republic.

(Signed)

P. H. PEARSE,

Commandant General.

The dating of this document, Thursday 28th April, is an error, for Thursday was the 27th. Diarmuid Lynch quotes Stanley, the printer, as stating that he received copy from Pearse

on Wednesday night or early Thursday morning and brought
printed copies to the G.P.O. just before Connolly was wounded.
Lynch quotes this as if it referred to the Manifesto (see below)
dated "28 Ap. 9.30 a.m." but is clearly in error as it must refer
to the War Bulletin. There is no evidence that the manifesto
was ever printed.

Manifesto issued from the General Post Office, 28 April, 1916

Headquarters, Army of the Irish Republic.
General Post Office,
Dublin.

28th April 1916.   9.30, a.m.

The Forces of the Irish Republic, which was proclaimed
in Dublin, on Easter Monday, 24th April, have been in
possession of the central part of the Capital, since 12 noon
on that day. Up to yesterday afternoon Headquarters was
in touch with all the main outlying positions, and, despite
furious, and almost continuous assaults by the British Forces
all those positions were then still being held, and the
Commandants in charge, were confident of their ability
to hold them for a long time.

During the course of yesterday afternoon, and evening,
the enemy succeeded in cutting our communications, with
our other positions in the City, and Headquarters is today
isolated.

The enemy has burnt down whole blocks of houses,
apparently with the object of giving themselves a clear field
for the play of Artillery and Field guns against us. We have
been bombarded during the evening and night, by Shrapnel
and Machine Gun fire, but without material damage to our
position, which is of great strength.

We are busy completing arrangements for the final
defence of Headquarters, and are determined to hold it
while the buildings last. I desire now, lest I may not have
an opportunity later, to pay homage to the gallantry of the
Soldiers of Irish Freedom who have during the past four
days, been writing with fire and steel the most glorious
chapter in the later history of Ireland. Justice can never be

done to their heroism, to their discipline, to their gay and unconquerable spirit, in the midst of peril and death.

Let me, who have led them into this, speak, in my own, and in my fellow-commanders' names and in the name of Ireland present and to come, their praise, and ask those who come after them to remember them.

For four days, they have fought, and toiled, almost without cessation, almost without sleep, and in the intervals of fighting, they have sung songs of the freedom of Ireland. No man has complained, no man has asked "why?". Each individual has spent himself, happy to pour out his strength for Ireland and for freedom. If they do not win this fight, they will at least have deserved to win it. But win it they will, although they may win it in death. Already they have won a great thing. They have redeemed Dublin from many shames, and made her name splendid among the names of Cities.

If I were to mention names of individuals, my list would be a long one.

I will name only that of Commandant General James Connolly, Commanding the Dublin division. He lies wounded, but is still the guiding brain of our resistance.

If we accomplish no more than we have accomplished, I am satisfied that we have saved Ireland's honour. I am satisfied that we should have accomplished more, that we should have accomplished the task of enthroning, as well as proclaiming, the Irish Republic as a Sovereign State, had our arrangements for a simultaneous rising of the whole country, with a combined plan as sound as the Dublin plan has been proved to be, been allowed to go through on Easter Sunday. Of the fatal countermanding order which prevented these plans from being carried out, I shall not speak further. Both Eoin MacNeill and we have acted in the best interests of Ireland.

For my part, as to anything I have done in this, I am not afraid to face either the judgment of God, or the judgment of posterity.

> (Signed) P. H. PEARSE, Commandant General, Commanding-in-Chief, the Army of the Irish Republic and President of the Provisional Government.

The whereabouts of the original of the above Manifesto is not known. The text was published in the *Sinn Fein Rebellion Handbook* compiled by the *Weekly Irish Times*. A photographic reproduction of a print-script version appeared in *The Sinn Féin Revolt*, published by Hely's of Dublin, probably in 1917. It was from a photograph taken by Mr. Thomas H. Mason some time before the end of August, 1916.

The print-script version was not in Pearse's handwriting but was on government stationery and perhaps prepared in this form when access to the printing works was no longer possible. The authenticity of the document is beyond dispute.

Internal evidence would indicate that the date (28th April) is here correct; that the "copy" was written not earlier than Thursday night—probably in the early hours of Friday morning. Pearse, for instance, speaks of the men having fought and toiled "for four days" and, again, tells that Connolly "lies wounded." Connolly did not "lie wounded" until Thursday evening.

Minute of Provisional Government decision, 29 April, 1916
H.Q. Moore St.

> Believing that the glorious stand which has been made by the soldiers of Irish freedom during the last five days in Dublin has been sufficient to gain recognition of Ireland's national claim at an international peace conference, and desirous of preventing further slaughter of the civil population and to save the lives of as many as possible of our followers, the members of the Provisional Government here present have agreed by a majority to open negotiations with the British Commander.
>
> P. H. PEARSE,
> Commandant General,
> Commanding in Chief
> Army of the Irish Republic.

29 April, 1916.

This minute was written by Pearse in pencil on a rectangle of card-board which had clearly been the backing of a framed picture. It records the decision reached at a meeting round the bedside of the wounded Connolly in 16 Moore St. at about

12.45 p.m. on the Saturday of Easter Week. The members of the Provisional Government present were Pearse, Clarke, Mac Diarmada, Plunkett and Connolly. The minute brings out two facts which are not clear from the subsequent surrender documents: the decision to open negotiations was not unanimous (Desmond Ryan's account of the meeting would suggest that Clarke for one had voted against it); and the reference to "recognition of Ireland's national claim at an international peace conference" supports the account (of which Ryan had carefully-reasoned doubts) of Pearse's speaking in similar terms to the G.P.O. garrison on Friday.

The   document was acquired by the National Library in 1966.

Following the meeting, Nurse Elizabeth O'Farrell was sent, under a flag of truce, with a verbal message from Pearse to Brigadier-General Lowe, Commander of the British Forces in the O'Connell Street area: a proposal to negotiate terms.

Lowe sent Nurse O'Farrell back with a written message that he would treat with Pearse provided only that he would surrender unconditionally.

To this message Pearse replied with a dispatch only part of which or of a draft for which has been recorded—in Joseph Mary Plunkett's Field Message Book (see below), though not in Plunkett's handwriting.

Fragment of Message to Brig. General Lowe, 29 April, 1916

> To the Commander
> I have recd your com sent by bearer of a flag of truce intimating your willingness to receive me should I surrender unconditionally. Lest any . . . [*illeg.* mistake? *Message breaks off.*]

Lowe's reply was a renewal of the demand for unconditional surrender, and that Connolly should follow on a stretcher. The members of the Provisional Government present held a short council and Pearse decided to accompany Nurse O'Farrell back to Lowe.

"Exactly at 2.30," said Major de Courcy Wheeler,[4] Staff Captain to Brigadier-General Lowe, "Commandant-General

Pearse walked up Moore Street, surrendered to General Lowe at the junction of Moore Street and Parnell Street and handed over his arms and military equipment to myself. These consisted of his sword, automatic pistol in holster, with pouch of ammunition, and his canteen, which contained two large onions. His sword was retained by General Lowe . . . . Two Army motor-cars were waiting. General Pearse, accompanied by the General's A.D.C., was driven in the G.O.C.'s car, preceded by the General and myself in the other car to Headquarters, Irish Command (Parkgate), to interview General Sir John Maxwell, the British Commander-in-Chief . . . ."

After this interview Pearse wrote, and when typed copies had been made, signed the order to the Commandants of the various districts in the City and Country to lay down their arms.

The Order for Surrender, 29 April, 1916

In order to prevent the further slaughter of Dublin citizens, and in the hope of saving the lives of our followers now surrounded and hopelessly outnumbered, the members of the Provisional Government present at Headquarters have agreed to an unconditional surrender, and the Commandants of the various districts in the City and Country will order their commands to lay down arms.

P. H. PEARSE.

29th April, 3.45 p.m., 1916.

Having signed the surrender order, Pearse, according to Major de Courcy Wheeler, "was conducted to a sitting-room[5] at Headquarters. I was ordered to keep guard over him. I was handed a loaded revolver with orders to keep it pointed at the General and to shoot if he made an effort to escape. I was locked in the room alone with General Pearse, who smiled at me across the table and did not seem in the least perturbed. I was on this duty for only fifteen minutes when I was sent for by General Lowe. Another officer was sent to relieve me. I did not see General Pearse again . . ."

Pearse was transferred on Saturday evening to Arbour Hill Detention Barracks.

Early on the morning of Sunday, 30 April, 1916, Father

Augustine and Father Aloysius, O.F.M.Cap., went to Dublin
Castle in quest of the surrender document as they felt that the
Volunteers in the Church Street area would not lay down
arms unless satisfied that the order was genuine. The priests met
General Lowe.

Father Augustine's statement[6] continues:

The General then, being still anxious as we were to get at least
a copy of the document so that it could be shown to the Volunteers who had not yet surrendered, placed his car and chauffeur
at our disposal and we drove at once to Arbour Hill Detention
Barracks to see Pearse who, after a short while, was ushered into
the room by a soldier who then stood at the end with a loaded
rifle. Pearse advanced with noble mien and such soldierly bearing
that the word "Napoleonic" shot at once through my brain. In
answer to my question he said he had signed a document of
unconditional surrender stating the reasons why he had done so,
but that one of our Fathers had been there a short time previously; as we assured him no copy of it could be found, he wrote
another of which the following is an exact copy:

In order to prevent further slaughter of the civil population and in the hope of saving the lives of our followers the
members of the Provisional Government present at Headquarters have decided on an unconditional surrender, and
Commandants or Officers commanding districts will order
their Commands to lay down arms.

P. H. PEARSE
30th April, 1916.

Note that Pearse's memorised version—the original MS of it
is lost—differs in some respects from the order signed the
previous day.

The Fifth Battalion of the Dublin Brigade, led by Thomas
Ashe, had over-run North County Dublin, capturing police
barracks and taking nearly a hundred prisoners, their greatest
achievement being a striking victory over superior forces at
Ashbourne, Co. Meath. At about 9 o'clock on the morning of
Sunday, 30 April, General Richard Mulcahy, who was second
in command to Ashe, was, with Ashe, on a tour of inspection
of sentry posts at Newbarn, Co. Dublin, where the Volunteers
were encamped, when news arrived of the previous day's surrender in the City. General Mulcahy says:[7]

".... Sentry post number four had intercepted a car coming from Dublin flying a white flag. In the car were a District Inspector of the R.I.C. and a Sergeant. They bore a message from Commandant Pearse to the O.C. of the Fingal men. The Inspector wished to meet Ashe. He had, in fact, come to deliver Pearse's order for a general surrender. . . .

Ashe decided to detain the District Inspector in the camp and to send me back with the sergeant to Dublin, there to make such contacts as would verify Pearse's order. . . .

We were soon in front of the large steps at British General Headquarters at Parkgate.

Without delay—I did not leave the car—a military officer sat in beside me and we proceeded to the military prison at Arbour Hill. Inside the prison, on the right, the door of the second or third cell was noisily opened by a soldier who shouted harshly 'Get up!' Pearse, in his uniform, was lying on bare trestle boards at the back of the cell; on a small table alongside was a glass of water and some biscuits. He arose and moved quietly a few steps towards us.

Slightly behind my left shoulder was the officer and, behind him, the soldier. When movement ceased I turned to the officer and said I wished to speak to Commandant Pearse alone. I was not surprised that this request was refused, and that in a manner which alerted me to the full realities of the position. I was in the presence of my Commander-in-Chief: both of us in the hands of the British Army authorities: I could be nothing but the most perfect soldier: it was a moment for standing to attention. . . .

'Is this your order, sir?' I asked, as I held it out before him.

Pearse answered 'Yes.'

'Does it refer to Dublin alone or to the whole of Ireland?'

'It refers to the whole of Ireland.'

'Would it be of any use,' I asked, 'if a small band of men who had given a good account of themselves during the week were to hold out any longer?'

And Pearse replied 'No.'

My lips moved to frame a 'Beannacht Dé agat' but the sound was stifled, absorbed in the solemnity of my salute which closed the scene . . ."

On Saturday, 29 April, a message was brought to the Volunteers holding Enniscorthy that Pearse had ordered a general surrender. The Wexfordmen refused to accept this without written confirmation from Pearse himself, and Captain Séamus Doyle and the late Captain Seán Etchingham were given a safe conduct by the Officer Commanding the British troops in

Wexford. On Sunday, 30 April, they were brought in a British military car to Arbour Hill Detention Barracks, Séamus Doyle records:[8]

".... The cell-door was banged open and we went in accompanied by a Tommy, while a group of officers waited in the corridor outside. ... just inside the door was a small table on which were a stetson hat, a pannikin of water and a broken military biscuit. At the far end, lying on a mattress, covered with a greatcoat was the first President of the Irish Republic. He rose up and advanced to meet us; it seemed to us that he was physically exhausted but spiritually exultant. His uniform was complete except for the Sam Browne belt which they had taken from him. The Dublin Brigade, he said, had done splendidly —'five days and nights of almost continuous fighting.' Amongst the dead, he told us, were the O'Rahilly and Tom Weafer (an Enniscorthy man). ... 'No,' he was not aware that we in Wexford were out.

Writing materials were brought in and the order to the Wexford men to lay down arms was written. While the Tommy was outside submitting the order for inspection to the officers Pearse whispered to us to hide our arms in safe places. 'They will be needed later,' he said.

The order was brought back and handed to us and we said farewell. ..."

The order—the original is preserved in Enniscorthy Castle Museum—read as follows:

> In order to prevent the slaughter of unarmed people and in the hope of saving the lives of our followers, the members of the Provisional Government present at Headquarters agreed last night to an unconditional surrender, and Commandants or commanding officers of districts will order their men to lay down arms or disband.
>
> P. H. PEARSE,
>
> 30th April, 1916.

There is an important difference between this and the original surrender document written only a day before. In this order Pearse tells the men "to lay down arms or disband."

The alteration seems to have been a deliberate one. When, in his cell in Arbour Hill, Pearse composed the order to the Enniscorthy men he must have been fully aware that it would be scrutinised by the British authorities. He must have realised that the chance of his being allowed to advise the Wexfordmen "to disband" was small. But he took the chance and the order was allowed to go through—surely a serious blunder on the part of some British officers.

Letter to his Mother, 1 May, 1916

Arbour Hill Barracks,
Dublin.
1st May, 1916.

My dear Mother,

You will I know have been longing to hear from me. I do not know how much you have heard since the last note I sent you from the G.P.O.

On Friday evening the Post Office was set on fire and we had to abandon it. We dashed into Moore Street and remained in the houses in Moore St. on Saturday evening.[9] We then found that we were surrounded by troops and that we had practically no food.

We decided in order to prevent further slaughter of the civilian population and in the hope of saving the lives of our followers, to ask the General Commanding the British Forces to discuss terms. He replied that he would receive me only if I surrendered unconditionally and this I did.

I was taken to the Headquarters of the British Command in Ireland and there I wrote and signed an order to our men to lay down their arms.

All this I did in accordance with the decision of our Provisional Government who were with us in Moore St. My own opinion was in favour of one more desperate sally before opening negotiations, but I yielded to the majority, and I think now the majority was right, as the sally would have resulted only in losing the lives of perhaps 50 or 100 of our men, and we should have had to surrender in the long run as we were without food.

I was brought in here on Saturday evening and later all the men with us in Moore St. were brought here.[2]

Those in the other parts of the City have, I understand, been taken to other barracks and prisons.

All here are safe and well. Willie and all the St. Enda's boys are here.[10] I have not seen them since Saturday, but I believe they are all well and that they are not now in any danger.

Our hope and belief is that the Government will spare the lives of all our followers, but we do not expect that they will spare the lives of the leaders. We are ready to die and we shall die cheerfully and proudly. Personally I do not hope or even desire to live, but I do hope and desire and believe that the lives of all our followers will be saved including the lives dear to you and me (my own excepted) and this will be a great consolation to me when dying.

You must not grieve for all this. We have preserved Ireland's honour and our own. Our deeds of last week are the most splendid in Ireland's history. People will say hard things of us now, but we shall be remembered by posterity and blessed by unborn generations. You too will be blessed because you were my mother.

If you feel you would like to see me, I think you will be allowed to visit me by applying to the Headquarters, Irish Command, near the Park. I shall I hope have another opportunity of writing to you.

Love to W.W., M.B., Miss Byrne,[11] . . .[12] and your own dear self.

P.

P.S. I understand that the German expedition which I was counting on actually set sail but was defeated by the British.

It is clear from this letter, written before his Court Martial, that Pearse had no illusions as to what the findings of the Court Martial would be.

The post-script, reinforced by his statement to the Court Martial (see below) that he "asked and accepted German aid in the shape of arms and an expeditionary force," seems to leave no doubt that Pearse had hopes of a German military expedition in addition to the cargo of arms dispatched on the ill-fated *Aud*.

We know that in the course of a message sent by Joseph Mary Plunkett to Roger Casement in Berlin early in April, 1916, Casement was advised that "German officers will be necessary for the Volunteer forces. This is imperative."

Pearse, when he wrote the letter on 1 May, may have assumed that the *Aud* carried military personnel as well as arms.

This letter was never delivered. It was given instead to Maxwell and used against Pearse at his Court Martial.

The text of the letter did not come to light until 1965 when a typed carbon-copy of it was discovered among Asquith papers in the Bodleian Library, Oxford, by Leon Ó Broin.[13]

In May, 1916, John Dillon, M.P. had made representations to the British Prime Minister to have made available to Mrs. Pearse papers written by her son while in prison. Maxwell, who was not in favour of releasing the documents, had forwarded to Asquith's Secretary, Mr. Bonham Carter, for the Prime Minister's information, "copies of all we have," pointing out that "some of it is objectionable." This explains how the copy-letter came to be among the Asquith papers. Pearse's original manuscript has never come to light. It can be taken that it is with the Court Martial documents which are preserved among the records of the British Judge-Advocate-General's Office held in the Public Record Office in London. Unfortunately, these records are closed to the public and facilities to inspect them cannot be granted until the records are a hundred years old.

In the British House of Commons on 29 May, 1916,[14] Mr. Laurence Ginnell asked the Under Secretary of State for War "whether the message to the Irish people written by P. H. Pearse between sentence and execution has yet been handed over to any person on his behalf and, if not, who holds it and when it will be given to those entitled to it?" The reply, by the Right Hon. Harold John Tennant was: "No message to the Irish people was received from P. H. Pearse. The letters and other documents addressed to his mother have been delivered." This was, of course, untrue.

Poems written in Arbour Hill Detention Barracks, 1 May, 1916

TO MY MOTHER

My gift to you hath been the gift of sorrow,
My one return for your rich gifts to me,
Your gift of life, your gift of love and pity,
Your gift of sanity, your gift of faith
(For who hath had such faith as yours
Since the old time, and what were my poor faith
Without your strong belief to found upon?)
For all these precious things my gift to you
Is sorrow. I have seen
Your dear face line, your face soft to my touch,
Familiar to my hands and to my lips
Since I was little:
I have seen
How you have battled with your tears for me,
And with a proud glad look, although your heart
Was breaking. O Mother (for you know me)
You must have known, when I was silent,
That some strange thing within me kept me dumb,
Some strange deep thing, when I should shout my love?
I have sobbed in secret
For that reserve which yet I could not master.
I would have brought royal gifts, and I have brought you
Sorrow and tears: and yet, it may be
That I have brought you something else besides—
The memory of my deed and of my name
A splendid thing which shall not pass away.
When men speak of me, in praise or in dispraise,
You will not heed, but treasure your own memory
Of your first son.   P. H. PEARSE.

Arbour Hill Detention Barracks,
1st May, 1916.

TO MY BROTHER

O faithful!
Moulded in one womb,
We two have stood together all the years,

B

All the glad years and all the sorrowful years,
Own brothers: through good repute and ill,
In direst peril true to me,
Leaving all things for me, spending yourself
In the hard service that I taught to you,
Of all the men that I have known on earth,
You only have been my familiar friend,
Nor needed I another.

P. H. PEARSE.

A MOTHER SPEAKS

Dear Mary, that didst see thy first-born Son
Go forth to die amid the scorn of men
For whom He died,
Receive my first-born son into thy arms,
Who also hath gone out to die for men,
And keep him by thee till I come to him.
Dear Mary, I have shared thy sorrow,
And soon shall share thy joy.

P. H. PEARSE.

Pearse was held in Arbour Hill Detention Barracks from the evening of Saturday, 29 April, 1916, until the morning of 2 May, 1916, when he was taken to Richmond Barracks to face his Court Martial. The Court Martial was held on the morning of Tuesday, 2 May, and that evening Pearse was transferred to Kilmainham. In a letter to Maxwell, written in Kilmainham on Tuesday (see below), Pearse asked that "the *four* poems which I handed to one of the soldiers on duty at Arbour Hill Detention Barracks this morning" be handed to his mother.

Only three poems—those reproduced above—written by Pearse in Arbour Hill, have come to light.

It is possible that, in fact, only three were written, for in his last letter to his mother (see below) Pearse spoke of "a *few* poems which I want added to the MS in the bookcase," and added: "You asked me to write a little poem which would seem to be said by you about me. I have written it and a copy is in Arbour Hill Barracks with the other poems. Fr. Aloysius is taking charge of another copy of it."

It is not clear from the letter if that poem, "A Mother Speaks," was in addition to, or included with the "other poems."

In 1946 Senator Margaret Pearse recalled[15] that, a few days after her brother's execution, she and her mother called to British Army Headquarters at Parkgate to try to get the poems which they knew from his last letter Pearse had written, "but," she said, "we only got 'A Mother Speaks.' When we asked for the others we were told: 'You shan't get them. They are seditious!' "

They had already received copies of "A Mother Speaks." (In 1962 Miss Pearse related[16] that when Fr. Aloysius called on 3 May, 1916, to tell herself and her mother of Patrick's execution he gave them three copies of "A Mother Speaks.")

There is a copy of it, in Pearse's handwriting, in the National Museum.

The text of the other two poems—"To my Mother" and "To my Brother"—did not come to light until 1965 when typed carbon-copies of them were discovered by Leon Ó Broin among the Asquith papers in the Bodleian Library, Oxford, referred to above.

"To my Mother" was dated "Arbour Hill Detention Barracks, 1st May, 1916." The originals, in Pearse's handwriting, of "To my Mother" and "To my Brother" have never come to light. Because they seem to have been regarded as "seditious" and because Maxwell recommended to Asquith that they be withheld from Mrs. Pearse it can safely be assumed that the two MSS are, like Pearse's letter of 1 May, 1916, to his mother, with the Court Martial documents preserved with the papers of the Judge-Advocate-General in the Public Record Office in London.

If Pearse did write a fourth poem while in Arbour Hill—and unless "four" in his letter to Maxwell is a mistake, he did—it is strange that Maxwell did not include a copy of it with the "copies of all we have" which he forwarded to Asquith.

The fourth Arbour Hill poem remains a mystery. See also "The Wayfarer" and note, below.

It is worthy of note that as the three poems reproduced above were written in Arbour Hill they were written before Pearse's Court Martial. They are further evidence that he expected only the death-sentence.

The well-known poem beginning *I do not grudge them, Lord*
appeared in Pearse's collected works (Maunsel, 1917). There is
no information on its date of composition and although in treatment and theme it seems to fit the requirements of the fourth
Arbour Hill poem, critics generally seem to agree that it belongs
rather to the prophetic mode and period of *The singer,* some
years earlier.

Three statements on business affairs, written in Arbour Hill Detention Barracks, 1 May, 1916

In a letter to Maxwell, written in Kilmainham on 2 May,
1916 (see below), Pearse asked that "the three statements on
business affairs (two with regard to my financial affairs and
one with regard to the publication of some unpublished books
of mine) . . . handed to one of the soldiers on duty at Arbour
Hill Detention Barracks this morning" be duly handed to his
mother.

The statements were, in fact, handed to Mrs. Pearse, but it
has not been found possible to come upon the full text of any
of them nor to locate the original manuscripts.

According to Louis N. Le Roux, who probably saw the
manuscripts, Pearse "gave, in writing, instructions about St.
Enda's College, the settlement of debts and tradesmen's
accounts. This done, he left a codicil to his last wishes about
his books and writings, manuscripts to be published or destroyed,
and naming Desmond Ryan to edit his writings about St.
Enda's with a view to publication in book form with an additional chapter."

In his preface to *The Story of a Success*, published by Maunsel
& Co. Ltd., in 1917, Desmond Ryan said :

The justification of "The Story of a Success" is to be found in
the following extract from Mr. Pearse's last instructions for the
publication of his writings given in Arbour Hill Military Detention Barracks, Dublin, 1st May, 1916 : —

The notes in An Macaomh, under the heading "By Way
of Comment" : I have revised a set of these which will be
found in the bookcase already referred to. As revised, they
form a continuous and more or less readable narrative of

St. Enda's College from its foundation up to May, 1913. I should like my friend and pupil, Desmond Ryan, to add an additional chapter describing the fortunes of St. Enda's since then, and the whole to be published as a book under his editorship.

Letter to General Sir John Maxwell, Commander-in-Chief of the British Forces in Ireland, 2 May, 1916.

Kilmainham Prison,
Dublin.
2nd May, 1916.

To the General Commanding
the British Forces in Ireland.

Sir,

I shall be grateful if you see that the three statements on business affairs (two with regard to my financial affairs and one with regard to the publication of some unpublished books of mine) and also the four poems which I handed to one of the soldiers on duty at Arbour Hill Detention Barracks this morning, are duly handed to my mother, Mrs. Pearse, St. Enda's College, Rathfarnham or Cullenswood House, Oakley Road, Ranelagh; or in her absence to my sister, Miss Margaret Pearse, same address.

I shall also be grateful if you see that the sum of £7 odd (a £5 Bank of England note and two gold sovereigns with some loose change) which were taken from me at Headquarters, Irish Command, on Saturday, be handed to my mother or sister, as also the personal effects taken from me on the same occasion, and the watch and whistle taken from me later at Arbour Hill.

I am, sir,
Yours, etc.,
P. H. PEARSE.

In 1946 a Mr. John O'Donovan of London presented to Senator Margaret Pearse a number of documents which had been in the possession of his sister-in-law, a Mrs. Norton of

Leeds. Mrs. Norton's late husband, a sergeant in the British Army, had been attached to the Records Department at Island-bridge Barracks and Kilmainham in 1916 and had, therefore, had access to the official files. He returned to England for de-mobilisation in 1918 and died four years later. The documents, found among his belongings, and presented to Miss Pearse, were :

(1) An original letter written by Pearse to Maxwell from Kilmainham on 2 May, 1916;

(2) An original note of acknowledgement from Maxwell to Pearse;

(3) A type-written file-copy of a statement written by Pearse in Kilmainham on 2 May, 1916, giving the substance of what he said when asked by the President of the Court Martial if he had anything to say in his defence (see below);

(4) A type-written file-copy of a note written by Pearse in Kilmainham on 3 May, 1916, to his brother, William (see below);

(5) A type-written file-copy of Pearse's poem " A Mother Speaks";

(6) A type-written file-copy of Pearse's letter to his mother, written in Kilmainham on 3 May, 1916 (see below); and

(7) A type-written file-copy of the manifesto issued by Connolly from the General Post Office on 28 April, 1916, with comments concerning its having been found on the body of The O'Rahilly (see below).

An exhaustive search has not revealed the present where-abouts of the documents presented to Miss Pearse and they must now be presumed lost.[17]

Fortunately, Desmond Ryan and Ciarán Ó Nualláin of *Inniu*, who consulted him as to the authenticity of the documents when they were brought to Dublin in 1946, had the foresight to have 'photostat' copies made. These (photostats) Mr. Ryan presented in 1964 to the Kilmainham Museum where they are now on exhibition.

The text of Pearse's original letter to Maxwell is reproduced above. The original came, obviously, from an official file. It was written on official paper bearing the embossed crown and embossed address "Detention Barracks, Kilmainham, Dublin," and franked "Detention Barracks, Kilmainham, 2 May, 1916."

The acknowledgement, in Maxwell's handwriting, read as follows :

To P. H. Pearse
I acknowledge receipt of your letter of 1st May, '16 which I have read.
                                                                J. G. Maxwell
Royal Hospital
May 2, 1916

Note that Pearse's letter to Maxwell was dated 2nd May, 1916, so that "1st May" in Maxwell's acknowledgement seems to be a slip. If it is not, then there was another letter from Pearse which has never come to light.

Address to Court Martial. Statement written in Kilmainham, 2 May, 1916

The following is the substance of what I said when asked today by the President of the Court Martial at Richmond Barracks whether I had anything to say in defence :

I desire in the first place to repeat what I have already said in letters[18] to General Sir John Maxwell and to Brigadier General Lowe. My object in agreeing to an unconditional surrender was to prevent the further slaughter of the civil population of Dublin and to save the lives of our gallant followers who, having made for six days a stand unparalleled in military history, were now surrounded and (in the case of those under the immediate command of Headquarters) without food. I fully understand now, as then, that my own life is forfeit to British law, and I shall die very cheerfully if I can think that the British Government, as it has already shown itself strong, will now show itself magnanimous enough to accept my single life in forfeiture and give a general amnesty to the brave men and boys who have fought at my bidding.

In the second place I wish it to be understood that any admissions I make here are to be taken as involving myself alone. They do not involve and must not be used against anyone who acted with me, not even those who may have set their names to documents with me. (The Court assented to this.)

I admit that I was Commandant General Commanding in Chief the forces of the Irish Republic which have been acting against you for the past week, and that I was President of their Provisional Government. I stand over all my acts and words done or spoken in those capacities.

When I was a child of ten I went down on my bare knees by my bedside one night and promised God that I should devote my life to an effort to free my country. I have kept that promise. As a boy and as a man I have worked for Irish freedom, first among all earthly things. I have helped to organise, to arm, to train, and to discipline my fellowcountrymen to the sole end that, when the time came, they might fight for Irish freedom. The time, as it seemed to me, did come, and we went into the fight. I am glad we did. We seem to have lost. We have not lost. To refuse to fight would have been to lose; to fight is to win. We have kept faith with the past, and handed on a tradition to the future.

I repudiate the assertion of the prosecutor that I sought to aid and abet England's enemy. Germany is no more to me than England is. I asked and accepted German aid in the shape of arms and an expeditionary force. We neither asked for nor accepted Germany [*sic*] gold, nor had any traffic with Germany but what I state. My aim was to win Irish freedom : we struck the first blow ourselves but should have been glad of an ally's aid.

I assume that I am speaking to Englishmen, who value their freedom and who profess to be fighting for the freedom of Belgium and Serbia. Believe that we, too, love freedom and desire it. To us it is more desirable than anything in the world. If you strike us down now, we shall rise again and renew the fight. You cannot conquer

Ireland. You cannot extinguish the Irish passion for freedom. If our deed has not been sufficient to win freedom,
then our children will win it by a better deed.

P. H. PEARSE,

Kilmainham Prison.   2nd May 1916.

The type-written copy which was among the documents presented to Senator Margaret Pearse in 1946 (see above) obviously
came from an official file. It was on official paper with embossed
crown on the first sheet and franked on the second sheet "Detention Barracks Kilmainham 3 May 1916." The manuscript is
on the recto and verso of a single sheet of the same paper.

That manuscript, the whereabouts of which had for years
been a mystery, was, in July, 1969, catalogued for auction at
Sotheby's, London. It aroused great interest in Ireland and the
(anonymous) owner withdrew it from the auction and presented
it to the Irish people. It is now in the National Library.

Careful revisions by Pearse throughout the text, which have
been followed in the version given above, indicate that he
intended or hoped that it might be published.

No doubt the Court Martial documents preserved with the
papers of the British Judge-Advocate-General's Office in the
Public Records Office in London contain a report of Pearse's
statement.

Poem written in Kilmainham, 2 (3?) May, 1916

THE WAYFARER

The beauty of the world hath made me sad,
This beauty that will pass;
Sometimes my heart hath shaken with great joy
To see a leaping squirrel in a tree,
Or a red lady-bird upon a stalk,
Or little rabbits in a field at evening,
Lit by a slanting sun,
Or some green hill where shadows drifted by,
Some quiet hill where mountainy man hath sown
And soon would reap; near to the gate of Heaven;
Or children with bare feet upon the sands

Of some ebbed sea, or playing on the streets
Of little towns in Connacht,
Things young and happy.
And then my heart hath told me:
These will pass,
Will pass and change, will die and be no more,
Things bright and green, things young and happy;
And I have gone upon my way
Sorrowful.

                                              P. H. PEARSE.

"The Wayfarer" is believed by some to be the last of the "four poems" written by Pearse in Arbour Hill and referred to in his letter to Maxwell (see above), but the available evidence seems to indicate that it was written in Kilmainham.

If it were written in Arbour Hill a copy of it would surely have been included among the "copies of all we have" forwarded by Maxwell to Asquith.

Desmond Ryan, whom Pearse appointed as his literary executor, believed that "The Wayfarer" was written in Kilmainham. He says so in a chronological note over his initials in *The Complete Works of P. H. Pearse: Plays, Stories, Poems,* originally published by Maunsel & Co. in 1917, reprinted by the Talbot Press in 1950.

Le Roux takes the same view.

Published in the Dublin *Evening Mail* shortly after the Rising, under the caption "Poem by Rebel Leader on the Eve of Execution," the poem was described as "an interesting literary contribution . . . composed by the late P. H. Pearse while awaiting the carrying out of the sentence of death." This would point, too, to the poem's having been written in Kilmainham rather than Arbour Hill.

The *Evening Mail* version contained a number of errors, e.g. "lit by a starring sun" instead of "slanting sun," "and some would reap" instead of "and soon would reap," and there was a footnote that the MS. was not quite clear and that transcription was possibly, therefore, incorrect. The MS. from which the transcription was made may have been Pearse's own. Its present whereabouts is unknown.

It has not been possible to ascertain if "The Wayfarer" was written on 2nd or 3rd May, 1916.

Letter to his Brother, 3 May, 1916

> Kilmainham Prison,
> Dublin.
> 3rd May, 1916.

To
William Pearse.

Dear old Willie,

Good-bye and God bless you for all your faithful work for me at St. Enda's and elsewhere. No one can ever have had so true a brother as you.

P.

The type-written copy, from which the above text was taken, was also among the documents presented to Senator Margaret Pearse in 1946 (see above). Typed on official paper bearing the embossed crown and Kilmainham frank, it, too, came from an official file.

The typed copy—it has been corrected in the reproduction above—showed the letter to have been addressed to "Dear old Billy" which was obviously a typist's error. William Pearse was never known as "Billy" but always as "Willie."

Again, it is unknown if the original manuscript, from which the typed copy was made, still exists, or, if it does, where it may be. The Public Record Office in London advise that letters of a personal nature written by, or to, persons detained by the military authorities after the Rising are not included in the files of Courts Martial proceedings among the Judge-Advocate-General's records, nor are they to be found among the Public Record Office Registered Papers.

Dated 3rd May, 1916, the note to his brother must have been written by Pearse some time between midnight and about 3.30 a.m. when he faced the firing squad.

(People, believing that it was still dark at 3.30 a.m., wonder how it was possible to carry out executions at such an hour. The explanation is simple. "Daylight Saving" did not come into operation until 21 May, 1916, and Greenwich Mean Time was not introduced into Ireland until 1917, so that, in 1916, it would have been as bright at 3.30 a.m. as it is today in May at 4.55 a.m.—i.e. 3.30 plus one hour, plus twenty-five minutes.)

The note to his brother and the statement in his last letter to his mother (see below) that "I hope and believe that Willie and the St. Enda's boys will be safe" leave no doubt that Pearse was unaware that his brother was to share his fate.

On the same page with the typed copy-note to William there was a typed copy of Pearse's poem, "A Mother Speaks." That, too, contained evidence of careless typing; e.g. "Dear many" for "Dear Mary."

Letter to his Mother, 3 May, 1916

> Kilmainham Prison,
> Dublin.
> 3rd May, 1916.

Mrs. Pearse,
  St. Enda's College,
    Rathfarnham;
or Cullenswood House,
  Oakley Road,
    Ranelagh.

My Dearest Mother,

I have been hoping up to now that it would be possible to see you again, but it does not seem possible. Good-bye, dear, dear Mother. Through you I say good-bye to Wow-Wow, M.B., Willie, Miss Byrne, Mícheál,[19] Cousin Maggie,[20] and everyone at St. Enda's. I hope and believe that Willie and the St. Enda's boys will be safe.

I have written two papers about financial affairs and one about my books, which I want you to get. With them are a few poems which I want added to the poems of mine in MS, in the large bookcase. You asked me to write a little poem which would seem to be said by you about me. I have written it, and one copy is at Arbour Hill Barracks with the other papers and Father Aloysius is taking charge of another copy of it.

I have just received Holy Communion. I am happy except for the great grief of parting from you. This is the death I should have asked for if God had given me the choice of all deaths,—to die a soldier's death for Ireland and for freedom.

We have done right. People will say hard things of us now, but later on they will praise us. Do not grieve for all this, but think of it as a sacrifice which God asked of me and of you.

Good-bye again, dear, dear Mother. May God bless you for your great love for me and for your great faith, and may He remember all that you have so bravely suffered. I hope soon to see Papa, and in a little while we shall all be together again.

Wow-Wow, Willie, Mary Brigid, and Mother, good-bye. I have not words to tell my love of you, and how my hearts yearns to you all. I will call to you in my heart at the last moment.

Your son,
PAT.

The last sentence of the first paragraph shows that Pearse had no idea that his brother was also to be executed.

It seems to the present writer that this letter was written in two instalments; that Pearse, having commenced the letter, laid it aside when Father Aloysius came to visit him, and completed it after the priest had left, either during the interval while Father Aloysius was with MacDonagh, or later, after the priest had been with him for the last time.

Father Aloysius has recorded (see his *Personal Recollections,* below, App. II) that when he visited Pearse in his cell, Pearse told him of his anxiety that his mother should get a letter "which he had just written." As Pearse had not been speaking to Father Aloysius prior to that—except in Arbour Hill before he had written "A Mother Speaks"—he could not have said about that poem in the letter that "Father Aloysius is taking charge of another copy of it." (He had, obviously, entrusted a copy of it to the priest); nor, until after Father Aloysius had ministered to him, could he have said : "I have just received Holy Communion. I am happy . . ."

The latter part of the letter must, therefore, have been written within an hour or less of his execution. (Father Aloysius left the prisoners "some time between 2 and 3 am.")

At Easter, 1966, when final preparations for the opening of the Kilmainham Museum were in hand, a copy of this letter, in manuscript, together with manuscript copies of the file-copies of Pearse's note to his brother (see above) and of his poem, "A Mother Speaks"—all written on official paper and bearing the frank "Detention Barracks Kilmainham 3 May 1916"— were received in Kilmainham, with no covering letter, in an envelope posted in England. The manuscript copies, now on display in the Kilmainham Museum, can have been made only by someone who had access to the British Army files in Kilmainham on 3 May, 1916, most likely a member of the British Army.

[1]J. J. Bouch, *Irish Press,* 16 Apr., 1936.

[2]*Sunday Press*, 22 April, 1962.

[3]Máire Nic Shiubhlaigh, who won fame as an actress in the early days of the Abbey Theatre, was herself on active service, as a member of Cumann na mBan, in Jacob's Factory, in 1916.

[4]*Irish Press*, 30 April, 1949. "2.30" conflicts with a statement from Nurse O'Farrell (*Irish Press*, 31 January, 1935). She says "3.30" but as it seems unlikely that the journey from Parnell Street to Parkgate, the interview with Maxwell, and the writing and typing of the surrender order could all have taken place within a quarter of an hour—Pearse signed the order at 3.45—"2.30" seems to be right.

[5]This is believed to be the room now occupied as his office by the Minister for Defence.

[6]Furnished to the Editor by Father Benedict, O.F.M.Cap., Archivist.

[7]In a written statement to the Editor.

[8]Do. See also *Irish Press*, 3 May, 1932.

[9]"on Saturday evening" is an error, possibly in the copying of the MS. It should read "on Saturday morning" or, more correctly, "until Saturday morning". By Saturday evening the men "in the houses in Moore St." had surrendered, the decision to negotiate terms having been taken, in No. 16 Moore Street, about midday.

[10]Pearse was, of course, mistaken in this. The men from Moore St., except those who were wounded, were taken to Richmond Barracks.

[11]W.W. was "Wow-Wow", a pet name of Pearse's sister, Margaret.

M.B. was his sister, Mary Brigid.

Miss Byrne was a family friend who lived with the Pearses.

[12]Illegible initials here were probably those of Pearse's cousin, Margaret Brady.

[13]See his *Dublin Castle and the 1916 Rising: the story of Sir Matthew Nathan* (Helicon, 1966).

[14]*Hansard*, Fifth Series, Vol. LXXXII.

[15]*Irish Press,* 17 August, 1946.

[16]*Sunday Press*, 22 April, 1962.

[17]Since the death, in November, 1968, of Senator Margaret Pearse, some, at least, of these documents have come to light in St. Enda's, Rathfarnham.—Ed.

[18]As stated above only one letter to Maxwell has come to light (and it does not refer to the surrender), and none to Lowe, unless Pearse was referring to the surrender order.

[19]"Mícheál"—Mícheál Mag Ruaidhri, the gardener at St. Enda's, a native speaker of Irish from Kilcummin, Killala Bay, Co. Mayo. He helped the students to improve their Irish.

[20]"Cousin Maggie"—Margaret Brady, a maternal cousin, who also lived with the Pearses at St. Enda's.

And see bibliographical note p. x.

Tomás Ó Cléirigh   Thomas J. Clarke

1858–1916

TOMÁS Ó CLÉIRIGH   THOMAS J. CLARKE

Tom Clarke, probably because of his age, was not asked to
march from Liberty Hall on Easter Monday, 24 April, 1916,
with the contingent of Irish Volunteers and Irish Citizen Army
who were to take over the General Post Office.

Instead, the frail Fenian veteran, fifty-eight years old, who
had spent more than a quarter of his life in English convict
prisons, went ahead with Seán Mac Diarmada who, limping,
carried a stick.

They were in O'Connell Street when the garrison arrived at
noon, entered the G.P.O. with the rest after Connolly's order to
occupy it, and took their places beside their comrades.

Clarke was at Pearse's side when, at 12.45 p.m., the latter
read the Proclamation of the Irish Republic outside the G.P.O.
To him, because he was the father of the revolution, the living
link with 1867, had been given, by common consent of the other
signatories, the honour of being the first to sign it.

Though he held no formal military rank, Clarke, recognised
by the garrison as one of the commanders, was active throughout the week in the direction of the fight, and shared the fortunes of his comrades.

On Easter Monday night Clarke wrote a letter to his wife.
The text of it is not available but we know that it was delivered
to Mrs. Clarke by Seán T. Ó Ceallaigh after he had, on the
instructions of Seán Mac Diarmada, called to Cabra Park to
release Bulmer Hobson. (See below.)

Deineann Seán T. tagairt don litir ina leabhar :

"Bhí dualgas eile le comhlíonadh agam fós sula bhfillfinn ar
Ardoifig an Phoist. Bhí litir agam i mo phóca, a scríobh Tomás
O Cléirigh chuig a bhean agus a thug sé dom nuair a bhí mé ag
dul amach go Páirc na Cabraí. B'onóir liom an teachtaireacht
seo a dhéanamh ar a shon óir ba sheanchara liom é agus bhí
meas as cuimse agam air.

Dá bhrí sin, nuair a dfhág mé slán ag Hobson, thug mé
m'aghaidh suas Bóthar Bhaile Phib, ar aghaidh liom ansin go
Bóthar Dhromchonnrach agus as sin go teach Uí Chléirigh in

aice le Bóthar Risteamain i bhFionnradharc. Bhí Bean Uí
Chléirigh sa bhaile agus thug mé an litir di. . . ."

Neither is the text available of another message which Clarke
asked Seán T. to deliver to Mrs. Clarke on Wednesday.

Deir Seán T.:

"Tráthnóna an lae sin d'iarr Tomás O Cléirigh orm teachtaireacht eile a thabhairt amach chuig a bhean ag Bóthar Risteamain. Bhí scéala faighte aige go raibh na Sasanaigh tagtha
chomh fada leis an gCuarbhóthar Thuaidh agus thuigfeadh sé
go maith, adúirt sé, mura n-éireodh liom dul tharstu. Dúirt mé
leis go ndéanfainn mo dhícheall an dualgas a leag sé orm a
chur i gcrích. . . ."

Seán T. did not succeed in reaching Richmond Road.

Dr. James Ryan, who was the Medical Officer attached to the
G.P.O. Garrison, recalled[1] that, on Wednesday (26 April),

"Tom Clarke came to the hospital (the G.P.O. casualty hospital) and sitting down quietly beside me began to talk. For no
apparent reason he launched into a full history of the I.R.B.
from the time of his release from prison (1898) up to 1911.
Then he gave me a detailed account of the events leading up
to the Rising. This talk lasted for two hours and at the end I
was aware of the reason for it. I was now Red Cross and so, he
said, I might possibly be spared by the enemy in the final
bayonet charge which was evidently expected by him as well as
the rest of us. If, therefore, I should survive, he hoped I now
understood and would make known the motives of those who
signed the Proclamation. He enumerated carefully the arguments
in favour of rising but, with characteristic chivalry, he gave the
most telling points advocated by those against rising at this
particular juncture. . . ."

On Friday night, when the Garrison were forced by flames to
evacuate the Post Office, Clarke dashed with them, under fire,
from the burning building. He was with them as they tunnelled
their way through the walls of the houses in Moore Street, as
they carried the wounded Connolly in a sheet. He was with
them when, some hours later, temporary headquarters were set
up in No. 16, and he was, of course, one of "the members of the
Provisional Government present at Headquarters" who, at
Connolly's bedside, decided, some time before noon on Saturday,

29 April, to negotiate terms and, a couple of hours afterwards, to surrender unconditionally.

Miss Julia Grenan, one of the three women who remained with the G.P.O. Garrison until the end, recalls[2] that, when the decision to seek terms was made, she and Winifred Carney, Connolly's secretary, were standing by the bed on which Connolly lay wounded, and that Clarke was standing at a window, looking out into Moore Street. When Seán Mac Diarmada asked Nurse O'Farrell to provide a white flag Clarke turned his face to the wall and broke down, sobbing. Miss Grenan and Miss Carney went across to him to try to console him but, instead, they themselves dissolved into tears and Clarke comforted them.

Dr. Ryan tells that when he heard of the surrender, he asked Clarke what terms Pearse and Connolly had agreed to, and that Clarke said in reply that he thought the signatories of the Proclamation would be shot, the rest set free.

Clarke was with the assembled Garrison when, some time after 4.30 p.m. on Saturday, Nurse Elizabeth O'Farrell returned to Moore Street with the written order to lay down arms, signed by Pearse and Connolly, and Brigadier-General Lowe's written instructions as to how the men should surrender.

Carrying a white flag they should "proceed down Moore Street, into Moore Lane and Henry Place, out into Henry Street and around the Pillar[3] to the right hand side of O'Connell Street, march up to within a hundred yards of the military drawn up at the Parnell Statue, halt, advance five paces and lay down arms."

Miss Grenan tells that a number of the members of the Garrison, still reluctant to surrender, spoke to Clarke. Having referred to his own years of effort—his whole life's struggle—for freedom, he told them he was satisfied and that they should be too. There was every reason to hope, he said, that the fight, short as it had been, had not been in vain and that Ireland would yet come victorious out of it.

Clarke marched out with the men. They were halted in front of the Gresham Hotel. When they had laid down their arms, their names and addresses were taken, they were searched and then marched to the small green plot in front of the Rotunda Hospital. There, surrounded by military and with machine-guns trained on them from the roofs all round, they spent the night in the open.

They were inhumanly treated, manhandled, insulted, threatened with hanging, shooting.

Brian O'Higgins, who was himself a prisoner there, has left an account of his experiences.[4]

He tells how the British Army officer in charge—"a demon in human form"—spoke to the soldiers under his command:

"While the prisoners were huddled up close together on the little patch of grass with orders not to stand up or put our feet on the gravelled path:
'Which are the Sinn Feiners or the Germans the worse, boys?'
'The Sinn Feiners, sir.'
'What should we do with these swine?'
'Shoot them, sir.'
'Aye, and shoot them we will.' " And so on.
"Later on, in the darkness, he came along with a group of brother officers . . . . and walked right round us while he kept up a running fire of insulting remarks, addressed to the others, but intended for our ears. Now and then he would strike a match, hold it close to the faces of the prisoners nearest to him and say:
'Does anybody want to see the animals? Now is the time. Aren't they beautiful specimens of Irish soldiers?' and other things that would not bear repetition. . . ."

Dr. Ryan recalled:

"The men were told to lie down, if we attempted to rise even to our knees we would be shot. It was very cold, but we were closely packed and managed to sleep fairly comfortably. One incident remains clear in my mind. I awoke towards morning and found my head was resting on Tom Clarke's shoulder. 'Are you awake?' he whispered. I said 'Yes.' 'I was waiting,' he said, 'for an opportunity to turn.' I shall always remember this consideration for a tired young man who indeed might easily have been disturbed without suffering any loss of sleep. . . ."

Brian O'Higgins's narrative continues:

"At dawn, a posse of the Dublin Metropolitan Police, unarmed, were marched in and placed around us in a cordon, between us and the soldiers . . . . Then . . the G-men . . recognised some well-known faces in our midst. Very soon Tom Clarke was pointed out to the British officer . . who immediately had him hauled off and searched in the usual British fashion, and the Dublin Castle history of his whole life was recounted for his benefit. He came back, cool, careless, dignified, a smile of contempt on his worn face. They hadn't overawed *him* at all events. Others were dragged out, ordered to take off their coats, vests, boots and socks, and searched from head to foot. . . ."

Éamonn Dore (Éamonn T. de hÓir), another member of the G.P.O. Garrison, who was also among the prisoners, refers[5] to the treatment meted out to himself and his comrades:

". . . . Most, if not all, of the Garrison had some kind of meal early on Friday. I, with Tom Clarke, Seán Mac Diarmada, Diarmuid Lynch and Seán McGarry—all now dead—had a meal about 3 o'clock. Just after this meal, I went, with Diarmuid Lynch, Frank Henderson, Pat Weafer, Paddy Murray (all dead) and one other, into the basement to shift bombs away from the track of the fire. When we finished we found all the Garrison lined up in the yard—it could be the sorting office—just behind where the present counters are and near the only door (Henry Street) not on fire. I was told they were waiting to get some biscuits before moving out. If they got them this was the last food anyone received—at least any one of those of us who went with O'Rahilly—until late on Sunday evening.

As for water we did not get a drink until about two hours after arriving at Richmond Barracks when we were almost mad from thirst. I saw John R. Reynolds part with his watch for one mouthful of water—a few others did the same. The prisoners, to my knowledge, had neither food nor drink—I speak of those of us who survived what is now known as 'The O'Rahilly Charge'; it is possible that those who left the G.P.O. after us and who were in Moore Street until the surrender had at least drink. If they had, it was the last they had—until the evening of Sunday. We were over two days without anything.

. . . . The night at the Rotunda was a bit of a nightmare and water and food did not trouble us. The officer in charge of the British military was a maniac. I saw Frank Henderson (R.I.P.) kneel to 'relieve' himself about day-break and the officer snatched a rifle from a Tommy and struck him on the head, knocking him back on the grass. We were not allowed to 'relieve' ourselves from the time we left our Garrison positions until about 3 o'clock or so on Sunday evening just before we got water to drink. This deprivation of sanitary process was much worse than the lack of either food or water and many of the prisoners fainted on the Richmond Barracks parade ground as they waited their turn to march forward in sections of four for searching. When finally we were allowed to 'relieve' ourselves in the room in Richmond Barracks—fifty or so to a room—we were given a large dust-bin to use. When we were finished the bin was removed and as far as I could see, the same bin was brought back full of water.[6] We were so mad with thirst by this time that we were not particular what was last in the bin so long as it contained water. This is no exaggeration. I could have killed anyone for a drink by this time.

About five o'clock on the morning of Sunday, after the officer had struck Henderson, he took Tom Clarke, Seán Mac Diarmada and Ned Daly into the street near the Rotunda Picture House (now 'The Ambassador') and stripped them down to their boots to search them. Near me at that time was Frank Thornton (R.I.P.) He said: 'If that bastard gets through the War and we get out, we'll get him!'[7] Tom Clarke had been wounded at the elbow-joint and his arm was in a sling so that he could not get his coat off quickly. The officer pulled the arm straight, opening the wound, and tore off his coat.'

It was approaching midday on Sunday, 30 April, when the prisoners, who, as we have seen, had had neither food nor drink since before the surrender, and who had been sitting or lying on the grass since about 8 o'clock the previous night, were ordered to stand up and were marched to Richmond Barracks.

On arrival there Clarke wrote what he believed would be his last message to his wife.

Message to his Wife from Richmond Barracks, 30 April, 1916

Dear K,

I am in better health and more satisfied than for many a day—all will be well eventually—but this is my good-bye and now you are ever before me to cheer me—God bless you and the boys. Let them be proud to follow same path—Sean[8] is with me and McG,[9] all well—they all heroes. I'm full of pride my love.

Yours

TOM

Love to John[10] & Madge[11] &c.

Written on the outside of the note, in pencil, were the words "Mrs. O'Toole, 32 King's Inn St., for Mrs. T. Clarke."

Referring to her husband's note Mrs. Clarke says:[12]

"The letter was written on their arrival in Richmond Barracks when they thought they would be shot at once, without trial. It was written in pencil but I went over it in ink fearing it would fade. My husband gave a British soldier his watch to bring the letter to me. A woman from Church Street brought it to me three weeks after the surrender."

Mrs. Clarke explains that Mrs. O'Toole was unknown to her and must have been a friend of the soldier to whom her husband entrusted the letter.

On the back of the note was a message to Mrs. Clarke from Seán Mac Diarmada. (See below.)

The letter is in the possession of John Daly Clarke.

Dé Domhnaigh, 30 Aibreán, tugadh an tOllamh Liam Ó Briain, a bhí tar éis páirt a ghlacadh san Éirí Amach, i bhFaiche Stiabhna, ina phríosúnach chuig Beairic Risteamain. Seoladh isteach é sa Gymnasium mar a raibh suas le ceithre scór príosúnach roimhe, a piocadh amach ag bleachtairí. Bhí Tomás Ó Cléirigh ina measc. Chaith an tOllamh cupla lá san chomhluadar agus thug cuntas faoi i leabhar a scríobh sé blianta ina dhiaidh sin:

". . . .Bhí Tomás Ó Cléirigh ina shuí ansin díreach mar chonaiceamar é fiche uair sa siopa i Sráid Pharnell, na héadaí céanna air, an chuma chéanna air, go ciúin, tostach, fríd an gháire ar a bhéal ó am go ham. Bhí Tom an-tsásta leis féin agus leis an saol. Tar éis ar chaith sé de bhlianta fada i bpríosúin Shasana bhí sé de shástacht aige urchar a chaitheamh le hArm Shasana nuair a tháinig na heachraí úd anuas Sráid Uí Chonaill Dé Luain roimhe sin; bhí de shástacht aige Óglaigh d'fheiceáil cruinn timpeall air ag tabhairt dúshlán an namhad ar feadh seachtaine, rud nár éirigh leis na Fíníní a dhéanamh leithchéad blian roimhe sin, ná lena chomhaimsirigh féin os cionn deich mblian fichead roimhe sin. Bhí seanchleachtadh aige ar phríosúntacht ach ba cheart an tuairim a bhí aige an tráthnóna Domhnaigh sin nárbh fhada an téarma a bhéarfadh sé an babhta seo, agus is é a bhí sásta a aghaidh a thabhairt ar an mbás gan scanrú roimhe. . . ."

Istoíche Dé Luain tugadh béile den bully-beef agus roinnt brioscaí do na príosúnaigh. Leantar le cuntas an Ollaimh:

". . . .Tar éis dom mo chéad bhéile den bully-beef d'ithe chuimhníos go raibh an dara todóg[13] i mo phóca agam. Suas liom go dtí an coirnéal den tseomra, mar a raibh an Pluingcéadach sínte . . . Tomás Ó Cléirigh lena ais go ciúin agus Seán Mac Diarmada agus Seán Mac Gadhra lena thaobh.

'Tom,' arsa mise leis, 'ar mhaith leat bronntanas?' 'Well, Liam,' arsa Tom agus an tseanchanúint Mheireacánach air, 'that depends on what the present is.' Tharraingeas an todóg as mo phóca agus thaispeánas dó é. 'O! Gee!' arsa Tom, agus rug sé ar an todóg go cíocrach. Ach mar sin féin dhiúltaigh sé é a chaitheamh leis féin. B'éigean dúinn suí thart air ar an urlár, Seán Mac Diarmada, Mac Gadhra, mé féin agus é féin, agus gachra gal an duine a bheith againn, ag síneadh na todóige ó dhuine go duine, mar a bheadh scata scoláirí ag síneadh toitín ó dhuine go duine i gcoirnéal de chlós scoile agus a gcúl leis an máistir!...."

"....Tar éis tamaill thit a chodladh ar Sheán (Mac Diarmada) a cheann in ucht Tom. Bhí an Piarsach óg (Liam) ag tiontó ó thaobh go taobh ar mo láimh chlé, agus é an-chorraithe cé go raibh sé ina chodladh. Ní dóigh liom gur thit aon chodladh ar Tom—ná orm féin ar feadh i bhfad. Ba léir go raibh an bheirt eile ar ais in Oifig an Phoist ina gcuid bhrionglóidí. Thugadh Seán léim bheag agus chloisfimis monabhar cainte uaidh ag rá 'The fire! The fire! Get the men out!' Ansin cloisfi glór beag caoin Tom ag rá: 'Quiet, Seán! We're in the barracks now. We're prisoners now, Seán!'...."

Clarke was tried by Court Martial in Richmond Barracks on the morning of Tuesday, 2 May. That evening he was transferred to Kilmainham.

At that time Mrs. Clarke was a prisoner in Dublin Castle. She was brought from there, after midnight, under military escort, to pay a farewell visit to her husband before his execution.

Describing her visit she states[14] that she spent an hour with her husband in his cell; that all during the interview a soldier holding a candle in a jam-jar was in the cell with them; that her husband condemned MacNeill's action, "a continuation of what he said to her about MacNeill on his return from the meeting in Liberty Hall on Easter Sunday" (the meeting of the Military Council); that her husband described the Court Martial as "a farce" and told her "he had made no speech from the dock or anything like that." He was "relieved," he told her, that he was to be executed, his one dread being that he would be sent to prison again. "He was in a most exalted frame of mind." He entrusted to her a message to the Irish people.

That message was circulated on an In Memoriam card in 1917.

Message to the Irish People, 3 May, 1916

I and my fellow-signatories believe we have struck the first successful blow for Freedom. The next blow, which we have no doubt Ireland will strike, will win through. In this belief we die happy.

THOMAS J. CLARKE.

Kilmainham Jail, 3 May, 1916.

In the death-cell Clarke was attended by Fr. Columbus, O.F.M.Cap.

---

[1]*Capuchin Annual*, 1966.

[2]In statements to the Editor.

[3]This was Nelson Pillar which stood in the centre of O'Connell Street, between Henry and North Earl Streets. It was partially demolished, by an explosion, by "a person or persons unknown" in the early morning of 8 March, 1966, and removed entirely, by Government order, a couple of weeks later.

[4]*Wolfe Tone Annual*, 1935.

[5]In a statement to the Editor.

[6]Richard P. Gogan, T.D., another prisoner, confirms this (in a statement to the Editor).

[7]Liam Tobin (R.I.P.), another prisoner, swore the same oath.

[8]Seán Mac Diarmada, no doubt.

[9]Probably Seán McGarry, a close friend of Clarke's, who had been with him in the G.P.O.

[10]John Daly, uncle of Mrs. Clarke.

[11]Madge Daly, one of Mrs. Clarke's sisters.

[12]In a letter to the Editor.

[13]Bhí an t-Ollamh tar éis cupla todóg a sciobadh as siopa i Sráid Ghrafton i rith na seachtaine.

[14]In letters and a statement to the Editor.

And see bibliographical note p. x.

Tomás Mac Donnchadha   Thomas MacDonagh
                         1876–1916

TOMÁS MAC DONNCHADHA
THOMAS MacDONAGH

Statement written at his home, Easter Sunday, 23 April, 1916

29 Oakley Road,
  Dublin.
23rd April, 1916.

I have now, at 8 p.m. returned from a visit to Eoin MacNeill at Woodtown Park, Ballyboden.

I have had a long conversation with MacNeill and Seán Fitzgibbon upon many aspects of the present situation. I hope that I have made clear to them my loyalty to Ireland, my honour as an Irish Volunteer, and also —a thing which I could not for obvious reasons state definitely—my intention to act with my own Council, and the position of that Council.

My future conduct may be different from anything now anticipated by MacNeill and Fitzgibbon, two honest and sincere patriots, though, I think, wrong in their handling of the present situation and in their attitude to military action. They and my countrymen must judge me on my conduct. I have guarded secrets which I am bound to keep. I have, I think, acted honourably and fairly by all my associates. I have had only one motive in all my actions, namely, the good of my country.

I now pray to God for the gifts of counsel and fortitude, and for His blessing on the cause of my country.

THOMAS MACDONAGH.

The original of this document is in the possession of Mrs. Michael Tierney (née Mac Neill). There is a microfilm copy in the National Library.

MacDonagh's Surrender

On consultation with Commandant Ceannt and other officers I have decided to agree to unconditional surrender
also.

THOMAS MACDONAGH.
30.IV.16
3.15 p.m.

Nurse Elizabeth O'Farrell, having brought the surrender
order, signed by Pearse and Connolly, to the G.P.O. and
Four Courts Garrisons, returned on Saturday evening, 29
April, to O'Connell Street. The British military arranged
accommodation for her for the night in the National Bank
premises at the corner of Parnell Street. She arose on Sunday
morning about 6 o'clock. The account which she wrote[1] of
her experiences continues :

"....I had only just finished dressing when I was told I was
wanted downstairs by Captn. Wheeler to take round the orders
to the other Commandants. Captain Wheeler had the type-
written copies and he took me to the middle of Grafton Street
in a motor car, and I had to walk from there to the College of
Surgeons with a white flag. Bullets were whistling round
Stephen's Green. There was no one in the streets and I saw
no dead or wounded. I got in at the side door in York Street
and asked for Commandant Mallin and was told he was sleeping
and that Countess Markievicz was next in command. I saw her
and gave her the order—she was very much surprised and she
went to discuss it with Commandant Mallin, whom I afterwards
saw. I gave her a slip with the directions as to how to surrender
—the southern sides being ordered to surrender at St. Patrick's
Park. (I don't think this was carried out and I don't know where
the College of Surgeons troops did actually surrender.[2]) I left
and went back to Grafton Street to Captain Wheeler who asked
me if I had seen Mallin and what he said about it—I said I saw
Mallin who had nothing to say. Captain Wheeler told me I
should have got him to say if he intended to surrender or not.
He next brought me in the car down to Trinity College into
which he went for a few minutes. Then he decided to take me
to Commandant de Valera at Boland's—for which purpose he
brought the car down Brunswick (now Pearse) Street, but the
barricades there blocked the way...."

After a hazardous journey during which Nurse O'Farrell
risked her life many times—a man crossing Grand Canal

Street Bridge about half a yard behind her was shot—she
reached Commandant de Valera. He said : "I will not take
any orders except from my immediate superior officer, Commandant MacDonagh."

"....I started off again towards the College where I was to
meet Captain Wheeler with Commandant de Valera's answer,
on receipt of which he said we would go up to Jacob's and see
MacDonagh. We went by Dame Street and the Castle Yard, into
which Captain Wheeler went for a short time. We then proceeded through Ship Street into Bride Street in the middle of
which he stopped the car. I got out and walked through the
firing line (through Golden Lane, Whitefriar Street and Peter
Street) to Jacob's. At 15 Peter Street I knocked and asked to see
Commandant MacDonagh. I was blindfolded and was walked
about for a few minutes. I then heard Commandant MacDonagh's
voice and the bandage was taken off my eyes. I gave him the
order from Commandant Pearse and told him of our position
in the G.P.O. and Moore Street. He brought me into a small
room and told me he would not take orders from a prisoner,
that he, himself, was next in command and he would have
nothing to say to the surrender until he would confer with
General Lowe, the members of the Provisional Government and
the officers under his command. . . ."

In the meantime Fathers Augustine and Aloysius had been
to Dublin Castle where they had met Brigadier-General Lowe
who had arranged for them to meet Connolly, in the Castle,
and Pearse, at Arbour Hill, to get confirmation of the surrender order from them. With this they had driven—the
General having placed his car and chauffeur at their disposal
—to Church Street, where they found that Father Columbus
had preceded them, and thence towards Jacob's Factory.

". . . .We left the car," said Father Aloysius,[3] "near the last
military barrier a little above Whitefriar Street and Father
Augustine and myself walked to the factory. We were admitted
through a door in Peter Street, and were brought through the
factory to Commandant MacDonagh. He took us to a room
where we met Major MacBride. (Miss O'Farrell had already
arrived with a copy of Pearse's letter similar to the one we bore.)
. . . .Thomas MacDonagh said that the letter of Pearse could
have no weight as he was in custody and not a free man when
he wrote it. As Pearse and Connolly were both under arrest
the chief command devolved on him, and no one else had any

right to issue commands or enter into negotiations. Although he was exceedingly courteous and agreeable with us he said he would not enter into negotiations with anyone except the General Officer Commanding the military. He was prepared to meet him in the factory or anywhere he might wish. MacDonagh also expressed the view that they could hold out for some weeks. They had ample provisions and ammunition and were well protected. He believed that a peace conference was being held or on the eve of being held and that Rumania had come in on the side of Germany; that the news was being kept from us; and that the fact of their continuing for a week or two to hold out would necessitate their case going before the peace conference. We undertook to convey his message to General Lowe, and returned in the car to the Castle. When we informed General Lowe of the result of our interview with Commandant MacDonagh, he asked us if we would accompany him to Headquarters. Accordingly we drove to the Infirmary Road Headquarters of General Maxwell. General Lowe, Father Augustine and, I think, another officer, occupied the interior. I sat outside with the chauffeur.

After consultation at Headquarters, General Lowe said he was prepared to meet MacDonagh, and gave us a letter expressing his readiness to meet him at the North East corner of St. Patrick's Park at 12 noon or 1 p.m. (I am not certain which hour)[1] and further undertaking to give MacDonagh safe conduct back to where he came from if he so desired. With this message we returned in the General's car to Jacob's. MacDonagh read the document and said he would meet the General. . . ."

Father Augustine, in his statement, says:

". . . .A Volunteer was then called and the four of us proceeded on foot. At the hour that had been arranged General Lowe, leaving his car, advanced, and MacDonagh and he met, each saluting the other in the usual military style. I could not help noticing the quiet matter-of-fact salute of the former, for of the two MacDonagh was certainly then the cooler man. I remained beside the Volunteer and kept my eye on both as they talked together outside the railing just at the corner of the Park. To the crowds that were gathering and pressing in Father Aloysius appealed and they withdrew at once, leaving the Square free. After a time the two retired to General Lowe's car and continued their parley for about ten or fifteen minutes, after which MacDonagh rejoined us and we walked back to the factory. He told us there was an armistice until 3 p.m., during which he was to see the garrisons at the South Dublin Union and Marrowbone Lane as well as his own. The General placed his car at our disposal, gave MacDonagh a special permit to visit the Volunteer centres and requested us to accompany him.

On returning to Jacob's MacDonagh consulted with his officers and then addressed his men. He was evidently suffering a great strain but still held up and spoke bravely for a few minutes telling the men, among other things, that the Volunteers had fought a good fight, held out for one glorious week, and achieved what they meant to accomplish. I listened with great sympathy and while I was wondering how he could speak so coolly under such circumstances, he used the word that my mind had conceived but my tongue never uttered—'surrender'—and then he burst into tears. Pulling himself together bravely after a very short time, and, I'm sure, feeling the difficulty of his position and the certainty of my opinion, he took the liberty of saying that I had advised them to surrender. Almost immediately he added, to my astonishment: 'Father Augustine will now address you.' I stepped forward from the side, faced the men, and felt that God would help me. Taking up MacDonagh's last word I said that our men everywhere had fought a brave fight, and, for the reasons mentioned by Pearse, the best thing to do now was to obey and to lay down arms. 'But they'll shoot us, Father,' cried out one of the boys, and, speaking the honest conviction of my soul at the time, I answered: 'Not at all, the thing is unbelievable.' After a few minutes I concluded, and then chatted with the boys, telling them amongst other things, that I would return before they left. Father Aloysius was all this time below with the chauffeur who was rather nervous in this area. MacDonagh and I joined him as speedily as we could and drove off, Father Aloysius sitting outside with a white flag,[5] and I inside chatting with MacDonagh. He was under the impression that the country was up and that the British wanted to quell us before attacking them. Near Basin Lane, because of a barricade across the street, we were obliged to leave the car and we then proceeded on foot to the South Dublin Union. . . .

After consultation with the officers, during which surrender was agreed upon, MacDonagh rejoined us and we walked along quickly. Soon a shot was fired in our direction, and speedily an English officer came forward to apologise and say that the soldier who fired it had been placed under arrest. I could not help noticing the nonchalant manner in which MacDonagh replied to the officer, saying ' I didn't notice it.' I did, and felt glad the soldier was such a bad shot!

Having regained the car we were soon at Jacob's and at 3 p.m. arrived again at St. Patrick's Park where MacDonagh informed General Lowe of the decision to surrender and handed his revolver and belt to an officer.[6] It was now decided that he should return to the two garrisons already named (Jacob's and South Dublin Union) and also to Marrowbone Lane to arrange details of the surrender. We were again requested to accompany him and General Lowe's son, with another officer, was also with us.

Father Aloysius remained outside with the chauffeur and I accompanied MacDonagh into the building (Marrowbone Lane Distillery) where we had a longer stay than I had anticipated. . . ."

"After what seemed a long time," said Father Aloysius,[3] "they returned to the car. I understood they had had some difficulty in persuading the Volunteers there to surrender. They were well fortified and had provisions to last for some time."

Séamus Ó Murchadha of the Marrowbone Lane Garrison recalls[7] the visit of MacDonagh:

". . . .I received a message from our unit stationed on the ' bridge' across Marrowbone Lane—the covered tunnel which joined the upper storeys of the Distillery—that Commandant MacDonagh, accompanied by a priest of the Franciscan Order, was approaching our outpost. The gates were opened and I went forward to meet them. MacDonagh was bare-headed and un-armed. Unlike him, his expression was grave and he seemed to be very weary. Firmly, however, he informed me of the General Surrender. . . ."

Continuing Father Augustine's statement:

". . . .We returned to the South Dublin Union where MacDonagh made final arrangements, and, walking back, he spoke more than usual. Amongst other things, he pointed out to me the place where they had held a large Volunteer recruiting meeting[8] some time previously, and, a little later, the spot near St. Catherine's Church where the scaffold was erected on which Robert Emmet was hanged.[9] I could almost feel his thoughts. Regaining Jacob's we were soon joined by Father Monahan of Francis Street who offered to do anything he could. But there was little now to be done. The boys gathered round me and asked me to take messages to their people. . . .I was filling every pocket I had with the messages. . . .mostly to their parents. These were delivered in the city on the following day by a few members of the Third Order. . . .After a time Father Aloysius and myself bade good-bye to the boys amid much bustle. . . ."

The men from Jacob's having assembled, according to Nurse O'Farrell,[1] at the corner of Bride Street and Ross Road, were disarmed.

One member of the garrison, Pádraig Ó Ceallaigh, recalled[10]:

". . . .We walked about half a mile before we met the British troops to whom we surrendered our guns and ammunition and who took our names and addresses. All the time a solitary sniper continued firing. We afterwards learned he was one of our own men—located in some high position in Jacob's factory—who had not heard of the surrender.

Before we reached the British, some of the boys just walked out into the crowd, which lined most of the way to the point of surrender, and escaped. The leaders who included Thomas MacDonagh, Major MacBride and Michael O'Hanrahan could as easily have escaped. However, they presumably thought they were in honour bound by their agreement to surrender...."

MacDonagh, with the rest of the garrison, was taken to Richmond Barracks.

Dispatch issued from Jacob's Factory, 30 April, 1916

> Army of the Irish Republic,
> Dublin Command,
> Battalion IV
> 30/4/16. 5.30 a.m.

To Commandant Mallon

(1) Dispatch received. I do not understand it. I have received no order from H.Q. re evacuation, and do not think it advisable or practicable. I have received order of personal nature but have been unable to obey. I have notified this to H.Q. I do not know where H.Q. is.

(2) I have been in touch this morning with Batt. IV at Thom's, Love Lane, Cork Street. They are very strong in numbers and in food. They have beaten off every attack with loss, and have lost no men.

(3) Good news of International situation. England is down and out. Enemy officers are uttering Proclamations full of falsehoods.

(4) Small actions seem to be developing against my right (Bride Street). Thank God, as we are tired of sniping.

(5) and (6) Torn in original and illegible.

> THOMAS MACDONAGH
> Commandant.

This, described as "Thomas MacDonagh's Last Despatch," was quoted (as above) in *Irish Life: A Record of the Irish Rebellion of 1916.* ("Irish Life," 1916.)

C

It seems to the present writer

(1) that the "dispatch received" from Mallin—it has not been possible to come upon the text of it—was sent to MacDonagh by Mallin *after* the latter had seen the surrender order brought to him on Sunday morning by Nurse O'Farrell, but *before* he had decided to lead the St. Stephen's Green Garrison out to surrender;

(2) that the "order of personal nature" which MacDonagh had been "unable to obey" was none other than the surrender order which Nurse O'Farrell had brought to him after she had been with de Valera who had told her he would take no orders except from MacDonagh, his immediate superior officer. MacDonagh, as we have seen, had stated that he would not take orders from a prisoner (Pearse), that he himself was next in command and would have nothing to say to the surrender until he could confer with the General Officer Commanding the British, the members of the Provisional Government already prisoners and the officers under his command. A message to this effect had been conveyed to General Lowe by Fathers Augustine and Aloysius;

(3) that it was while MacDonagh was awaiting the outcome of that message to Lowe that he wrote this dispatch to Mallin and that "5.30 a.m." is therefore a mistake for perhaps "10.30 a.m." or "11.30 a.m." just as "Batt. IV" is a mistake for "Batt II" and "Mallon" for "Mallin". The mistakes must, of course, be in the reproduction, not in the original manuscript, the whereabouts of which is unknown. MacDonagh's handwriting was far from clear.

MacDonagh was tried by Court Martial at Richmond Barracks on the morning of 2 May, 1916.

Address to the Court Martial, 2 May, 1916

Gentlemen of the Court Martial,

I choose to think you have but done your duty, according to your lights, in sentencing me to death. I thank you for

your courtesy. It would not be seemly for me to go to my
doom without trying to express, however inadequately, my
sense of the high honour I enjoy in being one of those pre-
destined to die in this generation for the cause of Irish
Freedom. You will, perhaps, understand this sentiment, for
it is one to which an Imperial poet of a bygone age bore
immortal testimony: " 'Tis sweet and glorious to die for
one's country." You would all be proud to die for Britain,
your Imperial patron, and I am proud and happy to die
for Ireland, my glorious Fatherland.

A member of the Court—You speak of Britain as our
Imperial patron.

The Prisoner—Yes, for some of you are Irishmen.

A member of the Court—And what of your Imperial
patron; what of Germany?

The Prisoner—Not if Germany had violated and de-
spoiled my country and persisted in withholding her birth-
right of Freedom.

The President—Better not interrupt the prisoner. (The
prisoner bowed.)

There is not much left to say. The Proclamation of the
Irish Republic has been adduced in evidence against me as
one of the Signatories; you think it already a dead and
buried letter, but it lives, it lives. From minds alight with
Ireland's vivid intellect it sprang, in hearts aflame with
Ireland's mighty love it was conceived. Such documents do
not die. The British occupation of Ireland has never for
more than 100 years been compelled to confront in the field
of fight a Rising so formidable as that which overwhelming
forces have for the moment succeeded in quelling. This
Rising did not result from accidental circumstances. It came
in due recurrent season as the necessary outcome of forces
that are ever at work. The fierce pulsation of resurgent pride
that disclaims servitude may one day cease to throb in the
heart of Ireland—but the heart of Ireland will that day be
dead. While Ireland lives, the brains and brawn of her
manhood will strive to destroy the last vestige of British rule
in her territory. In this ceaseless struggle there will be, as
there has been, and must be, an alternate ebb and flow.
But let England make no mistake. The generous high-bred

youth of Ireland will never fail to answer the call we pass
on to them—will never fail to blaze forth in the red rage
of war to win their country's Freedom. Other and tamer
methods they will leave to other and tamer men; but they
must do or die. It will be said that our movement was
doomed to failure. It has proved so. Yet it might have been
otherwise. There is always a chance of success for brave
men who challenge fortune. That we had such a chance
none knows so well as your statesmen and military experts.
The mass of the people of Ireland will doubtless lull their
consciences to sleep for another generation by the exploded
fable that Ireland cannot successfully fight England. We
do not profess to represent the mass of the people of Ireland.
We stand for the intellect and the soul of Ireland. To
Ireland's soul and intellect the inert mass, drugged and
degenerate by ages of servitude, must, in the distant day of
resurrection, render homage and free service—receiving in
return the vivifying impress of a free people. Gentlemen,
you have sentenced me to death, and I accept your sentence
with joy and pride, since it is for Ireland I am to die. I go
to join the goodly company of the men who died for
Ireland, the least of whom was worthier far than I can
claim to be, and that noble band are, themselves, but a
small section of the great unnumbered army of martyrs
whose Captain is the Christ who died on Calvary. Of every
white-robed knight in all that goodly company we are the
spiritual kin. The forms of heroes flit before my vision, and
there is one, the star of whose destiny sways my own; there
is one the keynote of whose nature chimes harmoniously
with the swan-song of my soul. It is the great Florentine,[11]
whose weapon was not the sword but prayer and preaching.
The seed he sowed fructifies to this day in God's Church.
Take me away, and let my blood bedew the sacred soil of
Ireland. I die in the certainty that once more the seed will
fructify.

*   *   *

The source of this document is unknown and there is doubt as
to its authenticity.

Its first appearance, in Dublin in June, 1916, led to four prosecutions under the Defence of the Realm Act.

Mr. J. M. Butler, a newsagent and former employee of the *Freeman's Journal,* carrying on a business at 41 Amiens Street, was fined £20 and bound over for: making a false statement in a printed publication likely to cause disaffection; having in his premises a large number of documents containing statements likely to cause disaffection to His Majesty; and doing an act preparatory to the commission of an offence against Regulation 27 of the Defence of the Realm Act by causing a number of these documents to be printed and published. Three printers, Peter Paul Curtis, 12 Temple Lane, Robert Latchford, Temple Bar, and W. H. West, 45A Capel Street, were each fined £5 for printing and publishing the document.

During the course of the trial of Mr. Butler, Mr. Robertson of the Chief Crown Solicitor's Office stated that "the document, headed 'The Last and Inspiring Address of Thomas MacDonagh' purported to be no doubt a statement made by this person but it was pure fiction and no such statement, as far as he could gather,[12] was ever made by this man. The conduct of the defendant in having the document which is absolutely bogus printed and published by other persons for circulation could only be for the purpose of causing disloyalty and disaffection in the country at the present time. . . ."

An Inspector of Police, Mills[13] who had seized 470 copies of the document in Mr. Butler's shop, deposed to Mr. Butler's having said, when asked where he got the documents, that he didn't know. Butler disclaimed authorship.

In the case against Curtis a Detective Inspector deposed that Curtis had told him that a man who gave his name as "James Smith" and his address as 50 St. Ignatius Road,[14] called on him and produced a printed leaflet "purporting to be the last address of Thomas MacDonagh" and asked him to print 2,000 copies of it and to insert a photograph of MacDonagh. Curtis had got the loan of a photograph from the Wood Printing Works and printed and supplied the copies in accordance with the order. He would not have printed the leaflets without making inquiries only that "Smith" had produced a printed copy of it and since it had already been printed he had assumed the authorities had not taken exception to it.

In the case against Latchford the Detective Inspector said the accused had told him that Butler had ordered, and he had printed, 10,000 copies of the document.

A police sergeant, in the case against West, said that West admitted having printed a number of copies of the document for a man "he didn't know" who had brought him a printed copy of it. When the Magistrate remarked that he had not heard anything of the genesis of the document the prosecutor said he could not prove that any of the three printers was the originator.

In all some 3,500 copies of the document were seized.

One account of the origin of the document—though it has not been possible to get confirmation of it—tells that a British Army officer present at the Court Martial, believed to be an Irishman and said to have been a journalist, gave to a newspaper reporter notes taken by him during the Court Martial proceedings and that the address was "put together" from those notes.

The first sentence of the address "Gentlemen . . . I choose to think you have but done your duty . . . in sentencing me to death" and the later sentence ". . . you have sentenced me to death" are held by many to prove the document false, as there is evidence from a number of sources that the findings of the courts martial were not made known to the prisoners at the conclusion of the trials but that, in accordance with established procedure, the prisoners were removed at the close of the trials and the verdicts conveyed to them some time afterwards. MacDonagh's own final statement confirms this.

President de Valera, Séamus Brennan (Secretary of the Kilmainham Restoration Society) and Maurice Brennan, all of whom were sentenced to death but whose sentences were commuted, state[15] that that was their experience.

Piaras Béaslai who was one of the first six to be court-martialled—while Pearse, Clarke and MacDonagh were being tried in one room at Richmond Barracks, he, Joseph McGuinness and Éamonn Duggan were being tried in another —has stated (see App. I) that no one was sentenced to death at his trial; that no judgment was given. Tried on the morning of 2 May, 1916, Béaslai did not hear the verdict until the following morning.

The same procedure applied, he said, when he was court-martialled again in 1919.

And in his last statement, which he commenced to write at midnight on 2 May, 1916 (see below) MacDonagh says: ". . . having now heard the sentence of the Court Martial held on me today . . ." which would seem to indicate that he had just then been apprised of the verdict.

There close the arguments against the validity of the document.

In support of its authenticity it can be adduced that MacDonagh did undoubtedly make a statement to the Court Martial. He refers to it in his last statement (see below).

Pearse has left on record (see above) the substance of a statement which he made when asked if he had anything to say in his defence.

Piaras Béaslai has stated (see App. I) that, at the conclusion of the evidence, each prisoner was asked the same question. It can be accepted that a similar inquiry was made of MacDonagh.

The sentiments expressed in the document, the style of composition and the words used, notably the reference in the final paragraph to "the great Florentine" give the document the ring of truth. (MacDonagh had a particular veneration for Savonarola who is mentioned on more than one occasion in his play "When the Dawn is Come.")

MacDonagh's son, the late D.J. Donagh MacDonagh, writing in 1956,[16] said "there are several points of internal evidence which would seem to indicate that it was his work, especially the reference to 'the great Florentine.'"

The late John MacDonagh, who was with his brother in Jacob's during Easter Week, could not make up his mind whether the document was genuine or not, but agreed that it rings true.[17]

If the document is not genuine and was, in fact, concocted by someone "for the purpose of causing disloyalty and disaffection" was it not strange that the author attributed it to MacDonagh, who had no reputation as an orator, rather than to, say, Pearse who had?

There is the possibility—though the reported "interruptions" during the address seem to discount it—that MacDonagh, expecting the death sentence (see his last statement, below, in which he said he knew the surrender would involve his death) and unaware of Court Martial procedure, prepared the address beforehand for use at his trial, but did not get an opportunity to use it.

The present writer believes—though time may, of course, prove him wrong—that MacDonagh did address the Court Martial in terms as in the document, but that the person who, after the event, used the notes (from whatever source they came) slightly amended them to suit the circumstances.

It is not without the bounds of possibility that a page was removed from an official file, as seems to have occurred in the case of Pearse's statement to the Court Martial.

The truth will not be known until the documents relating to the Court Martial, at present among the papers of the British Judge-Advocate-General's Office, held in the Public Record Office in London, are open to inspection.

Statement written in Kilmainham, 2/3 May, 1916

> Kilmainham Gaol,
> Midnight, Tuesday,
> 2nd May, 1916.

I, Thomas MacDonagh, having now heard the sentence of the Court Martial held on me today, declare that in all my acts—all the acts for which I have been arraigned —I have been actuated by one motive only, the love of my country, the desire to make her a sovereign independent state. I still hope and pray that my acts may have for consummation her lasting freedom and happiness.

I am to die at dawn, 3.30 a.m. 3rd May. I am ready to die, and I thank God that I die in so holy a cause. My country will reward my deed richly.

On April 30th I was astonished to receive by a message from P. H. Pearse, Commandant General of the Army of the Irish Republic, an order to surrender unconditionally to the British General. I did not obey the order as it came from a prisoner. I was then in supreme command of the Irish Army, consulted with my second in command and decided to confirm the order. I knew that it would involve my death and the deaths of other leaders. I hoped that it would save many true men among our followers, good lives for Ireland. God grant it has done so, and God approve our deed. For myself I have no regret. The one bitterness that death has for me is the separation it brings from my beloved wife, Muriel, and my beloved children, Donagh and Barbara. My country will take them as wards, I hope.

I have devoted myself too much to national work and too little to the making of money to leave them in competence. God help them and support them, and give them a happy and prosperous life. Never was there a better, truer, purer woman than my wife, Muriel, or more adorable children than Don and Barbara. It breaks my heart to think that I shall never see my children again, but I have not wept or mourned. I counted the cost of this, and am ready to pay it.

Muriel has been sent for here. I do not know if she can come. She may have no one to take the children while she is coming. If she does.

My money affairs are in a bad way. I am insured for £200 in the New York Life Co. but have borrowed £101, I think. I am insured for £100 in the Alliance Co., but have a bank debt for £80. That leaves less than £120 from these sources if they produce anything. In addition I have insured my two children for £100 each in the Mutual Co. of Australasia, payments of premiums to cease at my death the money to be paid to the children at the age of twenty-one. I ask my brother, Joseph MacDonagh, and my good and constant friend David Houston to help my poor wife in these matters. My brother John, who came with me and stood by me all last week has been sent away from here, I do not know where to.[18] He, if he can, will help my family too. God bless him and my other sisters and brothers. Assistance has been guaranteed from funds in the hands of Cumann na mBan and other funds to be collected in America by our fellow countrymen there in provision for the dependants of those who fall in this fight. I appeal without shame to the persons who control these funds to assist my family. My wife and I have given all for Ireland.

I ask my friend David Houston to see Mr. W. G. Lyon, publisher of my latest book, *Literature in Ireland* and see that its publication may be useful to my wife and family. If Joseph Plunkett survives me and is a free man I make him with my wife my literary executor. Otherwise my wife and David Houston will take charge of my writings. For the first time I pray that they may bring in some profit at last. My wife will want money from every source.

Yesterday at my Court-martial, in rebutting some trifling evidence, I made a statement as to my negotiations for surrender with General Lowe. On hearing it read after it struck me that it might sound like an appeal. It was not such. I made no appeal, no recantation, no apology for my acts. In what I said I merely claimed that I acted honourably and thoroughly in all that I set myself to do. My enemies have, in return, treated me in an unworthy manner. But that can pass. It is a great and glorious thing to die for Ireland and I can well forget all petty annoyances in the splendour of this. When my son, Don, was born I thought that to him and not to me would this be given. God has been kinder to me than I hoped. My son will have a great name.

To my son Don. My darling little boy, remember me kindly. Take my hope and purpose with my deed. For your sake and for the sake of your beloved mother and sister I would wish to live long, but you will recognise the thing I have done, and see this as a consequence. I think still I have done a great thing for Ireland, and, with the defeat of her army, won the first step of her freedom. God bless you, my son.

My darling daughter, Barbara, God bless you. I loved you more than ever a child has been loved.

My dearest love, Muriel, thank you a million times for all you have been to me. I have only one trouble in leaving life—leaving you so. Be brave, darling, God will assist and bless you. Goodbye, kiss my darlings for me. I send you the few things I have saved out of this war. Goodbye, my love, till we meet again in Heaven. I have a sure faith of our union there. I kiss this paper that goes to you. I have just heard that they have not been able to reach you. Perhaps it is better so. Yet Father Aloysius is going to make another effort to do something. God help and sustain you, my love. But for your suffering this would be all joy and glory. Goodbye.

Your loving husband,

THOMAS MACDONAGH.

I return the darlings' photographs. Goodbye, my love.[19]

(This document is in the possession of Barbara MacDonagh, Mrs. Liam Redmond.)

Father Augustine, O.F.M.Cap., wrote:

"....Wednesday, 3rd May, 1916. P. H. Pearse, T. MacDonagh and Tom Clarke were shot this morning about 3.25, the two former being attended by Father Aloysius and the last by Father Columbus. Father Aloysius was driven in an open motor car to Basin Lane Convent to fetch Sister M. Francesca, MacDonagh's sister, who, on leaving him for the last time, flung her Rosary round his neck. (Father Aloysius called for it on the following morning.)[20] That evening Father Albert and myself went to the house on the North Circular Road where we heard the chief English officers were staying and asked if there were to be executions on the following morning so that we might be prepared. We heard that there were to be four. . . ."

In *The Catholic Bulletin* of July, 1916, it was reported that a Catholic priest[21] had written about MacDonagh:

"He received the last rites of his Church with the utmost reverence from a priest who was his friend; he knelt for a long time in prayer on the bare floor of his cell in Kilmainham Jail with the Crucifix clasped in his hands....Thomas MacDonagh died as he had lived, with no rancour in his heart, with his courage high and unshaken, and with a firm faith in the Saviour by whose Precious Blood we are redeemed. May he rest in peace. . . ."

---

[1] *The Catholic Bulletin*, April-May, 1917.
[2] They surrendered at the College of Surgeons and were marched from there to Dublin Castle and thence to Richmond Barracks.
[3] In his "Personal Recollections", *Capuchin Annual*, 1966.

[4]Father Augustine says "12 o'clock noon".

[5]According to Father Aloysius ("Recollections"), an apron of one of the Jacob's workers tied to a brush-handle.

[6]It was at this stage—3.15 p.m.—that MacDonagh countersigned the surrender order, see above.

[7]Séamus Ó Murchadha, Captain, "A" Company, Adjutant, 4th Battalion, in the course of a statement, in response to enquiries by the Editor.

[8]This was The Fountain, James's Street.

[9]Father Augustine referred to this also when speaking of the death of Ceannt.

[10]In a statement to the Editor. See also *Capuchin Annual*, 1966.

[11]Savonarola.

[12]Unless Mr. Robertson had access to the Court Martial documents, which is unlikely, he could not have known if the statement was bogus or otherwise.

[13]Inspector Mills was killed, 10 June, 1917, by a blow of a camán, wielded by a Fianna boy, as police batoned crowds who protested at the arrest of Cathal Brugha and Count Plunkett, speakers at a meeting in Beresford Place in support of the 1916 prisoners' demands for political treatment.

[14]*Thom's Directory*, 1916, shows the occupant as Mr. Thomas Barber.

[15]In statements to the Editor.

[16]*Irish Press*, 6 April, 1956.

[17]In a statement to the editor.

[18]John MacDonagh was removed from Richmond Barracks on 2 May, and lodged in Knutsford Detention Barracks on 3 May.

[19]The manuscript is difficult to decipher in parts and some of the readings are doubtful.

[20]Sister Francesca later recalled this incident.

"Thomas kissed the beads," she said, "and placed them around his neck. As I turned to ask the British Officer, who was standing by, if I could get the beads back, Thomas said quietly: 'They will be shot to bits.'"

When Fr. Aloysius returned the Rosary to her six beads were missing.—Ed.

[21]Father Aloysius, no doubt, who attended MacDonagh.

And see bibliographical note p. x.

ÉAMONN Ó DÁLAIGH   EDWARD DALY

After Nurse Elizabeth O'Farrell had brought the surrender order to the G.P.O. Garrison in Moore Street on Saturday, 29 April, she proceeded towards the Four Courts. She was stopped several times on the way by British officers and, one officer having refused to let her pass on any condition, she was forced to return to Moore Street where she was provided with an escort. With the escort she got as far as a barricade in Little Mary Street from where she proceeded alone. In Chancery Street she met Father Columbus, O.F.M.Cap., of Church Street. Father Columbus accompanied her to a side entrance to the Four Courts.

"We called in for some Volunteers," Nurse O'Farrell recalled,[1] "and saw Captain ————.[2] We told him we had a message for Commandant Daly. He told us we would have to go round to the Quays to the corner of Church Street. This we did and found Commandant Daly firmly entrenched there. I gave him the order and told him of the Headquarters surrender. He was very much cut up about it but accepted his orders as a soldier should. He walked back with us to the side entrance. By this time the news had got about of the surrender and several officers of the Republican Army were down at the railings waiting for us. Having delivered the message I returned to O'Connell Street ....It was then about 7.15 p.m...."

Desmond Ryan recounts that at "about six o'clock on Saturday evening Daly told Piaras Béaslai with tears in his eyes that he had received orders from Pearse to surrender. When he announced it to his men there were cries of 'Fight it out!' Daly answered: 'That is what I would like to do but as a soldier I must obey Pearse's order'...."

Piaras Béaslai recalled the same incident:[3]

"....a priest arrived with the news of the surrender, and finally Pearse's signed order to surrender was conveyed to Commandant Daly. He showed it to me and his eyes filled with tears. He had borne himself like a gallant soldier through the week of fighting. Again he rose to this fresh test of soldiership. He checked the

65

Éamonn Ó Dálaigh   Edward Daly

1891–1916

murmurings of those who objected to surrender by an appeal to discipline. They must obey the orders of the Commander-in-Chief, however unwelcome. He impressed the English officers with his dignity. They permitted him to march at the head of his men as they brought us through the empty streets (where the few people we saw were those that cursed us) to where other bodies of prisoners were assembled in O'Connell Street. And when the English General asked: 'Who is in charge of these men?'—referring to his own officers—Daly proudly answered: 'I am. At all events I was'—a remark which, he must have known, signed his death-warrant."

Éamon Dore of the G.P.O. Garrison was already a prisoner and, with the other prisoners, was standing near the Parnell Monument facing down O'Connell Street, "when," he says,[4] "we saw a column of prisoners far down turning into O'Connell Street and marching towards us. As they came nearer we could see the men, with Commandant Daly in front, marching in perfect formation, rifles on shoulders, and quite calm-looking. As they came up towards us they were directed to the Gresham Hotel and lined up two deep. General Lowe and his aide, de Courcy Wheeler, were standing beside our group and Lowe told Wheeler to go over and order them to lay down their rifles. When he did so Daly stood in front of his men and we could hear his shout of command and his normal drill order which was carried out in such a perfectly soldierly manner that we were as proud as hell, and Wheeler, apparently, was so carried away that he and Daly exchanged salutes. I could hear Lowe saying, half to himself: 'God! Saluting a rebel!'"

Shortly afterwards Daly was ordered to march his men to join the men of the G.P.O. Garrison and, an hour or so later, all were marched to the plot in front of the Rotunda Hospital.

There, as has been stated, Daly, with Clarke and Mac Diarmada, was singled out for special ill-treatment.

Next morning he was marched with the rest to Richmond Barracks.

Bhí Éamonn Ó Dálaigh i measc na bpríosúnach ar cuireadh Liam Ó Briain isteach leo nuair a tógadh eisean go Beairic Risteamain an tráthnóna Domhnaigh sin. "Bhí Éamonn Ó Dálaigh ann," adeir sé, "as Luimneach, fear ceannais an Chéad Chatha . . . saighdiúir *debonair* ar chuma sa diabhal leis, déarfá,

céard a thiocfadh, bás nó beatha: bhí a dhualgas déanta, a
chuid orduithe comhlíonta aige, b'shin a raibh ann. . . ."

Chaith Liam Ó Briain an oíche sin leis an dream príosúnach
a raibh Éamonn ina measc, agus an oíche dar gcionn.

". . . .Ní raibh duine ba mhó a raibh iompar saighdiúra faoi
ná Éamonn Ó Dálaigh. . . .Shiúladh sé sráideanna na cathrach,
é féin agus comrádaí leis, Séamas Ó Súilleabháin, as Luimneach
freisin, agus éide oifigigh d'Óglaigh na hÉireann go péacach
orthu agus claidheamh feistithe go córach ar a gcliathán, agus
bheannaíodh saighdiúirí Sasanacha go míleata dhóibh ar an sráid
istoíche, mar cheapaidis go mba oifigigh dá gcuid féin iad! Bhí sé
tar éis bheith i gceannas ar na Ceithre Cúirteanna. Bhí troid
maith déanta aige agus bhreathnaigh sé anois agus é ina
phríosúnach go sásta leis féin agus leis an saol. Is meidhreach
meanmnach a thug sé amhrán dúinn an oíche sin, *When a man's
in love,* ceann de chuid Gilbert and Sullivan, agus is dearbh
liom gur bhreathnaigh sé chomh sásta céanna agus é ag siúl
amach chun a bháis cupla lá nó trí ina dhiaidh sin. . . ."

Tried by Court Martial in Richmond Barracks, probably on
3 May, Daly was transferred to Kilmainham that evening.

Towards midnight on 3 May, 1916, Daly's sister, Mrs. Tom
Clarke, received a message from Kilmainham:

> Kilmainham Prison,
> May 3rd, 1916.

Mrs. Clarke,
10 Richmond Ave.,
Dublin.
Madam,

I beg to inform you that your brother is a prisoner in the
above prison & would like to see you tonight. I am sending
a car with an attendant to bring you here.

> I am, Madam,
> Your obedient servant,
> W. S. Lennon
> Major
> Commdt.

In the early hours of the morning of 4 May, Mrs. Clarke, with
two of her sisters, Madge and Laura Daly, visited Edward Daly
in his cell.

Miss Madge Daly wrote an account of the visit, hitherto, so
far as the editor is aware, unpublished.

Because of the illness of our uncle,[5] and because the train services were dislocated, myself and my sister, Laura, could not get to Dublin until the afternoon of the 3rd May, 1916. We went to the residence of our sister, Kathleen,[6] in Richmond Avenue. When she opened the door to us she immediately burst out crying. She had prayed all morning, she said, for God to send her some of her own people—she had been alone all during her own trouble. She told us that Tom had been shot that morning and that Ned, Seán, and all our other friends would probably be shot too.

This was a stunning blow to us, but, somehow, my first feeling, on hearing that Ned would probably be shot, was one of relief— relief that his martyrdom would be short, and that he would not live to go through hell as an Irish political convict, as our uncle and his Fenian comrades, Tom Clarke and James F. Egan, had.

Our sister told us all that had happened and we consoled her as best we could. We were worn out when we got to bed that night but determined to save what strength we had so that we could face bravely whatever trials God had decreed for us.

Our test came sooner than we expected.

Shortly before midnight my sister jumped up and called to us that there was a military car outside. There was a knock at the door and when Kathleen opened it a policeman handed her a permit to visit her brother. We all got up. Myself and Laura seemed the veriest cowards. We were shaking all over. Our hands refused to work and it was only with the greatest difficulty and delay that we managed to get into our clothes. At last we were ready and were escorted by the policeman and two soldiers to the car, more dead than alive. The drive was terrible. It seemed endless. We were held up over and over again—every dozen yards or so, it seemed—and the car was surrounded by soldiers with fixed bayonets. They pointed their rifles into the car and put their lanterns to our faces to examine us. But we were not afraid of *them*. Our only fear was that we would not be able to bear up before our brother as would become the sisters of a hero and the daughters and nieces of Fenians. We prayed to God for strength, but, for all that, we were all the time trembling and could not keep back the tears.

God heard our prayers, for the minute we passed through the gates of Kilmainham and faced the soldiers there, our pride of race and our pride in the sacrifices of our heroes gave us strength. We walked in with heads erect and told our names with pride. We could have faced death—anything! As we were led into the entrance hall of the Jail a soldier called out: " Relatives of Daly, to be shot in the morning."

At first, the Commandant ordered that we should be taken in one at a time; so we decided that Kathleen should go first, then

I, and Laura last. She was Ned's special chum. But the Commandant changed his mind and we were let go in together.

We were escorted by five soldiers. One of them carried a candle-lantern. We were taken through a passage and up what seemed an endless stairs running up the centre of a big hall, then along a corridor to a cell with the number "66" on a tin or metal tab at the side of the door. I did not observe any other details at the time. One of the soldiers called "Daly!" in a gruff voice. Ned's voice answered "Yes" just as gruffly. As the door was opened our boy got up from the floor where he had been lying on a half-blanket or rug. He was dressed in his Volunteer uniform, minus cap, belt, bandolier, sword, etc., and looked so proud and strong and noble with eyes alert and full of the fire of enthusiasm that it was hard to believe that he was a captive doomed to be shot in a few short hours. He looked more like a brave young knight who had won some great victory. (And so he had, of course, for he and his comrades had saved the soul of Ireland.)

We rushed to him and twined our arms around him; and so stood in the centre of the cell all during our interview, surrounded by soldiers with their bayonets fixed. How long the interview lasted I do not know. The officer in charge told us that anything we might say would be regarded as private, but our talk, except in one or two instances, was all of Ireland.

My first words were: "Oh! Ned! Why are they giving you the highest honours? You must have done great work to earn a place with Tone and Emmet and all the others." He said: "I did my best." Then he spoke of the great fight and, in glowing terms, of all the men, especially those in his own command. Such soldiers, such heroes, never lived, he said. They never lost heart until the order to surrender came. Then big, strong men cried like children and rebelled too, against the order.

Speaking of himself, he said he was glad and proud to die for his country; that he knew that the week's fight would bring new life to Ireland; that he felt an absolute conviction, facing his God in a few hours, that the next effort would bring victory; that his only regret was that he would not be there to take part in it. I told him how proud our uncle, our mother and sisters would be when they heard that England had given him a martyr's crown. I said that his spirit and name would live on; that we would try to follow in his footsteps and that one day we would all be together in another world. He replied " Yes," that thought would give him added joy.

He spoke in the warmest terms of Tom Clarke, P. H. Pearse and Tom MacDonagh, for whom he had a particular admiration. When I told him that those three had gone that morning he said: "We'll have a glorious meeting in Heaven."

He gave us a copy of the charge at his Court Martial:

Did an act, to wit: Did take part in an armed rebellion
and in the waging of war against His Majesty the King, such
act being of such a nature as to be calculated to be prejudicial to the Defence of the Realm and being done with the
intention of and for the purpose of assisting the enemy.

He said he had protested strongly against the part of the charge
about "assisting the enemy"; that all he did, and he did his very
best, was for Ireland, his own land, to try to free her from the
only enemy he knew—England; and that he acted, as he was
bound to do, as a soldier of Ireland, in all matters under the
orders of his superior officers. He also added that he had only
one regret—the surrender; that if he had not understood it to
be an honourable one, he and his men would have fought on
to the end. He mentioned that he had had a large number of
English soldiers and some officers as prisoners and that he gave
them the best he had. Here Laura exclaimed: "Why didn't you
shoot them as they're shooting you?" "Ah no, Laura," he said.
"That wouldn't be playing the game. We got strict orders that
everyone captured was to be treated under the rules of civilised
warfare as a prisoner-of-war and as kindly as possible under the
conditions. In every case those orders were strictly carried out."
    He sent loving messages to his mother, to his aunt and to his
sisters. He said: "Tell Uncle John I did my best." Then he
gave us a small purse with a few coins, two pencils, and buttons
off his uniform as mementoes.
    We asked him had he been given food or drink and he said:
"Oh yes, I have food," and pointed to what, to me, looked like
dog-biscuits thrown on the floor.
    A soldier called "Time up!" and our interview was at an end.
We kissed and embraced our boy, once only, and walked from
the cell without a tear or moan, our heads up. Looking back
now I wonder how we bore up. But God helped us, and Ned
too, with his great courage and heart. The cell door banged
behind us and we walked down the endless stairs. I felt Laura's
steps faltering and, fearing she would faint, whispered to her:
"Keep up. You mustn't break down here." She answered, in a
whisper too, "I'll be all right."
    When we reached the entrance hall there were two pale girls
waiting there, seemingly on a like errand to ours. They rushed
to us and asked; "Who are you? Who have you been to see?"
    We told them. When they heard of Ned's fate one of them
moaned "Oh! Mícheál!" They were the O'Hanrahan sisters.
They had got a permit to visit their brother and understood
he was being deported. They were quite unprepared for his
death. I learned afterwards that they bore themselves bravely
until they left their brother. Then one of the sisters fainted.
    Before leaving the Jail we put in formal claims for the bodies

of Tom Clarke and Ned. We asked if they could not be given
to us if we sent in coffins, so that they could be identified and
laid to rest with their own. We also claimed our men's tunics
and belongings.

We later received a formal refusal to our request for the bodies
but no reply at all to our other request.

When we got to the Jail gate, escorted by an officer, the car
to take us home could not be got, so we were taken back into
an office to wait. The officer there—he was kind—told us we
had his deepest sympathy but said he could not understand
our outlook or that of the prisoners.

I replied that he was probably English and loved his country
and I asked him how would he feel if Germany won the War and
took possession of England. If he could vision that, I said, he
would understand how we felt about the conquerors of our
country.

After a short delay the car arrived and we were led out to it by
some soldiers and then driven back to our sister's home.

The rest of that night is our own—and God's, but we did not
miss one moment of agony. We counted every second until dawn
when our hero's soul flew to its reward.

In an account of the visit, with her two sisters, to her brother,
Mrs. Tom Clarke says:[8]

". . . .When I saw Ned I had two of my sisters with me and we
got only a quarter of an hour with him. Five young army officers
accompanied us to his cell and seemed very hostile to him. The
interview was so short we had no time to do much more than
kiss Ned good-bye. . . .My sister, Madge, may remember more
than I as she had more opportunity to speak to Ned, because
when the officers tried to get into the cell with us I blocked the
door for a few minutes to give Ned a chance to say anything
he might want to say that he wouldn't want the officers to hear.
I did hear Ned say: 'It doesn't matter—we had planned to go
out on a job on Saturday night[9] in which we all (1st Battalion)
expected to go down'. . . .

When I was kissing Ned good-bye he said: 'Have you got
Tom's body?' I said: 'No, but I have made a request for it and
have told Madge to do the same for you.'

She did make the request and, about a week later, received
a letter from the British saying they could not accede to it as
the body was then already buried. Ned was alive when Madge
made the request. . . ."

Another sister, Nora (Mrs. Éamon Dore), had been in the
G.P.O. until the Wednesday of Easter Week when she was sent

to Cork with a message to the Volunteers there. As it was then impossible for her to get back to Dublin she made her way to Limerick. She was there when her sisters, Madge and Laura, set out for Dublin on the morning of 3 May, 1916.

She recalls[10] what her sisters told her of their visit to Kilmainham :

"They got the first train out of Limerick to Dublin on the morning of 3 May to try to get some news. We had had no news from Dublin while the Rising was on as Dublin had been cut off from the rest of the country. (I was in Dublin until Wednesday morning, 26 April.)

When they arrived in Dublin they got a cab to my sister's house in Fairview. The cabman had to get a permit from the British military to drive across the city. . . .That night a military car came to Mrs. Clarke's house and she was given a permit to see her brother. My two other sisters insisted on going too. They had a long fight as the permit was for one only. When they arrived at Kilmainham there was a long delay. At first they were told they could see my brother only one at a time. Then the military changed their minds and let them in together. When they went into the cell Ned was asleep on the floor with what looked like a dog-biscuit beside him. (There was no place to sleep but on the floor.) The soldier who led them in had to shake Ned by the shoulder to waken him. He had got no sleep for the week of the fighting and so was exhausted.[11] He seemed as cool as ever he was. He told them that he had given the large sum of money he had in gold—which our uncle had insisted on giving him—to Captain Lindsay to give to our mother. He had given Captain Lindsay his watch as a reward. Ned had in his pockets only two pencils which he had used during the week, a note-case and a pipe. He took the buttons off his sleeves and gave them to my sisters with the other things. I have one of the buttons and one of the pencils still. . . .They talked calmly and said 'Good-bye' when it was time to leave, without anyone breaking down.

Madge, my eldest sister, on the drive over to Kilmainham, had asked Our Lady to give them the grace she had got at the foot of the Cross and Our Lady must have answered her prayer, for Laura was a very excitable girl, and she adored Ned, but even she remained calm. I think it was a minor miracle.

Laura asked the British authorities to be allowed send in a coffin but was refused. She then asked if she could have Ned's uniform but was told he was to be buried in it. Captain Lindsay did not send the money to my mother. My sister, Madge, went to British Headquarters and threatened, if the money was not returned at once, to have leaflets printed and handed out telling of the lack of honour in the British Army. The money was returned but not in gold. . . ."

Another sister, Carrie, has confirmed[12] that Madge and Laura told of finding Ned asleep on the floor of his cell.

"He was apparently worn out after his very strenuous week," she says. "He was full of pride of the week's work and of all the men who had fought with him. He had no illusions about what would be his fate after the surrender. Tom Clarke had told his wife the night before when she visited him that Ned would be the next to go."

A "Catholic Priest"[13] writing in July, 1916,[14] gave the following account of his meeting with Daly immediately before his execution:

". . . .I remember well seeing him coming down from the prison cell where he had been to Confession and received Holy Communion. He was calm and brave as when he was with his men in the Church Street area and wished to be remembered to the Sisters of Charity, Brunswick Street, who were known to him and had been very kind. As I shook his hand for the last time I felt intensely all that was meant by marching out blindfolded to his death, such a gentle, noble, brave young Irishman."

---

[1] *The Catholic Bulletin*, May, 1917.
[2] Possibly Captain Frank Fahy.
[3] *Dublin's Fighting Story*. (Kerryman, 1949)
[4] In a statement to the editor.
[5] John Daly, veteran Fenian.
[6] Mrs. Tom Clarke.
[7] Seán Mac Diarmada.
[8] In a letter to the Editor.
[9] The reference to "Saturday night" here is obscure. Perhaps it should read "Sunday," the day originally fixed for the Rising.
[10] In a letter to the editor.
[11] Others would attribute his sound sleep to his serenity and lack of concern for his fate.
[12] In a letter to the Editor.
[13] This was either Father Albert, O.F.M.Cap., or Father Sebastian, O.F.M.Cap. There were four priests in Kilmainham that morning—Fathers Augustine, Columbus, Albert and Sebastian. Father Augustine did not see Daly; Father Columbus attended him.
[14] *The Catholic Bulletin.*
And see bibliographical note p. x.

LIAM MAC PIARAIS   WILLIAM PEARSE

The Pearse brothers were inseparable.

Le Roux, describing the events of Easter Sunday, records that "Willie had never been out of his brother's sight for a fortnight." The brothers were together at the fateful meeting in Liberty Hall that morning and, on Sunday afternoon, went together to St. Enda's to bid a last farewell to their mother. In the General Post Office, William, a Staff Captain attached to the Headquarters Staff, acted as aide-de-camp to his brother, the Commander-in-Chief. Éamon Dore tells[1] that Willie never left his brother's side all that week. Diarmuid Lynch records, in respect of Wednesday, 26 April, that "frequent visits were made to the G.P.O. parapet by Willie Pearse, to whose Company[2] most of the defenders belonged, and by the Commander-in-Chief." And, referring also to Wednesday, Desmond Ryan had this to say :

"Pearse and his brother pass along the roof after their return from a tour of the O'Connell Street positions, where they both had some close escapes from flying bullets. As they arrive a Volunteer officer, Lieutenant Michael Boland, has just issued an order for the hundredth time in genial tone to his men to keep under the cover of planks and sandbags. . . .Pearse, impassive and confident, in his green uniform, grows so absorbed with a survey of the Volunteers visible on guard in the Imperial[3] and Metropole and adjoining houses, at the hostile and noisy nests of snipers and machine-guns beyond the Liffey, at mounting flame and debris from the Parnell Monument to O'Connell Bridge that Boland in alarm raps out a special appeal to Pearse himself to keep under cover. Pearse smiles, thanks him, promises the men on the roof who had been on duty without sleep since Monday afternoon that they will be relieved shortly, and passes on. 'A curious business,' comments William Pearse in his slow, lisping voice as he looks in passing at the fires and chaos in view, 'I wonder how it will end? I know a lot of good work has been done but there is a great deal more to do.' There is a melancholy and patient look in his sensitive dark brown eyes . . . ."

It was at this stage—Wednesday evening—that Patrick wrote

Liam Mac Piarais   William Pearse
1881-1916

a message to his mother (see above) and William added a footnote.

Message to his Mother from the General Post Office, 26 April, 1916

Have really nothing to say. We are still here. Don't worry. I saw a priest again (Confession) and was talking to Fr. Bowden also.

WILLIE

William, ever at his brother's side, was one of the group around the bed of the wounded Connolly in 16 Moore Street when on Saturday afternoon it was decided to seek terms.

He came out of the room and told Desmond Ryan of the proposal—" 'to save the men from slaughter, for slaughter it is.' He shook his head sadly, and then sighed with relief at the thought that the men might be saved. . . . 'Say nothing yet,' says William Pearse, 'as it may not come to anything.' He returns and asks for a safety razor for his brother. Pearse arrives. He looks firm and sad and cannot speak. His brother gives him a razor. . . ."

When finally the G.P.O. Garrison marched out from Moore Street to surrender, they were headed, Ryan says, by William Pearse and Joseph Plunkett "with waving white flags as if they were banners of victory."

William Pearse spent Saturday night with his comrades outside the Rotunda Hospital and, on Sunday morning, marched with them to Richmond Barracks.

Casadh Liam Ó Briain leis ansin tráthóna an lae chéanna:

". . . .Cé eile a bhí ann?" adeir sé, "Fear óg a raibh gruaig sách fada air, féachaint bhrionglóideach ina shúile, cuma an calaíontóra air agus é ag caitheamh culaith na nÓglach: Liam Mac Piarais, deartháir Phádraic. . . ."

Chodail siad in aice lena chéile an oíche sin:

". . . .Tháinig Liam Mac Piarais agus luigh sé síos ar thaobh mo chiotóige agus a cheann ar an urlár. Chuaigh sé a chodladh ar an bpointe. . . .Bhí an Piarsach óg ag tiontó ó thaobh go taobh ar mo láimh chlé, agus é an-chorraithe cé go raibh sé ina chodladh. . . .ar ais in Oifig an Phoist ina chuid bhrionglóidí. . . . thugadh sé scread beag 'The fire! The fire! anois agus arís. . . ."

Scaradh ó chéile iad an lá dar gcionn agus ní fhaca siad a
chéile riamh arís.

It seems that Patrick Pearse, having despaired of meeting his
mother (see his last letter, above) or, possibly, having been
advised by the British military that their efforts to bring her to
him had failed,[4] asked that his brother be sent for, for William
was, in fact, brought to Kilmainham and was there at the time
of his brother's execution. (See his statement to his sister and
his mother, below.) He did not meet his brother, however, and
heard only the volley which sent him into eternity.

It is more than likely that William Pearse had, at that stage,
already been courtmartialled and that he would have been
brought to Kilmainham later the same day in any event, as
happened in the case of Joseph Mary Plunkett who, tried on
2 May, was executed with William Pearse on 4 May.

Leon Ó Broin tells[5] that William Pearse "insisted at the Court
Martial that he had been immersed in the plans of the Rising
from the beginning." And Ó Broin quotes Desmond Ryan as
having heard from eyewitnesses that "Willie Pearse practically
condemned himself to death by the exultant attitude he
adopted at the Court Martial."

Only an examination of the Court Martial documents, held
with the papers of the British Judge-Advocate-General's Office in
the Public Records Office in London, will reveal the date and
what actually took place at the trial of William Pearse.

*   *   *

In the early hours of the morning of 4 May, William Pearse
was visited in his cell in Kilmainham by his mother and sister.

His sister, Senator Margaret Pearse, wrote an account[6] of
the visit:

"....On the morning of Low Sunday we heard of the sur-
render, and then no news whatever until the following
Wednesday, 3rd May, when at about ten o'clock a.m. the Rev.
Father Aloysius arrived to break to us the terrible news that
Pat had made the supreme sacrifice—that he had died that
morning at a quarter to four.

I cannot describe how we received the news more than to say
that all the light and joy of life seemed to have gone from us

in those few moments. Father Aloysius consoled, advised and strengthened us. He gave us details of the last hours, told us how bravely Pat, Tom Clarke and Thomas MacDonagh had died. He mentioned also that Pat had asked that he (Father Aloysius) should be sent for to minister to them, and that a farewell letter written in his last moments was in the prison and would be given to mother.

The day passed somehow and towards midnight we were aroused from an attempt to get a few hours' rest by the arrival of a military lorry. I went to the hall-door and was given a note saying that the prisoner, William Pearse, desired to see us. At once I realised we were to lose Willie. I returned to the bedroom and said to mother: 'More bad news. Willie wants to see us, so he is going too.'

We dressed and accompanied the soldiers. The lorry broke down at Terenure; it seemed hours whilst it was being repaired. At last we arrived at Kilmainham. Another long delay before we were allowed up to the cell. We were given to understand that we must remain below until relatives of other prisoners should leave.

When our turn came we entered the cell and found Willie, standing, ready to receive us. There were three military officers with him, each holding a candle, the only available light. We talked quietly, calmly, and chiefly on personal matters—some letters and books about which Willie was anxious. We told him how proud we were of him and of Pat, and that we were satisfied they had done right.

One touching incident he told us. 'Last night,' he said, 'I had a terrible experience. I was in prison over there (indicating across the road) when a guard of soldiers came and brought me here. About half way over we heard shots. The men looked at each other, and one said: "Too late." I think they were bringing me here to see Pat, but we heard only the volley that took him.'

I asked him if the priest had been with him, telling him that Father Aloysius had been there on the previous night. Willie replied that he had asked for a priest but that so far none had come. When I mentioned Father Aloysius one of the officers immediately said: 'Yes, that clergyman is coming.' His reply was so quick that I felt it was not true, and that he was merely trying to reassure us. Our interview ended. We bade Willie a last good-bye, and left him gazing after us, one longing, sad look, till the cell door closed.

When we came down to the prison hall the letter from Pat was given to mother, together with a note concerning his books and manuscripts. Several things he had written on the previous night were withheld. These we never got.[7]

As I passed out I turned to the several officers who were in the

hall and said: 'Men, you will lose no time in sending for a
priest. There is only an hour now. Lose no time.' They assured
me they would send at once, which they did, to the Capuchin
Friary, Church Street. I understand they asked for four priests
and that four went to Kilmainham. However, I know for certain
that Father Augustine was with Willie until the end and that
Father Albert was also there.

There is no more for me to tell. . . .Though our sorrow and
our loss were very great indeed we were resigned. Pat and Willie,
so wonderfully united in life, were also united in death. We knew
that God in His loving mercy had reunited them in an eternity
of happiness, and that He, in His own good time, would grant
from the sacrifice of 1916 a glorious fruition."

A few weeks before she died, in 1932, Mrs. Margaret Pearse,
mother of the Pearses, recalled[8] the "touching incident" referred
to above by Senator Miss Pearse.

According to Mrs. Pearse: "Willie said: 'O Mother! You
have come. A terrible thing happened here last night. I was
brought across a yard. When we came to a gate the man with
me knocked, and the answer we got was: " You are too late."
On the minute the spirit in me grew strong. I never shed a tear.
There were seven men there and one officer. They had candles
in their hands.'

I spoke to Willie and said: 'Never mind, my boy. You will
soon be with Pat. Tell him that Mother will be braver than ever
and that she will carry her cross.'

That was my second and supreme sacrifice. Maggie and I
came home and we knelt in prayer until we knew all was over."

Father Augustine, O.F.M.Cap., wrote:

Thursday, 4th May, 1916: This morning, before 3 a.m., we
heard loud knocking at the Bow Street gate.[9] I went down at
once and the first words one of the soldiers said were: "You've
got to hurry, Sir, as we have but little time." I quickly called
Fathers Albert, Columbus and Sebastian and we started for
Kilmainham where the Governor told us that four were to be
executed—Edward Daly, Michael O'Hanrahan, Joseph Mary
Plunkett and Willie Pearse. The Governor told us that there
was not much time, but he had got a slight postponement of the
fixed hour so as to give us an opportunity of attending to the
men. Father Columbus, having met him before at the surrender,
naturally went to the first, Father Albert to the second, Father

Sebastian to the third and I to Willie Pearse whose hands were already tied behind his back.

He was beautifully calm, made his Confession as if he were doing it on an ordinary occasion, and received Holy Communion with great devotion. A few minutes later he stood before the firing squad and, with Our Lord in his heart, went to meet his noble brother in a better land.

Edward Daly I did not meet at all and he was, I feel sure, the first shot on this hurried morning. Willie Pearse was the second, Michael O'Hanrahan the third and Joseph Mary Plunkett the last.

---

[1]In a letter to the Editor.

[2]This was E Company of the 4th Battalion of the Dublin Brigade. To that Company, which included a number of senior students of Scoil Éanna (Pearses' bilingual school for boys), William Pearse belonged before his appointment as Staff Captain. Desmond Ryan was a member of the same Company.

[3]Now Clerys.

[4]Father Aloysius tells in his "Personal Recollections" (see App. II) that the military bringing him to Kilmainham late on the night of 2 May proposed to call, on the way, for Mrs. Pearse and Mrs. MacDonagh but were forced to turn back; and Mrs. Tom Clarke has stated (in a letter to the editor) that the driver of the car which brought her and her sisters to Kilmainham on the night of the 3rd to see their brother, Edward Daly, told her that he had tried to get to Mrs. Pearse the previous night "but was unable to reach Rathfarnham owing to continuous sniping."

[5]*Dublin Castle and the* 1916 *Rising: the story of Sir Matthew Nathan* (Helicon, 1966).

[6]*Capuchian Annual,* 1942.

[7]The above was written in 1942.

[8]*Irish Press,* 4 April, 1932.

[9]Of the Capuchin Friary, Church Street.

And see bibliographical note p. x.

Mícheál Ó hAnnracháin   Michael O'Hanrahan
1877–1916

MÍCHEÁL O hANNRACHÁIN
MICHAEL O'HANRAHAN

Michael O'Hanrahan, a member of Jacob's Garrison, surrendered with them, on the afternoon of Sunday, 30 April, 1916, and was taken to Richmond Barracks.

There John McDonald, another member of the Garrison, recalls[1] having seen the O'Hanrahan brothers[2] "crying together, locked in each other's arms."

Tried by Court Martial on either the 2nd or 3rd May—more likely the 2nd, the day on which Plunkett, who was executed, with him, on the 4th, was tried—he was transferred to Kilmainham and was visited there, in the early hours of the morning of 4 May, by two of his sisters, one of whom, Eily, now Mrs. O'Hanrahan O'Reilly, has written an account of the visit.

It was after midnight, the early hours of Thursday, the 4th of May, 1916, when I was awakened by the ringing of the doorbell of our home at 67 Connaught Street, Phibsboro, where I lived with my mother, two sisters and my two brothers, Mícheál and Harry, all of us sharing with each other the joys and sorrows of life as they came—a happy, happy home.

There, when the call came, a little over a week previously—it seemed an eternity ago to us—Mícheál and Harry had donned their uniforms and gone out to join in the fight for Ireland's freedom. They were with the Jacob's Garrison and surrendered with Tom MacDonagh and the rest. (Mícheál and Tom MacDonagh were intimate friends.)

As the ringing of the bell continued I jumped from my bed and ran to the window. Outside—I shall never forget it!—were lorries full of English soldiers and D.M.P. men.

We opened the door and a note was handed in: "Mr. O'Hanrahan, a prisoner in Kilmainham, wishes to see his mother and sisters before his deportation to England."

This was a terrible shock to us, particularly to Mother, as we had no idea where my brothers had been since the surrender.

We decided that two of us—one of my sisters and myself—would go to Kilmainham.

There was curfew. We were driven to Kilmainham Jail through pitch-black streets, halted constantly all along the route by British soldiers on guard.

After a terrifying drive we arrived at the Jail and were conducted to a room off the front hall, to the left. The room, lit by a flickering, naked gas light, had once been white-washed but now looked grey and dirty. We were told to wait there. After about half an hour we saw, through the door, which was open, three young women on their way out—Mrs. Tom Clarke and her sisters who had been to see their brother, Ned Daly. They told us Ned was to be shot at dawn.

We were horror-stricken, overcome, as we realised that the same fate must await our own brother.

It took us some time to regain our composure. Then six soldiers arrived, one of them carrying an old lantern. In darkness, except for the light of the lantern, they conveyed us along some corridors and up an iron stairs to the cells on the second floor of a large hall. On the way one of the soldiers told us that Mícheál was to be executed.

Mícheál's cell—it was No. 67—was in absolute darkness and was empty except for a bucket and a sack on the floor in one corner. We rushed forward into Mícheál's outstretched arms.

He asked us if we knew why we had been brought there. We told him we had just heard from a British soldier.

Mícheál was his usual calm gentle self. He seemed to have no fear of the death awaiting him. His chief concern was his mother and us, his sisters. He asked us to try to find out where Harry was and, through us, sent to him, to Mother, and to our sister, who had stayed behind with her, " his heart's love and his promise to remember them in God's home above."

We had been warned that we must speak only of personal matters, but several times I tried to slip out little bits of information to him. Each time I was immediately cautioned—"Just a few minutes! "

However, I did get to tell him that Pat Pearse, Tom Clarke and Tom MacDonagh had gone on the morning of the 3rd, and managed to say quietly: "Ned Daly is going with you, Mícheál, at dawn."

Time was running out we were curtly told. Mícheál said he wished to make his will. A broken old table and chair and a stump of a candle were brought in by two soldiers and the will was written by Mícheál and witnessed by two of his jailers. I have it still.

Then I asked Mícheál had he had anything to eat. He said he had been given bully-beef at 4 o'clock. (That was some ten hours before.) I asked had he even had a drink of water. He hadn't. Though I was myself at the point of collapse at the strain I demanded—I was desperate—that a drink of water be brought to him. I was surprised at the speed with which my request was answered. One of the soldiers rushed off and came back in no time with water in a black billy-can. Mícheál drank it from the can.

Our chief worry, before leaving him, was that a priest should be with him. He assured us that he had already asked for a priest and was expecting one at any moment. This was a great, great comfort to us.

Then we bade Mícheál good-bye. We had been with him only a few minutes in all.

We were driven home through the dark streets again, and when we got there Mother's one question was: "When will I hear from my boy?" We could not bring ourselves to tell her the real truth, so, later in the morning, said we were going to Mass in St. Peter's but, instead, rushed over to Church Street to get Father Augustine to come to break the awful news to her. We met him in Church Street on his way to our home and he, like the wonderful priest, patriot and friend that he was, brought us back with him to the Friary and tried to console us. Then, when we did control our sorrow, he walked back home with us. We waited outside, on his instructions, until he had told all to Mother.

Then we went in, mo bhrón, to a home of mourning.

It will be noted that the message brought to the O'Hanrahan home told that " Mr. O'Hanrahan, prisoner in Kilmainham, wishes to see his mother and sisters before his deportation to England."

The O'Hanrahan sisters had no idea that their brother was about to be executed until they met, at Kilmainham, Madge and Laura Daly and Mrs. Tom Clarke, who were leaving the Jail having bade farewell to their brother, Edward. (See Miss Madge Daly's account, above.) It was only when they heard that Edward Daly was to be executed that it struck them that the same fate awaited Michael. (Mrs. Tom Clarke has told[3] of the efforts of herself and her sisters, distressed though they themselves were, to prepare the O'Hanrahan sisters "for something worse than deportation" for Michael.)

The wrong message was an extraordinary as it was an inexplicable error. None of the deportees, even those whose death sentences had been commuted to penal servitude, some for life, was given an opportunity to meet his people.

Confirming that the cell in which Michael O'Hanrahan spent his last hours in Kilmainham was No. 67, Mrs. O'Hanrahan O'Reilly writes:[4]

Yes. "67" seems to have always been mixed in and out of our

D

lives. Father was a '67 man. 67 Connaught Street was our home up to the Rising. Mícheál was executed from Cell No. 67, and, after sentence was passed on Harry, he was put into the same cell from which Mícheál had been taken to be shot. The late Tom Hunter[5] was in the next cell and he "tapped" on the wall in code a message to Harry that Mícheál had been taken from there for execution. When they were released from Portland poor Tom came straight to visit us and told us the same.

The Will of Michael O'Hanrahan, written in Kilmainham, 4 May, 1916

I, Micheal O hAnnrachain, give and bequeath all my rights in "A Swordsman of the Brigade"[6] to my mother & after her to my sisters.

MICHEAL O HANNRACHAIN
Kilmainham
4/5/16

May 4th, 16

T. Wright,[7] S.M.
M.P.S.C.
B. L. Barnett[7] Lieut.
59th Sig.Co.R.E.

Father Augustine, O.F.M.Cap wrote :

"....After I had left Willie Pearse I saw O'Hanrahan in his cell, and I now write here again what I wrote of him in another place shortly after he had laid down his life for Ireland: — 'He was one of the truest and noblest characters that it has ever been my privilege to meet. His last message to me before he went out into the dark corridor that led to the yard where he was shot was: "Father, I'd like you saw my mother and sisters and consoled them." I promised him I would, and, whispering something in his ear, I grasped the hands that were tied behind his back. In his right he pressed mine most warmly; we exchanged a look and he went forth to die.'
Turning from him I caught sight of Joseph Mary Plunkett who was standing....
We returned to the Friary after the executions and offered up Mass for the dear departed.
About 10.30, as I was going to fulfil my promise to Michael O'Hanrahan, I met his sisters in Church Street. They were

coming to see me. I returned with them and, in one of our parlours, tried to console them for the loss of such a brother. They were very brave and grateful, especially when I promised that I would call as soon as possible to see their mother.[8]

That afternoon I went to see their brother, Harry, in his cell at Kilmainham.

He asked me if I had seen his brother and I answered 'Yes.' 'Where is he, Father?' was the next question, and when I replied haltingly, while my heart stirred within me, that he was well, he suspected something and I then said I would tell him all; that I felt sure he would be man enough to bear it.

When I mentioned the first scene he leant his head against his right arm which was pressed against the wall and burst into tears and sobs.

It was perfectly natural, of course, and with a few cheery words from me, he quickly pulled himself together. I spoke on, and after some time, I promised to see him soon again and we parted.

The good God gave me the privilege of attending him later during his last illness in the Mater Misericordiae Hospital and of anointing him before his happy death. . . ."

---

[1]In a statement to the Editor.

[2]Michael and Henry. Henry was also sentenced to death but, in his case, the sentence was commuted to penal servitude for life.

[3]In a letter to the Editor.

[4]In a letter to the Editor.

[5]Thomas Hunter, of the Four Courts Garrison, was also sentenced to death but in his case, too, the sentence was commuted to penal servitude for life.

[6]*The Swordsman of the Brigade* is a book written by O'Hanrahan. He wrote others, e.g. *When the Normans Came* and *Irish Heroines*, which were published after his execution.

[7]Efforts have been made to trace Sergeant Major T. Wright and Lieut. B. L. Barnett, the witnesses to the Will, who might have been able to throw some light on events in Kilmainham in 1916. The British Army Records Centre, Hayes, Middlesex, advise that Lieutenant and Quartermaster Thomas Wright (formerly Sergeant Major, M.P.S.C.) died in 1960 and that Lieut. B. L. Barnett left the service with the rank of Captain in 1919. His last known address, 15 Aberdeen Road, Highbury Road, London N5, is, New Scotland Yard advise, now a derelict building.

[8]Father Augustine, in fact, returned home with the sisters and broke the sad news to their mother. (See Mrs. O'Hanrahan O'Reilly's account.)

And see bibliographical note p. x.

Íoseph Ó Pluingcéad   Joseph Mary Plunkett

1887–1916

IOSEPH Ó PLUINGCÉAD

JOSEPH MARY PLUNKETT

The Will of Joseph Mary Plunkett, 23 April, 1916

Will of Joseph Mary (Patrick) Plunkett made this day April 23rd 1916.

I give and bequeath everything of which I am possessed or may become possessed to Grace Evelyn (Mary Vandeleur) Gifford.

> Signed JOSEPH MARY PLUNKETT
> Witnessed George Oliver Plunkett.

The Will, it will be noted, was written on Easter Sunday, 1916, most likely some time after the momentous meeting of the Military Council in Liberty Hall at which it was decided, MacNeill's order cancelling the "manoeuvres" for Easter Sunday having totally disrupted the plans for a Rising that day, to strike at noon on Easter Monday, a decision which was tantamount to the signing of their own death-warrants by the members of the Military Council. They were also, of course, the signatories of the Proclamation and, when it was read by Pearse, the members of the Provisional Government.

The will is in the possession of Miss Maeve Donnelly.

Plunkett, who left a Mountjoy Square nursing home on Good Friday or Holy Saturday after an operation, on Easter Monday, though a very sick man—Éamon Dore says[1] "he looked dying"— marched from Liberty Hall with Pearse and Connolly at the head of the contingent of Irish Volunteers and Irish Citizen Army who took over the General Post Office.

In the Post Office he wrote notes during the week in his Field Message Book (now in the National Library). The book is composed of numbered leaves perforated for tearing. Pp. 1-52, 54-56, 61-64 have been removed, perhaps used for messages sent. Pp. 57 and 58 have been transposed in the course of a repair while the book was in private hands.

Entries in Field Message Book

(52) Easter Monday 1916.

GPO occupied in the name of the Republic shortly after noon (about 12.15 p.m.) Republic proclaimed.

About one hour later a detachment of enemy Lancers attempted to rush O'Connell Street. They were opposed at the Parnell Statue. A small number (described as "about 20") succeeded in advancing as far as the GPO but on our opening fire they retired in confusion leaving a few casualties. Simultaneously with our operation positions were successfully taken up in the front and rear of Dublin Castle, and troops in that stronghold prevented from coming out . . .

(58) 3rd Day.

Garriston[2] Police Barracks taken. No guns or ammunition. P.O. wrecked. 40 I.R.A. under Commandant Ashe (5th Batt.) moving on railway N of Gormanstown.[3]
Finglas   News from Navan says 200 I.R.A. moving on Dublin.

(57) Thursday, 4th Day of the Republic.

About one o'clock Commandant General Connolly was wounded in the left arm and ten minutes later in the left leg (by a sniper). The leg wound is serious as it caused a compound fracture of the shin bone.[4]

Thursday, 4th Day. One o'clock

The Linenhall Barracks, in the possession of the enemy, is on fire.

(59).

Signal to Imperial.

Cut way to Liffey St.

Food to Arnotts.

Order to remain at posts unless summoned.

Barricades in front.

(60).

Henry St.

Food.

There follow (66) an incomplete copy in Plunkett's handwriting of Lowe's message dated "29 April 1916 1.40 p.m." con cerning the surrender negotiations and (65) the incomplete copy or draft of a reply thereto. (See above.)

Some pages of the Field Message Book bore the "Circle and Sword" symbol rather like a Celtic cross, which Plunkett had used in his literary work.

Though Diarmuid Lynch records that "Plunkett lay seriously ill most of the week," Desmond Ryan tells that "during the worst stages of the shelling no one was more assiduous in keeping up the spirits of the defenders. He walked past the long line of men at the front windows, smiling carelessly, his sabre and pistol dancing merrily, calling out at intervals: 'one of the enemy's barracks is on fire!' He looked out at the raging conflagration which swept closer and closer in glaring circles, laughed and announced: 'It is the first time it has happened since Moscow, the first time that a capital has been burned since then!'"

On Friday night Plunkett rallied the men as they dashed from the blazing G.P.O. amid a hail of machine-gun and rifle bullets.

"Plunkett," says Ryan, "orders a van to be dragged across one of the lanes down which the machine-guns rattled, a feeble screen enough, but it served its turn while Plunkett stood there shouting: 'Don't be afraid. Don't be cowards any of you. On! On! On!'"

On Saturday forenoon Plunkett was with Patrick and William Pearse, Clarke and Mac Diarmada when, in 16 Moore Street, in consultation with the wounded Connolly, it was decided to negotiate terms for a surrender.

More than likely, it was immediately after that decision was taken that Plunkett wrote to his fiancée.

Letter to Grace Gifford, 29 April, 1916

To Miss Grace Gifford, 8 Temple Villas,
Palmerston Road

6th Day of the Irish Republic
Saturday April 29th 1916. About noon.
Somewhere in Moore St.

My Darling Grace,

This is just a little note to say I love you and to tell you that I did everything I could to arrange for us to meet and get married but that it was impossible.

Except for that I have no regrets. We will meet soon.

My other actions have been as right as I could see and make them, and I cannot wish them undone. You at any rate will not misjudge them.

Give my love to my people and friends. Darling, darling child, I wish we were together. Love me always as I love you. For the rest all you do will please me. I told a few people that I wish you to have everything that belongs to me. This is my last wish so please do see to it. Love x x x x

JOE.

Before his signature Plunkett drew his tiny Celtic cross.

This letter, according to the late Mrs. Grace Plunkett,[5] was entrusted by Plunkett to Winifred Carney, Connolly's secretary, Plunkett hoping, no doubt, that Miss Carney would not be taken prisoner. She was, and was not released until Christmas, 1916, when she delivered the letter. It is now in the possession of Miss Maeve Donnelly.

The closing sentences of the letter give the impression that Plunkett had little hope that he would survive the surrender, an impression which seems to be confirmed by the reply he gave, shortly afterwards, to an inquiry from Dr. Ryan as to the surrender terms to which Pearse had agreed. He told Dr. Ryan that he thought the signatories of the Proclamation would be shot, the rest set free.[6]

Some hours later, Brigadier-General Lowe's instructions as to how the men should surrender having been brought to Moore Street by Nurse Elizabeth O'Farrell, the Garrison marched out, led, as Desmond Ryan has said, by Plunkett and William Pearse "waving white flags as if they were banners of victory."

That night Plunkett spent in the open, with over six hundred of his comrades of the G.P.O. and Four Courts Garrisons, on the grass forecourt of the Rotunda Hospital, and the following morning he marched with them to Richmond Barracks.

Miss Julia Grenan, of the G.P.O. Garrison, who was also

taken to Richmond, recalls[7] seeing Plunkett collapse from sheer exhaustion and being carried into the Barracks.

On Sunday evening Plunkett wrote a message to his family.

Message to his Family, 30 April, 1916

Sunday, 30 April
6.25 p.m.
Joe, George and Jack[8] well and happy but detained at Richmond Barracks.
Plunkett,
Larkfield,
Kimmage.

Professor Liam Ó Briain, soon after he was brought into Richmond Barracks, a prisoner, on Sunday afternoon, 30 April, 1916, met Plunkett among the prisoners already there.

Ó Briain, taking at his word the British soldier who first entered the College of Surgeons after the surrender of the St. Stephen's Green Garrison and who told the men to take with them any bedclothes they could lay their hands on as "there'll be none in the place you're going," had brought with him a quilt on which wounded members of the Garrison had lain. When Seán Mac Diarmada, who was also a prisoner, saw Ó Briain with the quilt he promptly told him to give it to Plunkett who was very sick.

Leanann cuntas an Ollaimh :

"....Bhí Ióseph Ó Pluingcéad ina luí sínte ar an urlár....ag iarraidh suaimhneas d'fháil agus é ag cinnt air. Bhí an tseanchuilt sin aige ar feadh cupla lá ina dhiaidh sin, mar leaba faoi, scaite, agus scaite eile, craptha suas mar philiúr faoina cheann. Bhí an Pluingcéadach ag caitheamh culaith na nóglach agus bróga arda air; fearacht sin ag a bheirt deartháir, Seoirse agus Seán....

Bhí sé tinn—an-tinn—agus níor lig an tinneas dó, dar liom, aon mhachnamh a dhéanamh ar cad a bhí i ndán dó féin agus dúinn uile, ná oiread agus suim a chur sa scéal. Bhí comhrá agam leis faoin amhantar mór—ar tÉirí Amach—....ach ní chuimhin liom anois den mhéid adúirt sé ach na focail seo: 'Nothing was overlooked; nothing was forgotten'...."

Plunkett was tried by Court Martial in Richmond Barracks

on Tuesday, 2 May, 1916, as the following extract from the statement of Father Augustine confirms.

Father Augustine, O.F.M.Cap., wrote:

". . . .On Tuesday afternoon Father Albert and myself went to Richmond Barracks. . . .
In another part of the grounds of the Barracks is a fairly large building opposite which is a piece of land on which the grass was delightfully green. This sunny day a few tired Volunteers were resting on it and one of these I recognised as Joseph Mary Plunkett who lay there in a sitting posture with his body thrown slightly back supported by his two hands which pressed against the ground. He was, I was told, awaiting his turn for Court Martial, with his back turned towards us and his face towards the building he was soon to enter. My heart went out to him, but I did not then know I was to see him so soon again. . . ."

On the same day Plunkett wrote a further letter to his fiancée.

Letter to Grace Gifford from Richmond Barracks, 2 May, 1916

Richmond Barracks,
Tuesday, May 2nd, 1916.

My darling child,

This is my first chance of sending you a line since we were taken. I have no notion what they intend to do with me but have heard a rumour that I am to be sent to England.

The only thing I care about is that I am not with you —everything else is cheerful. I am told that Tomás[9] was brought in yesterday. George and Jack (Plun) are both here and well. We have not had one word of news from outside since Monday 24th April except wild rumours. Listen— if I live it might be possible to get the Church to marry us by proxy—there is such a thing but it is very difficult I am told. Father Sherwin might be able to do it. You know how I love you. That is all I have time to say. I know you love me and so I am very happy.

Your ————[10]

JOE.

Miss Grace M. V. Gifford,
8 Temple Villas,
Palmerston Rd., Rathmines.

This letter was, according to the late Mrs. Grace Plunkett,[11] given by Plunkett to a British soldier who delivered it to her.

It was written on the back of the Will which Plunkett had written on 23 April (see above) so that Plunkett had kept the Will in his pocket for nine hectic days.

The statement, "I have no notion what they intend to do with me," would seem to indicate that the letter was written after Plunkett had faced his Court Martial but before the verdict of the Court was communicated to him.

Arrangements were, in fact, made for Plunkett and Grace Gifford to be married. They were married on the night of 3 May in Kilmainham,[12] Plunkett having been transferred there some time that day.

"John Brennan" (Mrs. Sidney Czira née Gifford) has given the following account[13] of her sister's wedding :

"Joe had been engaged to Grace since December and they were to be married on Easter Sunday. MacNeill's orders counter-manded not only the Rising but also the wedding, for Joe was so involved in Military Council affairs that morning that he had time for nothing else. Grace and he agreed that if he were arrested she would marry him in prison.

At dawn on Wednesday, 3 May, 1916, Grace's brother-in-law, Thomas MacDonagh, had been executed in Kilmainham. At 6 o'clock that evening she was summoned to the Jail. For two hours she walked up and down, alone, in a prison yard, while Joe, she was told, waited in a cell.[14] At 8 o'clock she was taken to the prison chapel and, as she entered, her fiancé was led in by a party of soldiers with fixed bayonets. The soldiers remained in the chapel while, at the altar, Father Eugene McCarthy, the prison chaplain, read the marriage service by the light of a candle (the gas supply having failed). Two soldier witnesses shifted their rifles from hand to hand as they assisted at the ceremony. Immediately after-wards the newly-married couple were separated. Grace was taken to lodgings found for her by Father McCarthy in Thomas Street and Joe was escorted back to his cell.

They met only once again. Grace was brought to the Jail from Thomas Street in the early hours of Thursday morning. Soldiers with fixed bayonets stood by while she spoke to her husband in his cell. 'Your ten minutes are up,' said the officer in charge, glancing at his watch, and they parted for ever."

When she left Kilmainham Grace Plunkett brought with her her husband's keys and a lock of his hair.

Plunkett was the last of the four men executed on 4 May, 1916. He was attended by Father Sebastian, O.F.M.Cap., to whom he gave his spectacles, for his mother, and his ring, for his wife. Father Sebastian stated[15] that while Plunkett waited, with his hands tied behind his back, to be called to the place of execution, he said: "Father, I am very happy. I am dying for the glory of God and the honour of Ireland."

Plunkett used almost the same words to Father Albert, O.F.M.Cap., who was also in Kilmainham that morning. (He attended Michael O'Hanrahan.)

Plunkett's mother, the late Countess Plunkett, recalled, in 1942,[16] a conversation she had had with Father Albert.

"....He told me how four priests from Church Street were sent for in the early hours of the morning of May 4th, 1916, and in twenty minutes the four had arrived at Kilmainham Jail to find Joseph and three others (Edward Daly, William Pearse and Michael O'Hanrahan) were about to be executed. One priest and a prisoner were sent to a nearby cell. The prisoner had his hat on and the priest wondered to see a man going to confess and wearing his hat. A jailer put his head into the cell, and then entering, undid the handcuffs behind the man's back and allowed him to remove his hat. It was nearly dark and there was only a candle for light.

The three other prisoners were together in an adjoining room, among them Joseph, to whom Father Albert was attracted. Joseph, seeing him looking at him, walked across the room to Father Albert and said: 'Father, I want you to know that I am dying for the glory of God and the honour of Ireland.' 'That's all right, my son,' answered Father Albert. In a few minutes the firing squad carried out their orders. And that was Joseph's first —and last—meeting with Father Albert on earth. God grant they have met in heaven."

And Father Augustine, O.F.M.Cap., who also saw him in Kilmainham before he was led out to die, told the late Professor McBrien of Plunkett's last moments.[17]

"He was there, his hands tied behind his back, waiting to face the firing squad. I noted his courteous 'Thank you, Father'; his face reminded me of St. Francis and 'Welcome, Sister Death.' He was absolutely calm, as cool and self-possessed as if he looked

on what was passing and found it good. No fine talk. No heroics.
A distinguished tranquillity—that came from his nobility of soul
and his faith—nothing more."

[1]In a statement to the Editor.

[2]*recte* Garristown.

[3]*recte* Gormanston.

[4]Diarmuid Lynch records (Report of Operations, Easter Week, 1916, *The
I.R.B. and the 1916 Insurrection*) that Connolly was wounded in the arm at 4 p.m.
on Wednesday and, seriously, in the leg on Thursday afternoon; but Dr. Ryan's
account (*Capuchin Annual,* 1966) confirms Plunkett's, as do Connolly's own
statements.

[5]In a statement made in June, 1949.

[6]*Capuchin Annual,* 1966.

[7]In a statement to the Editor. See also *The Catholic Bulletin,* June, 1917.

[8]George and Jack were Plunkett's brothers who had been with him in the G.P.O.
Both were sentenced to death—commuted to ten years' penal servitude.

[9]"Tomás" was Thomas MacDonagh who was married to Grace Gifford's
sister, Muriel. The word "Tomás" was written in Gaelic script in the original.
If by "brought in" Plunkett meant "arrested," he had been misinformed about
MacDonagh, for MacDonagh was "brought in" to Richmond Barracks, on his
surrendering, on Sunday, 30 April.

[10]"Your own" or "Yours ever." The manuscript, in copying-ink pencil, is not
clear.

[11]In a statement made in June, 1949.

[12]The altar, from the Chapel in Kilmainham, at which the wedding ceremony
took place, is now in the Military Church of the Sacred Heart, Arbour Hill.

[13]In a written statement to the Editor.

[14]See below for discussion of the number of Plunkett's cell later occupied
by Ceannt.

[15]*The Catholic Bulletin,* July, 1916.

[16]*Capuchin Annual,* 1942.

[17]Quoted in an article by Mary Purcell in *The Belvederian,* 1966.
And see bibliographical note p. x.

Seán Mac Giolla Bhríde   John MacBride

1865–1916

SEÁN MAC GIOLLA BHRÍDE   JOHN MacBRIDE

John MacBride held a commission as a Major not in the Irish
Volunteers—in which, incidentally, no one held such a rank—
but in the Irish Brigade which, organised by himself and other
Irish exiles in South Africa, fought with gallantry on the side
of the Boers against the invading British during the Boer War
(1899-1900).

It is not clear how MacBride came to be attached to the
Jacob's Garrison in 1916.

One account[1] tells of his having left the group with whom
he had been mobilised at 41 Parnell Square—Headquarters of
the First Battalion, Dublin Brigade—and gone from there,
apparently of his own accord, to join up with MacDonagh at
Jacob's.

Another account[2] quotes the late John MacDonagh as having
asked his brother, Thomas, " Who is the man in the blue
suit?" when MacBride appeared at the head of the Jacob's
Garrison as they marched from their mobilisation point in St.
Stephen's Green to the Factory. " That's Major MacBride,"
Commandant MacDonagh is reported to have replied. "He
walked up to me and said 'Here I am if I'm any use to you.' Of
course I am delighted to have him."

Still another account[3] tells that MacBride, unaware of the
plans for the proposed Rising, had come into town to attend a
wedding and "finding a rebellion on decided to take part in it
as I always detested British rule."

As MacBride was a member of the Irish Republican Brotherhood it is most unlikely that he was entirely in ignorance of the
proposed Rising.

He was seen at 41 Parnell Square on Easter Sunday morning
by Séamus Brennan[4] who had gone there on the instructions of
Seán Heuston after Séamus had shown to Heuston the *Sunday
Independent* containing MacNeill's countermand.

And it is known that Seán Mac Diarmada wrote a "most
urgent" message to MacBride on Easter Monday morning.[5]

Desmond Ryan told[6] that "MacDonagh was joined by

MacBride who came straight into Dublin and joined in the fight which broke out as he happened to pass Jacob's as it was being taken over . . . the occasion found the man and MacBride threw himself enthusiastically into the fray as MacDonagh's second-in-command and he led in addition several dangerous raiding parties during the week."

Father Aloysius, O.F.M.Cap., has told that when he and Father Augustine came to Jacob's with Pearse's surrender order "Major MacBride said that if any attempt were made to counsel surrender he would oppose it with all the strength he could command," and Father Augustine has recorded[7] that when General Lowe agreed to meet MacDonagh to discuss terms MacBride volunteered to accompany his Commandant but that he (Father Augustine) dissuaded him "remembering the fine part he had played in the Boer War" and fearing, no doubt, that the British, remembering too, would be ill-disposed towards him.

After the surrender MacBride was taken to Richmond Barracks. Pádraig Ó Ceallaigh, another member of Jacob's Garrison, recalls[8] having seen him there "on the first or second day after we were brought in. I can see him still, sitting on a long form in one of the rooms jingling a few coins in his hand as I passed. 'I suppose that's some of the German gold,' I said. He smiled a wry smile in response."

MacBride was tried by Court Martial in Richmond Barracks on 4 May, 1916.

Victor Collins, writing to John Devoy from an address in Paris in June, 1919,[9] refers to MacBride's Court Martial:

"Charles Wyse Power, the barrister," he says, "told me that he was at a luncheon in a mess-room at a camp during a court martial and heard Major Blackadder who presided at John's 'trial' say: 'All the men behaved well, but the one who stands out as the most soldierly was John MacBride. He, on entering, stood to attention facing us and in his eyes I could read: "You are soldiers. I am one. You have won. I have lost. Do your worst." ' "

And again:

"Mrs. Allan, whom he called as a witness, tells me when she entered. John was seated facing the Court, but seeing no chair was put for her he jumped up and handed her his chair return-

ing to his place and standing until an orderly brought him
another chair. . . ."

T. M. Healy, who was not, however, an entirely reliable witness, told[3] that "MacBride's speech to the Court Martial was
repeated to him (Healy) by the Crown Prosecutor somewhat as
follows:

I was never a Sinn Féiner. I knew nothing of the plan to start
an insurrection. I came into Dublin on Easter Monday from
Kingstown to attend the wedding of a relative. Finding a rebellion on I decided to take part in it as I always detested British
rule. I thank the officers of the Court for the fair trial I have
had and the Crown Counsel for the way he met every application
I made. I have looked down the muzzles of too many guns in the
South African War to fear death, and now please carry out your
sentence."

The last sentence alone seems to discount the authenticity of
this statement for, as we have seen, Courts Martial did not
pronounce sentences but these were conveyed, afterwards, to
the prisoners. And Major MacBride himself told Seán T. Ó
Ceallaigh (see below) that he would not be told his sentence
"until later tonight."

The truth about what transpired at this and the other Courts
Martial must remain a secret until the Court Martial documents, preserved with the papers in the British Judge-Advocate-
General's Office in the Public Records Office in London, can
be examined.

Bhí Seán T. Ó Ceallaigh ina phríosúnach i mBeairic
Risteamain an lá a tugadh an Méidsear os comhair an Chúirt
Airm.

"Is cuimhin liom go maith," adeir sé, "é a fheiceáil á mháir-
seáil trasna chearnóg na beairice an lá a tugadh os comhair an
chúirt airm é. Bhí triúr nó ceathrar príosúnach eile in éineacht
leis. Bhí urraim mhór againn go léir dó ach, ag cuimhniú dúinn
ar an 'stair' a bhí aige, ba bheag dóchas a bhí againn go dtiocfadh
sé slán. Throid sé féin agus a Bhriogáid Éireannach go cróga in
aghaidh na Sasanach i gCogadh na mBórach agus ba rud é sin
nach ligfí i ndearmad. Bheadh fonn ar an namhaid an scór a
ghlanadh.
An lá úd ar cuireadh an chúirt airm ar Mhac Giolla Bhríde
leanamar linn ag faire gur tugadh amach ar an chearnóg arís é

féin agus na príosúnaigh eile a bhí leis. Timpeall a cheathair a
chlog tráthnóna a bhí ann, agus cén áit ar mairseáladh iad ach
go dtí ball a bhí go díreach faoin fhuinneog s'againne....
D'ardaigh mé comhla íochtarach na fuinneoige agus chuir mé
forrán orthu. Labhair mé go speisialta le Seán Mac Giolla Bhríde
agus d'fhiafraigh mé de ar cuireadh triail air fós. Dúirt sé gur
cuireadh.
    'Agus ar insíodh toradh na trialach díbh fós?' arsa mise.
    'Níor insíodh,' ar seisean. 'Tá sé le hinsint dúinn níos déanaí
anocht. Ach i mo chás féin de, is maith atá fhios agam cén breith
a thabharfar agus cad a dhéanfar.'
    Shín sé a chorrmhéar i dtreo a chroí agus bhí sé an-dáiríre
faoinar dhúirt sé:
    'Gheobhaidh mé anseo é ar maidin,' ar seisean.
    'O, ná habhair sin, a Sheáin,' arsa mise. 'Tá Dia láidir. Ní fios
cad a tharlódh a shábhálfadh thú.'
    'Ní shábhálfaidh dada mé, a Sheáin T. Seo é an deireadh.
Cuimhnigh gurb é seo an dara huair a pheacaigh mise ina
n-aghaidh.'
    Labhramar cupla focal eile le chéile agus ansin tháinig
oifigeach fhad linn agus roithleán ina láimh. Dhírigh sé ormsa
é agus d'ordaigh dom an fhuinneog a dhúnadh. Rinne mé sin,
ach leanamar linn ag breathnú ar Mhac Giolla Bhríde agus a
chairde go dtí gur greadadh ar shiúl iad go dtí a n-áit féin san
fhoirgneamh. Nuair a bhíodar ag imeacht d'osclaíomar an
fhuinneog arís agus ghlaomar slán agus beannacht orthu.
Shnaidhm Seán Mac Giolla Bhríde a dhá láimh ina chéile faoi
mar bheadh sé ag croitheadh láimhe leis féin. Ansin d'ardaigh
sé iad faoi mar bheadh sé ag croitheadh láimhe linne.
    'Slán agaibh, a fheara, agus rath Dé oraibh. Agus slán go deo
agatsa, a Sheáin T. Ní fheicfidh mé níos mó thú.'
    Bhí an ceart aige. Ní fhacamar a chéile ní ba mhó...."

Very soon after he bade farewell to Seán T., MacBride was
taken to Kilmainham.
    He was attended there by Father Augustine, O.F.M.Cap.

Father Augustine, O.F.M.Cap., wrote:

Friday morning, May 5th, 1916.
    After two o'clock this morning a loud knocking was heard
at the Bowe Street gate.[10] I went down and a soldier told me I
had been asked for by one of the prisoners at Kilmainham.
I was prepared, owing to information received the previous
evening at the Officers' quarters on the North Circular Road,
and went at once.
    On reaching the prison I was immediately shown to a cell

and on its being opened I gripped the hand of Major MacBride. He was quiet and natural as ever. His very first words expressed sorrow for the surrender, and then he went on quickly to say that on his asking for water to have a wash a soldier had brought him a cupful. "I suppose," he added with a smile, "they think I could wash myself with that much." He then emptied his pockets of whatever silver and coppers he had and asked me to give it to the poor.

Finally, placing his Rosary tenderly in my hand, he uttered a little sentence that thrilled me: "And give that to my Mother."

Then, having given me a message for another that convinced me he was a man of very deep faith, he began his Confession with the simplicity and humility of a child. After a few minutes I gave him Holy Communion and we spent some while together in prayer.

I told him I would be with him to the last and that I would anoint him when he fell.

When the time was up a soldier knocked at the door and we went down together to the passage where final preparations were made. (I seem to see it all now vividly again, and as I write I feel naturally stirred.)

He asked quietly not to have his hands bound and promised to remain perfectly still.

"Sorry, Sir," the soldier answered, "but these are the orders."

Then he requested not to be blindfolded, and a similar answer was given. Turning slightly aside, he said to me, quite naturally, in a soft voice: "You know, Father Augustine, I've often looked down their guns before."

Later a piece of white paper is pinned above his heart, and, inspired by the Holy Spirit, I whisper into his ear: "We are all sinners. Offer up your life for any faults or sins of the past." And this brave man, fearless of death, responds like a child, yet firmly: "I'm glad you told me that, Father. I will."

The two soldiers and myself now move along the corridor, turn to the left and enter a yard where the firing squad of twelve is already waiting with loaded rifles.

Six now kneel on one knee and behind them six stand. He faces them about fifty feet from the guns, two or three feet from the wall.

The two soldiers withdraw to the left, near the Governor and the Doctor, and I, oblivious of all but him, stand close at his right, in prayer.

The officer approaches, takes me gently by the arm and leads me to a position below himself at the right.

He speaks a word. The prisoner stiffens and expands his chest. Then quickly, a silent signal, a loud volley, and the body collapses in a heap.

I moved forward quickly and anointed him, feeling the mean-
ing of the beautiful words of the Liturgy as, I think, I never felt
them before, and the certainty of the consoling thought that
the soul of the dear one who had fallen was already on its way
to God and His Blessed Mother.

Victor Collins, in the letter to John Devoy, previously mentioned, tells also of MacBride's last moments:

"....I must first tell you," he says, "of the noble end of
John MacBride as I heard it from the lips of Father Augustine
who attended him at his martyrdom for Ireland. Early on the
morning he prepared John for death, and as soon as their
devotions were ended John said: 'Father, I would like to wash.'
The priest went to the door of the cell and told a warder that
Major MacBride would like to wash. The warder brought a
cup of water. John looked at it, laughed and said: 'I can't do
much washing with that, but never mind.' He then dipped his
fingers in the cup and wet his eyes, which he wiped with his
handkerchief. His ablutions ended, he put his hand into the
right pocket of his trousers and pulled out his money which he
gave to the priest for the poor. Then, putting his left hand into
the left pocket, with a sad note in his voice, he said: 'And,
Father, when I am dead—hello, what is this?' and pulled out a
crumpled paper which he smoothed out and exclaimed: 'A
Treasury note for 10/-! I did not know I had this; put it with
the rest,' and gave it to Father Augustine. Again diving into his
pocket he drew out his rosary, which he always carried, and said
to his confessor: 'When I am dead, give that from me to my
dearest mother.'
Shortly afterwards he was called to execution. With the priest
he descended some stone stairs, passed along a passage, and
came to a door leading to a yard. As soon as he was in the open
air he looked upwards and remarked casually: 'It's a fine
morning, Father.' Father Augustine tells me he rather was
shivering, and replied: 'Major, I find it rather cold.' John just
smiled as if to say—warm or cold will soon make no difference
to me—wished Father Augustine good-bye, walked to the wall,
faced the soldiers, and fell dead like the gallant Irishman he
was, without a sign of either fear or bravado. God rest his
gallant soul."

The accounts of Father Augustine and Victor Collins differ,
it will be noted, in some slight particulars, but no more than
can be expected in a record of events, occurring in times of
great stress, remembered after a lapse of some years.

In June, 1916, Father Augustine wrote to John MacBride's mother.

Franciscan Capuchin Friary,
Church Street,
Dublin.
13/6/'16

Dear Mrs. MacBride,

I had intended writing to you long before this, but I have been very busy.

To your son, however, who called here, I gave all information about Major MacBride, and I am sure it reached you long since.

He was a gentle, noble character, and his last thoughts were about you, God's poor, his friends and God whom he went to meet in a most beautifully Catholic spirit.

I was with him in good time on the morning of his death. We said prayers together in his prison cell; he went to Confession, received Holy Communion and prepared for the last like a good Catholic. He knew no fear. When, standing together at the entrance to the corridor through which he was soon to pass out to die, I whispered in his ear to offer up his life in atonement for any frailties or transgressions of the past, he replied most sweetly: "Yes, I will. I'm very glad you told me that."

I was with him to the last and he knew I was by his side. The moment he fell I rushed over and anointed him. I feel God was kind and merciful to him.

He spoke of you and sent you his watch and beads which I'm sure you received. He also gave me a £1 note and some shillings for bread for the poor.

I hope I may meet you some day, but let me say now that you have reason to be proud of your brave son. We shall meet him again in heaven, please God.

May he rest in peace and may God console you.

Very sincerely yours,
F. Augustine, O.S.F.C.

This letter is in the National Museum.

---

[1] Brian O'Higgins in the *Wolfe Tone Annual*, 1960.

[2] "John Brennan" in *Dublin's Fighting Story* (Kerryman, 1949).

[3] T. M. Healy in *Letters and Leaders of My Day* (Butterworth, 1928).

[4] In a statement to the Editor.

[5] See below.

[6] "Personal Recollections," *Capuchin Annual*, 1966.

[7] In his statement.

[8] In a statement to the Editor.

[9] Quoted in *John Devoy's Post Bag*, 1871-1928. Ed. by William O'Brien and Desmond Ryan, Vols. I–II (Fallon, 1948).

[10] Of the Capuchin Friary, Church Street.

And see bibliographical note p. x.

Seán Mac Aodha   Seán Heuston

1891–1916

SEÁN MAC AODHA   SEÁN HEUSTON

"On Wednesday morning, 26 April, 1916, two Volunteer
dispatch carriers hurried from the Mendicity Institution near
Usher's Island on the Liffey's southern quays through barricades
and dangerous streets and lanes past the Four Courts and the
duels of British and Republican snipers with a very urgent
message from Seán Heuston, Commandant of their post, to James
Connolly at headquarters, informing him that Heuston and
some twenty men were still holding out after a terrific fight
against some hundreds of British troops who had then nearly
completely surrounded them, and were raking their fortress with
machine-gun fire on all sides. Moreover, an all-out assault was
expected almost immediately; food supplies were exhausted and
ammunition was almost spent. The dispatch carriers. . . P. J.
Stephenson and Seán McLoughlin. . . reached the General Post
Office and noticed at once that Connolly grew unusually ani-
mated and excited as he read Heuston's dispatch. . . .There was
an immediate and obvious reason for Connolly's emotion: his
orders to Heuston had been to hold up any troops moving
towards the Four Courts for three or four hours, and by this
delay give the garrisons there and in headquarters itself time
to establish their defences. . . .Heuston had not only held his fort
for the few hours specified, but was still there, a very hornet's
nest for the enemy, after nearly fifty hours. . . ."

—from *The Rising* by Desmond Ryan.

Soon after sending that "dispatch"—it was, in fact, a verbal
message—Heuston decided to surrender.

As one member of the Garrison has said :[1]

"Our tiny garrison—now twenty-six—had battled all morning
against three or four hundred British troops. Machine-gun and
rifle fire kept up a constant battering of our position. Seán
visited each post in turn, encouraging us. But now we were
faced with a new form of attack. The enemy, closing in, began
to hurl grenades into the building. Our only answer was to try
to catch these and throw them back before they exploded. Two
of our men, Liam Staines and Dick Balfe, both close friends
of Seán's, were badly wounded doing this.
We had almost run out of ammunition. Dog-tired, without
food, trapped, hopelessly outnumbered, we had reached the limit

of our endurance. After consultation with the rest of us, Seán decided that the only hope for the wounded and, indeed, for the safety of all of us, was to surrender. Not everyone approved but the order was obeyed and we destroyed as much equipment as we could before giving ourselves up. One of our party went out into the yard behind the Institution waving a white flag and we followed. As we crossed the yard we were fired on by a British sniper and one of our men, Peter Wilson of Swords, was shot dead.

The British were infuriated when they saw the pigmy force that had given them such a stiff battle and caused them so many casualties. They screamed at us, cursed us, manhandled us. An officer asked who was in charge and Seán stepped out in front without a word.

We were forced to march to the Royal (now Collins) Barracks with our hands up, held behind our heads.

In the Barracks we were lined up on the parade ground. Here we were attacked by British soldiers, kicked, beaten, spat upon. (This stands out very clearly in my memory.)

Then we were marched under heavy guard, by an underground passage, to Arbour Hill Detention Barracks where we were searched and everything we had, even our handkerchiefs, were taken from us.

We were placed in the Gym—all of us except Seán who was led away, I assume to a cell. We never saw him again. The last words he spoke to us were those he used when deciding to surrender. He got no chance to speak to us after that."

In Arbour Hill, according to his brother, Father John M. Heuston, O.P.,[2] Heuston wrote to the Adjutant a letter the contents of which are unknown apart from the fact that a certain Lieut. Mount is mentioned.[3]

Heuston was transferred to Richmond Barracks on 4 May, 1916, and tried there by Court Martial the same day.

He wrote notes on the Court Martial charge sheet.

Notes written on Court Martial charge sheet

Copy of Charge.

Did an act, to wit: Did take part in an armed rebellion and in the waging of war against His Majesty the King, such act being of such a nature as to be calculated to be prejudicial to the Defence of the Realm and being done with the intention of and for the purpose of assisting the enemy.

War commenced Monday, 24 April, 1916 at noon,
surrendered to vastly superior numbers and armament
Wednesday April 26, lodged in Arbour Hill Detention
Barracks until Thursday May 4th.
Tried at Richmond Barracks May 4th
Lodged in Kilmainham Prison May 4th.

Desmond Ryan tells, though he quotes no source—but he
was a reliable and painstaking historian—that on the day before
his execution a friend asked Heuston if he had heard the result
of his Court Martial and Heuston replied quite calmly that he
had not, adding: "There is no hope for me. I expect to be shot."

In Kilmainham, again according to his brother, Heuston
wrote a letter[3] to the Commandant in Charge. Again the text
is unavailable, but the letter is believed to have concerned the
disposal of some small items of personal property which were
in his possession when he was taken prisoner.

On the evening of Sunday, 7 May, 1916, the verdict of the
Court Martial was conveyed to him—that he had been sentenced to death and would be shot the following morning at
dawn. He sent for his mother, his sister and his aunt who lived
with them.

> Detention Barracks
> Kilmainham
> 7th May, 1916.
>
> Madam,
>
> John Heuston, your son, desires to see you and also his sister,
> Theresa, and his aunt, Theresa McDonald. I am sending a motor
> car to convey you and his sister & aunt here.
>
> > Yours faithfully,
> > (Sgd.) W. S. Lennon Major
> > Commdt.
>
> Mrs. Heuston,
> 20 Fontenoy St., Mountjoy St.

He wrote to his brother, Michael, who was studying for the
priesthood at the Dominican Priory, Tallaght—Michael's name
in religion was "Brother John"—asking him to come to see him.

Letter to his Brother, Michael, 7 May, 1916

> Kilmainham Prison,
> Sunday, May 7th, 1916.

My Dearest M.,

I suppose you have been wondering why I did not communicate with you since Easter but the explanation is
simple. I have been locked up by His Britannic Majesty's
Government. They have just intimated to me that I am
to be *executed* in the morning.

If the rules of the Order allow it I want you to get
permission *at once* and come in here to see me for the last
time in this world. I feel quite prepared to go—thank God,
but want you to get all the prayers you can said for me.
You will probably be able to come in the motor which takes
out this note.

I have sent for Mother, Duckie[4] and Teasie[5] also.

> Affectionately,
>
> JACK.

And while he waited for his visitors he wrote to his sister,
Mary, who was a Dominican nun in Taylor's Hill Convent,
Galway.

Letter to his Sister, Mary (Mother Bernard, O.P.), 7 May, 1916

> Kilmainham Prison,
> Dublin.
> Sunday, May 7th, 1916.

My dearest Mary,

Before this note reaches you I shall have fallen as a
soldier in the cause of Irish Freedom. I write to bid you
a last farewell in this world, and rely on you to pray
fervently and to get the prayers of the whole community
for the repose of my soul. I go, I trust, to meet poor
Brigid[6] above and am quite prepared for the journey. The
priest was with me and I received Holy Communion this

morning. It was only this evening that the finding of the Court Martial was conveyed to me.

Poor Mother will miss me but I feel that with God's help she will manage to pull along. You know the Irish proverb : "God's help is nearer than the door." The agony of the past few days has been intense, but I now feel resigned to God's Holy Will. I might have fallen in action as many have done and been less well prepared for the journey before me. Do not blame me for the part I have taken. As a soldier I merely carried out the orders of my superiors who should have been in a position to know what was best in Ireland's interest. Let there be no talk of foolish enterprise. I have no vain regrets. Think of the thousands of Irishmen who fell fighting under another flag at the Dardanelles, attempting to do what England's experts now admit was an absolute impossibility.

If you really love me teach the children in your class the history of their own land, and teach them that the cause of Caitlín Ní Uallacháin never dies. Ireland shall be free from the centre to the sea as soon as the people of Ireland believe in the necessity for Ireland's Freedom and are prepared to make the necessary sacrifices to obtain it. Ireland cannot be freed by strong resolutions or votes of confidence, however unanimous.

It may be that the struggle we have made will lend strength to Ireland's claim for representation at the Great Peace Conference when the map of Europe is being redrawn. Let us pray that Ireland will benefit from it ultimately.

Let you do *your* share by teaching Ireland's history as it should be taught. Mary, pray for me and get everybody to pray for me.

Your loving brother,
JACK.

Heuston was visited in his cell in Kilmainham by his mother, his sister, Theresa, his aunt, Miss Theresa McDonald, a first cousin, Miss Lil Heuston, who was also staying with the Heustons at the time, and by his brother, Michael, who was accompanied by the Master of Novices and Professed Students at Tallaght, Father Michael (now Cardinal) Browne.

Miss Theresa Heuston (in whose possession the above letter remains) recalls the visit :[7]

A policeman called to 20 Fontenoy Street on Sunday night, 7 May, 1916, and handed to Mrs. Heuston the message quoted at page 109, from the Commandant of Kilmainham.

A car waited outside.

Seán's cousin, Lil, insisted on accompanying the three mentioned in the permit.

The night was dark and it was raining heavily.

The car, driven by a soldier, was stopped several times on the journey to Kilmainham. Each time two soldiers, with fixed bayonets, examined the car and occupants and questioned the policeman and the driver before allowing them to proceed. Their answer to inquiries each time was a cryptic "King's messenger!"

When they arrived at the Jail there was some delay about their admission because of the presence of Miss Lil Heuston, but eventually she was allowed to accompany the others to Seán's cell, which was on the ground floor, on the left-hand side, at the far end of the Central Hall.[8] On their entering the cell Seán begged them not to break down.

In the cell there was a table with a stump of a candle—not lighting—on it. On a shelf attached to the wall was a heel of dry bread, partly eaten. There was a chair and, on the floor, near the door, what appeared to be a ground-sheet, rolled up.

One soldier, holding a lighted candle, was in the cell with them. He was young and deeply affected. He was crying.

During the interview there were constant visits to the cell by other soldiers. Miss Heuston overheard one officer say: "These men must be got away by three."

When the time came for the visitors to leave, the soldier locked the cell-door, leaving Seán in darkness.

Seán called out: "Won't you leave the light?" and Michael, turning to the soldier, said: "Will you bring back the light? He wants to write a letter."

Michael Mallin's cell was "further on" than Seán's.[9] Miss Heuston saw the Mallin party leaving. She has a dim recollection of Mrs. Mallin's having a baby in her arms.[10]

Cardinal Browne has given an account[11] of the visit as he remembers it :

In the late evening of May 7th, 1916, a military car arrived at St. Mary's Dominican Priory, Tallaght, Co. Dublin, with a message for Brother John (Michael) Heuston, that he had permission to come to Kilmainham Prison to visit his brother, Seán Heuston, who was to be executed the following morning.

I was at the time Master of Novices and Professed Students, one of whom was Brother John Heuston, at Tallaght Priory. I accompanied him to Kilmainham.

On arrival we were brought to a waiting-room near the prison entrance, where we found Mrs. Heuston, Seán's mother, his aunt, Miss McDonald, his sister, Miss Theresa Heuston, and a cousin of his.

After a brief delay the members of the Heuston family were admitted to the interior of the prison. I, at first, was not admitted, but after insistence on my part on account of my relationship with Brother John Heuston, I was allowed to enter.

I was brought to Seán Heuston's cell where his family had already arrived. Seán came forward to meet and welcome me. He was quite serene, and for a short time I joined with the members of his family in conversation with him. I then withdrew a little to allow them to be alone together. . . .

(Cardinal Browne, at this stage, visited Michael Mallin in his cell. See below.)

I bade good-bye to Michael Mallin and returned to the cell of Seán Heuston. His family were still in conversation with him, but time was running on and the guards let us know that the end of the visit was near at hand so we had to prepare to leave. I embraced him, promising our prayers and the celebration of Mass in the early morning. Each member of his family, which, as I have said, included his mother, bade him a long and fond good-bye, and so we left him, serene as he had been during the whole time of our visit.

The letter, referred to by Brother John, which Heuston wanted to write must have been that to Mr. Walsh, a colleague in the Great Southern and Western Railway.

Letter to Mr. Walsh, 7 May, 1916

Kilmainham Prison,
Sunday, May 7th.

Dear Mr. Walshe,

Before this note reaches you I shall have said farewell to this Vale of Tears, and have departed for what I trust will prove a much Better World. I take this last opportunity of thanking you and all my railway friends for the kindnesses of the past years. I ask all to forgive me for any offences which I may have committed against them and I ask all to pray fervently for the repose of my soul. Whatever I have done I have done as a soldier of Ireland in what I believed to be my country's interests. I have, thank God, no vain regrets. After all, it is better to be a corpse than a coward.

Won't you as a last favour see that my mother gets whatever assistance you can give in obtaining whatever salary is due to me, and whatever refund is due from the Superannuation Fund? She will stand badly in need of it all.

Gratefully yours,

J. J. HEUSTON.

A photocopy of this letter is in the National Library, made from the original lent by a private owner to the Bureau of Military History. The other Heuston documents cited are in private possession.

He wrote another letter also, after midnight, to his mother.

Letter to his Mother, 8 May, 1916

8/5/'16

My dear Mother,

I forgot to mention to you that a refund of 5/- (five shillings) is due to young D. O'Sullivan of Glengarriff Parade (I think the number is 33). He paid me the money for the proposed Easter Camp. Give him back the money and ask him to pray and get all the Fianna to pray for me.

Your affectionate son,

JACK.

Father Albert, O.F.M.Cap., who attended him, has left an account[12] of the closing scenes of Seán Heuston's life :

On Sunday night, May 7th, 1916, Father Augustine and myself were notified that we would be required at Kilmainham Jail the following morning as four of the leaders in the Rising were to be executed.

At 1.30 a.m. a military motor car came for us to Church Street,

and on our arrival at Kilmainham we were brought to the wing
of the Jail in which our friends were confined. Father Augustine
went to Éamonn Ceannt's cell and I to Commandant M. Mallin's.
Having visited Con Colbert and Éamonn Ceannt, I went to
Seán Heuston's cell at about 3.20 a.m. He was kneeling beside a
table with his Rosary beads in his hand. On the table was a little
piece of candle, and some letters which he had written to near
relatives and friends. He wore his overcoat, as the morning was
extremely cold, and none of these men received those little
comforts that are provided for even the greatest criminals while
awaiting sentence of death. During the last quarter of an hour
we knelt in the cell in complete darkness, as the little piece of
candle had burned out; but no word of complaint escaped his
lips. His one thought was to prepare with all the fervour and
earnestness of his soul to meet his Divine Saviour and His
sweet Virgin Mother, to whom he was about to offer up his
young life for the freedom and independence of his beloved
country. He had been to Confession and had received Holy
Communion early that morning, and was not afraid to die. He
awaited the end not only with that calmness and fortitude which
peace of mind brings to noble souls, but during the last quarter
of an hour he spoke of soon meeting again Pádraic Mac Piarais
and the other leaders who had already gone before him.

We said together short acts of faith, hope, contrition and love;
we prayed together to St. Patrick, St. Brigid, St. Colmcille, and
all the saints of Ireland; we said many times that beautiful
little ejaculatory prayer: "Jesus, Mary and Joseph, I give you my
heart and soul," etc., which appealed very much to him. But,
though he prayed with such fervour for strength and courage in
the ordeal that was at hand, Ireland and his friends were close
to his soul. He loved his own unto the end.

In his last message to me he said: "Remember me to the
boys of the Fianna. Remember me to Mícheál Staines and his
brothers,[13] and to all the boys at Blackhall Street."[14]

At about 3.45 a.m. a British sentry knocked at the door of the
cell and told us the time was up. We walked out together, down
to the end of the large open space from which a corridor runs
to the Jail Yard; here his hands were tied behind his back, a
cloth placed over his eyes and a small piece of white paper, about
4 ins. or 5 ins. square, pinned to his coat over his heart. Just
then we saw Father Augustine with Commandant M. Mallin
coming towards us from the cell where they had been. We were
now told to be ready. I had a small cross in my hand, and though
blindfolded, Seán bent his head and kissed the Crucifix; this
was the last thing his lips touched in life. He then whispered to
me: "Father, sure you won't forget to anoint me?"—I had told
him in his cell that I would anoint him when he was shot.
We now proceeded towards the yard where the execution was

to take place; my left arm was linked in his right, while the British soldier who had handcuffed and blindfolded him walked on his left. As we walked slowly along we repeated most of the prayers that we had been saying in the cell. On our way we passed a group of soldiers; these I afterwards learned were awaiting Commandant Mallin; who was following us. Having reached a second yard I saw there another group of military armed with rifles. Some of these were standing, and some sitting or kneeling. A soldier directed Seán and myself to a corner of the yard, a short distance from the outer wall of the prison. Here there was a box (seemingly a soap box) and Seán was told to sit down upon it. He was perfectly calm, and said with me for the last time: "My Jesus, mercy." I scarcely had moved away a few yards when a volley went off, and this noble soldier of Irish Freedom fell dead. I rushed over to anoint him; his whole face seemed transformed and lit up with a grandeur and brightness that I had never before noticed. . . .

Never did I realise that men could fight so bravely, and die so beautifully, and so fearlessly as did the Heroes of Easter Week. On the morning of Seán Heuston's death I would have given the world to have been in his place, he died in such a noble and sacred cause, and went forth to meet his Divine Saviour with such grand Christian sentiments of trust, confidence and love.

---

[1]Séamus Brennan, Secretary of the Kilmainham Jail Restoration Society, in a statement to the Editor.

[2]In a written statement to the Editor.

[3]Exhaustive inquiries have failed to discover any trace of the survival of either the letter to the Adjutant in Arbour Hill or that to the Commandant in Kilmainham. Neither the British Ministry for Defence, the Home Office nor the London Public Record Office have any record of them. The Public Record Office advise that the letters "are not included in the files of Courts Martial proceedings held with the British Judge Advocate General's records" preserved there, "nor are they to be found among the Registered Papers of the appropriate period."

[4]"Duckie" was a pet-name for his sister, Theresa.

[5]"Teasie" was his aunt, Theresa McDonald.

[6]Brigid McDonald, his mother's sister, died in 1906.

[7]In a statement to the Editor.

[8]It was Cell No. 19. Maurice Brennan, who was in Cell No. 16, remembers seeing "Heuston, with his back to me, being led into the third cell from the 'porch'."

[9]It was Cell No. 18. Éamonn Ceannt was in Cell No. 20.

[10]Mrs. Mallin did have her baby, Joseph, with her.

[11]In a written statement to the Editor.

[12]Quoted in John McCann's *War by the Irish* (Kerryman, 1946).

[13]Michael Staines fought with the G.P.O. Garrison. His brother, Liam, was wounded in the Mendicity Institution.

[14]The Gaelic League Hall, 5 Blackhall Street, was the meeting-place of A and D Companies of the First Battalion of the Dublin Brigade.

And see bibliographical note p. x.

MÍCHEÁL Ó MEALLÁIN   MICHAEL MALLIN

It seems that, after Nurse Elizabeth O'Farrell had delivered to him (see below) the surrender order, signed by Pearse and Connolly, Michael Mallin, in the College of Surgeons, St. Stephen's Green, sent a dispatch to MacDonagh in Jacob's Factory.

It has not been possible to come upon the text of that dispatch, nor is it clear, indeed, if MacDonagh's reply acknowledging it (see above) ever reached Mallin.

It is certain, however, that having sent the dispatch to MacDonagh, Mallin decided to surrender.

Liam Ó Briain, who was attached to the St. Stephen's Green Garrison all during the week, has written an account of the surrender.[1]

He tells that about 11 o'clock on Sunday morning Lieut. Bob de Coeur of the Irish Citizen Army, in charge of the outpost in York Street to which he (Ó Briain) was attached, received orders to bring his men back to the College of Surgeons.

"In the College the men were gathering from all sides; from the roof, from the top rooms, from the various sentry posts at the back and both sides of the building, from the positions occupied in the houses towards Grafton Street....There was great excitement and anger, a general query of why? Of course none of us had any idea what had happened in the other areas of the city. Some of the women were weeping. Mallin addressed us...."

"....Labhair sé den ghuth íseal ciúin sin a chualas uaidh ó thús go deireadh na haithne a bhí agam air. Bhí scéal brónach le hinsint aige, dúirt sé. Bhí na taoisigh, an Piarsach agus an chuid eile sa Cheanncheathrú, is é sin le rá, in Ardoifig an Phoist, tar éis éirí as an troid, ar son na ndaoine i mBaile Átha Cliath. Bhí ordú faighte aige uathu agus ordú fé leith óna cheannfort féin, Séamas Ó Conghaile, go gcaithfí géilleadh; nárbh ar a son féin amháin a bhíodar ag géilleadh in Ardoifig an Phoist ach in ainm agus ar son saighdiúirí na Poblachta ar fud na hÉireann; dá bhrí sin go mbeimisne ag leagan síos na n-arm agus ag dul amach inár bpríosúnaigh nuair a thiocfadh na saighdiúirí inár gcoinne. D'iarr sé orainn go léir glacadh leis seo mar a dhéanfadh fíorshaighdiúirí; d'iarr sé ar an I.C.A. muinín a bheith acu as

E

Mícheál Ó Mealláin   Michael Mallin

1874–1916

a dtaoiseach féin, Séamus Ó Conghaile; thug sé buíochas dúinn
uile; dúirt sé nár shíl sé go bhféadfadh fir bheith chomh dílis,
chomh seasmhach, chomh daingean is bhí gach duine san áit i
rith na seachtaine; go mba mhór ar fad an onóir leis bheith i
gceannas orainn; gur....gur....gur....ansin, tháinig tocht air;
chonaiceamar na deora ina shúile; chrom a cheann ar an
mbord...."

Major de Courcy Wheeler, who was Staff Captain to
Brigadier-General Lowe in 1916 and who accepted the surrender of the St. Stephen's Green Garrison, has left an account[2]
of what occurred :

"....I went to the Castle and obtained information from the
Garrison Adjutant that a telephone message had been received
from the O.C. Troops, Shelbourne Hotel, stating that the
Republican Flag over the College of Surgeons had been hauled
down and that troops were required to take over the College and
the surrender of the Garrison.

I motored back at once to Trinity College and ordered the
officer in charge of the military escort, which was in waiting, to
proceed up Grafton Street as far as possible and to keep his
men out of view of Stephen's Green as there was still sniping
from various points.

From there I motored to the Kildare Street entrance to the
Shelbourne Hotel and interviewed the O.C. Troops, who pointed
out the position from the top window where he had his Maxim
gun placed.

Having ordered him, and telephoned the O.C. Troops in the
United Services Club, not to open fire under any circumstances
as I was about to receive the surrender of the Garrison, I returned
to Grafton Street, picked up the Sergeant Major and drove to
the front door of the College of Surgeons.

I ordered the Sergeant Major to bang on the door and, after
I had waited for a reasonable time without getting any response,
a civilian signalled that there was something going on down in
York Street. I went there and saw a white flag hanging out of
the side door of the College. Two of the officers came out,
advanced and saluted.

The Commandant stated that he was Michael Mallin and that
his companion was Countess Markievicz and that he and his
followers wished to surrender....Commander Mallin was not
armed but carried a walking-stick which he gave to me as a
personal memento. . . .The walking-stick was stolen from me
....I requested Commandant Mallin to order his men to lay
down their arms in the College, march out and form up in front
of it. While they were doing so, I sent a message to the escort

in Grafton Street to come up . . . I then inspected the Garrison
in the College, ascertained that they had disarmed, and inspected
the arms in a large room in the upper part of the building. . . .
Commandant Mallin and Countess Markievicz accompanied me
during my inspection. . . .Having completed the inspection I
ordered the Commandant to march out his followers who, he
informed me, numbered 109 men, 10 women, Countess
Markievicz and himself. I telephoned, from the nearest instru-
ment available, to Headquarters to inform the General of the
surrender. . . ."

From the College of Surgeons, led by Mallin and Countess
Markievicz, his second-in-command, the Garrison were taken,
under heavy guard—". . . saighdiúirí timpeall orainn . . . sáirsint
ag siúl síos suas go bagarthach ag iarraidh eagla a chur
orainn . . ."—to Dublin Castle and thence to Richmond
Barracks.

Liam Ó Briain has recorded several conversations he had
with Mallin while both were prisoners there:—

Speaking of the plan of the Rising Mallin said: "Nuair a
taispeánadh an plean dom—plean an Éirí Amach—dúras ar an
bpointe boise: 'Cá bhfuil an dara plean, an plean ionaid
(alternative plan) a thiocfas i bhfeidhm nuair nach n-oibreoidh
an plean seo? Plean ar nós oibriú cloig (clock-work) an plean
seo agus tá chuile sheans go dtitfidh sé as a chéile.' Ní raibh aon
phlean ionaid ann."
The same day Mallin remarked to Ó Briain: "Taking him
all in all, the average Tommy Atkins is not a bad fellow!" Dar
le Ó Briain, "ní raibh fuath ar bith ná gangaid i gcroí Uí Mheal-
láin d'éinne. Ní raibh aon am aige dá leithéid mar ba léir gurbh
ar a theaghlach féin agus a anam a bhí a intinn leagtha."

Rumours of executions were rife in Richmond Barracks but
the prisoners, including Mallin, were loath to believe them until,
one day, a British soldier gave to Ó Briain a portion of the
Evening Mail which contained a list of men executed that morning. He showed the paper to Mallin who said: "That proves
that the rumours are true."

"Ó shin amach," adeir Ó Briain, "go dtí gur tógadh uainn é,
bhí sé níba chiúine, dá mb'fhéidir, agus bhíodh an paidrín ina
láimh aige ar feadh an lae beagnach. . . .
An lá d'imigh sé uainn chraitheamar lámh leis agus ghuíomar
sonas air. Rinne sé meangadh beag gáire linn agus shiúil amach

i ndiaidh na saighdiúrí. Dar liom bhí sé chomh suite is bhí an
Méidsear Mac Giolla Bhríde ar céard a bhí i ndán dó. . . ."

Mallin was probably tried on the same day as Heuston
(4 May).

"When I was giving evidence before the Field General Court
Martial of the surrender of Commandant Michael Mallin," said
Major de Courcy Wheeler "the President of the Court asked
him did he wish to put any questions to me. Commandant
Mallin said: 'No' but (turning to me) 'I would wish it placed on
record how grateful my comrades and myself are for the kindness
and consideration which Captain Wheeler has shown to us
during this time.' The President of the Court said that his wish
would be carried out."

And it is more than likely that Mallin was taken to Kilmainham, as was Heuston, on the day of his trial.

On Sunday, 7 May, he was told the verdict of the Court
Martial—that he was to be shot on Monday at 3.45 a.m.
He wrote a letter to his wife.

Letter to his Wife, 7 May, 1916

My darling Wife Pulse of my heart, this is the end of all
things earthly; sentense of Death has been passed, and a
quarter to four tomorrow the sentence will be carried out
by shooting and so must Irishmen pay for trying to make
Ireland a free nation, Gods will be done. I am prepared
but oh my darling if only you and the little ones were
coming too if we could all reach Heaven together, my
heartstrings are torn to pieces when I think of you and them
of our manly James happy go lucky John shy warm Una
dadys Girl and oh little Joseph my little man my little man
Wife dear Wife I cannot keep the tears back when I think
of him he will rest in my arms no more, to think that I have
to leave you to battle through the world with them without
my help . . . . . With Gods help I will be always near you
If you can I would like you to dedicate Una to the service
of God and also Joseph, so that we may have two to rest on
as penance for our sins try and do this if you can pray to
our Divine Lord that it may be so, Fr. McCarty has just

been in with me and heard my Confession and made me
so happy and contented. he will see to the Education and
General welfare of our dear ones; you must go and see him
my darling Fr. McCarty James St God Bless him as well
you will go and see Alderman T. Kelly, he is a good God
fearing man and will be able to help you for my sake as
well as yours he will know what to do, it is due to you
as the Wife of one of the fallen, when I left Richmond
Barracks to come he (Kilmahainm) the only one of my
household that I could cast my longing Eyes on was poor
Prinie the *dog* she looked so faithfull there at the door;[3]
are you sure you left nothing in the house you know the
Police broke in and made a thorough search, however those
are mear earthly things let me get back to you and I
we have now been married thirteen years or so and in all
that time you have been a true loving wife too good
for me, you love me my own darling think only of the
happy times we spent together forgive and forget all else,
I am so cold this has been such a cruel week, Mr. Partridge[4]
was more than a Brother to me kept me close in his arms
so that I might have comfort and warmth his wife[4] is here
under arrest if he gets out and you see him tell him I met
my fate like a Man, I do not believe our Blood has been
shed in vain. I believe Ireland will come out greater and
grander but she must not forget she is *Catholic* she must
keep her Faith. I find no fault with the soldiers or Police
I forgive them from the Bottom of my heart, pray for all
the souls who fell in this fight Irish & English God and his
Blessed Mother take you and my dear ones under their
care a husband's blessing on your dear head my loving wife,
a father's blessing on the heads of my children James John
Una Joseph my little man my little man my little man, his
name unnerves me again all your dear faces arise before me
God bless you God bless you my darlings . . . . . .

God and his Blessed Mother guard you again and again,
Pulse of my heart good by for a while, I feel you will soon
be in heaven with me. I am offering my life in atonement
for all my sins and for any debts due.

Give my love to your dear Mother Josephine[5] Mr.
Farrell[5] and all the children, they must all pray for my

poor soul. You will have a Mass said for me loved wife, my life is numbered by hours now darling I am drawing nearer and nearer to God to that good God who died for us you and I love and our children and our childrens children. God and his Blessed Mother again and again Bless and protect you Oh Saviour of man if my dear ones could die and enter heaven with me how Blessed and happy I would they would be away from the cares and trials of the world Una[6] my little one be a *Nun* Joseph[6] my little man be a Priest if you can James & John to you the care of your mother make yourselves good strong men for her sake and Remember *Ireland* good By my wife my darling. Remember me, God again Bless and Protect you and our children. I must now Prepare these last few hours must be spent with God alone. Your loving Husband MICHAEL MALLIN

Commandant

Stephens Green Command

I enclose the Buttons off my sleeve keep them in memory of me

MIKE xxxxxx

The original of this letter is in the possession of Michael Mallin's son Séamus.

Letter to his Mother and Father, 7 May, 1916

Kilmainham Prison,
May 7th, 1916.

My dear Mother and Father,

Forgive your poor son who is soon to meet his death. I am to be shot tomorrow at a quarter to four. Forgive him all his shortcomings towards you—this applies especially in the management of my father's business.

Dear father, forgive me all, and you, dear mother, the pain I give you now.

Pray for me. Give my love to Tom, May, John, Bart, Katie and Jack Andrews.[7] They must all pray for me.

I tried, with others, to make Ireland a free nation and

failed. Others failed before us and paid the price and so
must we.

Good-bye until I meet you in Heaven.

Good-bye again. A kiss for you, dear mother. God bless
you all.

I have now but a few hours left. That I must spend in
prayer to God, that good God who died that we might be
saved. Give my love to all. Ask Uncle James[8] to forgive me
any pain I may have caused him. Ask Tom Price[9] and all
in the trade to forgive me. I forgive all who may have done
me harm. God bless them all.

Good-bye again, Mother dear, and Father, God bless
you.

                    Your loving son,
                                   MICHAEL MALLIN.

A manuscript copy of this letter—not in Mallin's handwriting—is held in the National Library. The original cannot be
traced. Although the copy-manuscript bears the wrong date—
9th instead of 7th May—and contains some misspellings (corrected in the reproduction) the text has every appearance of
authenticity; and Mallin's son, Séamus, confirms[10] that there
was such a letter.

On the night before he was executed Mallin was visited in
his cell in Kilmainham by his wife and four children, John,
James, Una and Joseph—Joseph was an infant in arms—two
of his brothers, Tom and Bart, and a sister, Katie.

Séamus, the eldest of the four children—he was twelve years
of age at the time—has written the account which follows[11] of
the visit as he remembers it.

"Bhíomar ceathrar de chlann ann faoi Bhealtaine, 1916: níor
rugadh Maura Constance, an cailín is óige, go ceann ceithre mhí
tar éis a hathair do lámhachadh. Lenár seanmháthair i dtigh
beag ar thaobh an bhóthair, timpeall cúpla céad slat ó Phríosún
Chill Maighneann, a bhí mé féin agus Seán, an deartháir is
cóngaraí dom in aois, ag cur fúinn.

Bhíomar tar éis Seachtain na Cásca féin a chaitheamh lenár
n-aintín, Jane Thewlis, deirfiúr ár máthar, a raibh teach aici i
Séipéal Iosóid ag bun an chnoic mhóir ar a dtugtar "Guinness's
Hill." Ní chuimhin liom mórán faoin seachtain ach an aimsir
a bheith go breá grianmhar agus an bia, an t-arán ach go háir-

ithe, a bheith gann, ceal plúir. Nuair a bhí an tÉirí Amach thart, d'aistríomar go dtí an teach beag i gCill Maighneann. Bhí mo mháthair agus an bheirt pháiste eile, Úna agus Seosamh, ag fanacht ag Cros an Araltaigh le Tom Mallin, deartháir m'athar. Ach b'shin rud nach raibh ar eolas agam san am. Bhí mo mháthair tar éis Seachtain na Cásca a chaitheamh ag cuardach na cathrach ar lorg eolais faoina fear céile, ach tásc ná tuairisc ní bhfuair sí air.

Bhí mé féin agus mo dheartháir inár gcodladh nuair a tháinig an carr. Bhí giota páipéir, ordú de shaghas éigin, i láimh póilín a bhí sa charr. Thaispeáin sé do mo sheanmháthair é. "Tá ré Mhaidhc caite," ar sise.

"Níl, ní féidir sin a bheith fíor," arsa m'aintín Katie. D'imigh an bheirt acu sa charr. Ní raibh mo sheanathair inár bhfochair; bhí sé thall i Léarpholl ag obair sa mhonarcha nua a bhí bunaithe ag Muintir Jacob ansin. Nuair a d'fhill an bheirt bhan dúradh linne ár gcuid éadaigh a chur umainn agus imeacht sa charr. Ní dúradh a dhath eile, ach, cé nach raibh deoir le feiceáil ar ghrua na seanmhná, thuigeamar go maith go raibh rud éigin uafásach ag titim amach, rud nárbh fhéidir é a mhíniú dúinn. Bhí m'aintín Katie ag osnáil os íseal. Cuireadh isteach sa charr sinn. Tháinig m'uncal Bart in éineacht linn. Sílim go ndeachamar ar dtús go Cros an Araltaigh faoi choinne mo mháthar agus na beirte páiste óga. Níl me cinnte faoi sin amach is amach. B'fhéidir go ndeachaigh carr eile faoi choinne mo mháthar. Ní raibh mé féin, an páiste ba shine, ach dhá bhliain déag d'aois. Rud eile de, bhí sé mall san oíche agus gan sinne, na páistí, inár ndúiseacht i gceart.

Ach bhí mo mháthair linn ag dul isteach sa phríosún dúinn. Halla mór leathdhorcha a bhí ann; póilíní agus saighdiúirí timpeall orainn. Ar éigin a labhair duine ar bith focal, agus nuair a labhair ba i nguth íseal a labhraítí. Treoraíodh ar aghaidh sinn thar dhoirse ísle ar thaobh na láimhe clé, gach doras acu cosúil lena chéile. Thug mé solas faoi deara, mar a bheadh solas buí coinnle ann, taobh thiar de dhoras a bhí ar leathoscailt; agus chuala mé monabhar mar a bheadh an Paidrín Páirteach á rá.

Osclaíodh an chéad doras eile agus ligeadh isteach i seomra beag sinn. Bhí m'athair ansin romhainn ina sheasamh os ár gcomhair amach, é díreach mar ba chuimhin liom i gcónaí é, aoibh bheag an gháire ar a éadan, ach gan sult ann; ach gan é bheith searbh ach oiread. Bhí blaincéad beag thart ar a ghualainn air. Ní dóigh liom go raibh seaicéad air; ach sin rud eile nach bhfuil mé cinnte faoi. Thug mé faoi deara sagart ard maorga a raibh culaith fhada a bhí dubh agus bán air. Blianta ina dhiaidh sin chuala mé gurbh é an tAthair Mícheál de Brún, O.P., a bhí ann. Bhí sagart eile ann freisin, sílim;[12] ach ní fhaca mé i ndáiríre ach m'athair agus mo mháthair.

"Tá mé le bás a fháil amárach le breacadh an lae," arsa m'athair. Níl mé chun aon rud a rá faoin mbriseadh croí a bhí ar mo mháthair. Ní chreidfeadh sí é. Cheap sí i gcónaí go n-éalódh na Volunteers agus an Irish Citizen Army amach as an gcathair. Deireadh m'athair roimh an Éirí Amach gurbh é sin an rud ba chóir a dhéanamh, agus gur cheart cath a chur ar an namhaid faoin tuath faoi mar a tharla a cheathair nó a cúig de bhlianta ina dhiaidh sin. Ní raibh mo mháthair in ann a chreidiúint gurbh é seo an deireadh. Maidir linne, na páistí, ní móide gur bhaineamar ciall cheart as a raibh ag titim amach. Roimh an Éirí Amach ba ghnách le m'athair labhairt liomsa mar a labhródh sé le duine fásta; ar ndóigh, cheap mé gur dhuine fásta mé féin cheana féin. Ach anois ní raibh ionam ach páiste beag arís gan aon tuiscint agam ar chúrsaí an tsaoil, agus gan ach an t-aon smaoineamh amháin i m'intinn, nach bhfeicfinn m'athair arís, rud nach raibh inchreidte agam.

Ní cuimhin liom mórán eile faoin oíche sin. Ach d'fhan rud amháin go soiléir i mo mheabhair. Bhí pictiúr againn sa bhaile in Inse Chora, pictiúr a rinne m'athair agus é san India. D'olann a bhí sé déanta agus mheasamar gur phictiúr breá é, ní mar gheall ar an rud a thaispeáin sé ach mar gheall ar chomh cliste is a rinneadh é. Séard a bhí ann macasamhail de bhratacha agus drumaí na Royal Scottish Fusiliers, reisimint leanar chaith m'athair dhá bhliain déag ina dhrumadóir. Dúirt sé anois go mba cheart an pictúir a dhó. "B'fhearr gan é sin a dhéanamh," arsa an sagart ard. "B'fhearr gan ach smaointe na carthanachta a bheith i d'intinn agus i do chroí agus tú ag dul i láthair ár dTiarna." D'aontaigh m'athair leis ar an bpointe, agus rinne sé gáire beag. Ar ndóigh, séard ba mhó a bhí ag déanamh buartha dó, an riocht ina raibh mo mháthair agus gan aon duine againn in aois le cúnamh a thabhairt di slí mhaireachtála a bhaint amach.

Ach labhair sé faoi na daoine a raibh sé i gceannas orthu i rith na Seachtaine i bhFaiche Stiabhna agus i gColáiste na Máinlia, go háirithe na fir a fuair bás; ina measc siúd bhí fear óg, Jimmy Fox, aonmhac baintrí fir ar bheag an bhaint a bhí aige go foirmiúil leis na Volunteers nó leis an Irish Citizen Army. Ach theastaigh ón mhalrach óg a chuid féin a dhéanamh ar son na tíre agus chuaigh sé amach chun troda in éineacht le m'athair. Maraíodh ar an dara lá é i bhFaiche Stiabhna. Labhair sé freisin faoi William Partridge, Comhairleoir de Bhardas na Cathrach. "Ba gheall le dearthaáir ionúin dom é an t-am ar fad," ar seisean. Agus leis an bhfírinne a rá ba dheacair teacht ar fhear ba chneasta ná é. Cheap m'athair gur bheag seans a bhí aige éaló ón bhású ach oiread leis féin. Ach tháinig sé slán an t-am seo cé nárbh fhada a mhair sé ina dhiaidh sin."

Cardinal Browne, who had accompanied Michael (then

Brother John) Heuston on the latter's visit to his brother, Seán, in the adjoining cell, recalls[13] having visited Mallin's also.

".... After some time I heard sounds of weeping from outside. I spoke to the cell-guard about them, and he told me they came from the cell next door,[14] which was that of Michael Mallin who was also under sentence of death and whose family had just arrived to visit him.

As the weeping was intense I said to the guard that I should like to enter Michael Mallin's cell to help to console his family. He said, however, that I had no permit and that he could do nothing about it. As the weeping continued as before I spoke to him again, and he, as if also very moved, said to me: 'Just walk in.'

I was dressed in my white religious habit, and my entrance causing surprise, the weeping momentarily ceased.

The cell-guard made no difficulty, and Michael Mallin came forward to meet and welcome me. He was serene though very much affected. I remained with him and his family for some time.

I cannot now remember the details of our conversation but one of them has never left my mind. Having said that a baby was soon to be born to Mrs. Mallin, he said to her that if that child should be a boy she should direct him towards the priesthood, and if it should be a girl,[15] he asked that she be called 'Mary' in Baptism in honour of the Blessed Virgin. Having done what I could during my visit, under feelings of deep emotion I bade good-bye to Michael Mallin and returned to the cell of Seán Heuston...."

---

[1]*Capuchin Annual*, 1966, and *Cuimhní Cinn*.

[2]*Irish Press*, 30 April, 1949.

[3]Mallin's home was "cúpla céad slat ó Phríosún Chill Maighneann." (See below.) He passed by it on the way from Richmond Barracks to Kilmainham. He had passed it too on Sunday, 30 April, when the St. Stephen's Green Garrison were being led, under escort, from the Castle to Richmond Barracks. As Liam Ó Briain said (*Cuimhní Cinn*): " . . . agus leanamar ar aghaidh thar Ard-Teampall Chríost, tré Shráid Thomáis, Sráid Shéamais, agus amach Cill Maighneann. Bhí níos mó daoine anois amuigh ag breathnú orainn agus bhí cuma eile orthu. Cé nár dhúradar tada, ba léir duinn go rabhadar cairdiúil linn. Ag dul i méid a bhí an chairdiúlacht agus sinn ag siúl Bóthar Emmet. Ní raibh aon eolas agamsa ar an taobh seo den chathair ach dúirt duine éigin liom gur thart anseo a bhí cónaí ar an gCeannfort Mallin agus thugas fá deara gur aithnigh go leor é, agus go rabhadar á thaispeáint dá chéile." "Prinie," the family pet, was a great favourite with Mallin—"mada," dar le Séamus, mac Mhichíl, (i litir don Eagarthóir) "a shábháil mo dheirfiúr ó chapall a bhí anuas uirthi, ar cosa in airde, bliain go leith roimhe sin.'

[4]William Partridge, Irish Citizen Army, a member of Dublin Corporation, was with Mallin in St. Stephen's Green, in the College of Surgeons and in Richmond

Barracks. He was sentenced to 15 years' penal servitude (five years remitted) for his part in the Rising. His wife, Mary, was detained in Kilmainham for a few weeks after the surrender.

[5]Josephine was Mallin's sister-in-law. Mr. Farrell was her husband.

[6]Una became a Loreto nun; Joseph became a Jesuit priest, as did John also.

[7]Tom, John and Bart were Mallin's brothers. May and Katie were his sisters. Jack Andrews was May's husband.

[8]Uncle James (Dowling) was Mallin's mother's brother.

[9]Tom Price was a weaver, a friend of Mallin, who was himself a weaver.

[10]In a statement to the Editor.

[11]*Inniu*, 23 Meán Fómhair, 1966.

[12]Bhí. An tAthair Aguistín, O.F.M.Cap. a rinne friotháil ar Ó Mealláin.

[13]In a written statement to the Editor.

[14]Cell No. 18.

[15]It was a girl—Maura Constance.

ÉAMONN CEANNT

As we have seen above, MacDonagh, in Jacob's Factory, had refused to accept the surrender order, signed by Pearse and Connolly, brought to him on the morning of Sunday, 30 April, 1916, first by Nurse Elizabeth O'Farrell and later, by Fathers Aloysius and Augustine; he would discuss terms only with the General Officer commanding the British military.

Fathers Aloysius and Augustine having advised Brigadier-General Lowe of this, a parley was arranged between Lowe and MacDonagh. This took place at midday and a truce was arranged to allow MacDonagh to consult the Garrisons of the South Dublin Union and Marrowbone Lane Distillery as well as the Garrison of Jacob's Factory.

The two Capuchin Fathers accompanied MacDonagh. They went first to the South Dublin Union where Éamonn Ceannt was in command.

"There," says Father Aloysius, "we were admitted and saw Éamonn Ceannt. After consultation between Thomas MacDonagh and the officers it was agreed that surrender was the wisest plan."

MacDonagh having returned and having informed Lowe of the decision to surrender, and having formally surrendered himself, it was agreed that he should go back to the South Dublin Union and call also to Marrowbone Lane Distillery to arrange the surrender of those Garrisons. " When we returned to the South Dublin Union," continues Father Aloysius,[1] "Éamonn Ceannt, speaking to the officer at the door of the Union, remarked that it would surprise him to see the small number who had held the place."

Desmond Ryan, referring to this incident, quotes Sir Francis Vane, who was in command of the British forces in the area, as having asked Ceannt "in amazement whether the main buildings had been held with only forty men" and Ceannt as having replied gently: "No. Forty-two."

Ceannt marched with his men to Marrowbone Lane Dis-

Éamonn Ceannt
1881–1916

tillery. Séamus Ó Murchadha of the Garrison there has described[2] the arrival of Ceannt:

Even though MacDonagh had told us of the surrender we had had no word from our own Commandant—we had not heard from him all during the week—and felt that it was still necessary to be on the alert. Somewhat late on the previous day, Saturday, an unofficial report had reached us that surrender had taken place. We had had doubt as to its genuineness. It must have been very early on Sunday morning that I wrote a dispatch to Commandant Ceannt referring to the report and requesting his orders. It never reached him. . . . In all, we felt doubt and uncertainty at that time.

But our doubts and uncertainties were dispelled by the arrival of Commandant Ceannt leading the South Dublin Union Garrison. He halted them outside the Marrowbone Lane outpost and came in accompanied by a British officer. He was bareheaded as well as I remember, but still armed. I can remember noticing a tear in his uniform. There was dignity in his bearing. He came over to where I waited for him, informed me of the General Surrender and told me to have the Garrisons assembled and formed up. With the assistance of Con Colbert who, with his men had moved from Ardee Street about the middle of the week and joined our Garrison, the units were summoned to the Distillery yard and formed up. We marched out of the Distillery and joined the South Dublin Union Garrison at "Halt!" outside.

The two priests, having called with MacDonagh to the South Dublin Union, to Marrowbone Lane and then to Jacob's, returned to St. Patrick's Park "hoping," as Father Augustine has said, "to see the boys there again."

Father Augustine wrote:

They did not arrive and I began to wonder what was causing the delay. In about fifteen minutes, however, we saw the South Dublin Union Garrison marching in, and at once my eye caught sight of the   [3] figure of the leader.

The whole column marched splendidly with guns slung from their left shoulders and their hands swinging freely at their sides. They wore no look of defeat, but rather of victory. It seemed as if they had come out to celebrate a triumph and were marching to receive a decoration. Ceannt was in the middle of the front   [4] with one man on either side. But my eyes were riveted on him so tall was his form, so noble his bearing, and so manly his stride. He was indeed the worthy captain of a brave band who had fought a clean fight for Ireland.

They drew up just opposite us as we stood at the corner where ⁵ Street meets ⁵ Street and grounded their guns at his command. Father Aloysius and myself looked on in silence. We saw Éamonn give up his gun and then his belt to an English officer. But when I saw them taking off his Volunteer uniform I said at once to Father Aloysius: "I can't stand this any longer. Come along and we'll let them see what *we* think of those men." We walked across the street, shook hands warmly with Éamonn and with a "Good-bye and God bless you" just looked at the officers and departed for Church Street after a tense and trying day.

After the surrender Ceannt was taken to Richmond Barracks. Séamus Ó Murchadha has described[2] the journey there:

From Marrowbone Lane to Bride Street; halted there east side of Street and turned, facing opposite side. A large force of British military and Army covered lorries. After a while we were ordered to place all arms and equipment at our feet. (I am sure we looked sadly down at our hard-bought arms and equipment.) Then soldiers came, collected them in handcarts and brought them to the lorries. On the march again from Bride Street: destination unknown. Ceannt was at the head of our Garrison. I was beside him. A tall soldierly figure, he was resolute in expression; pallid of countenance as usual. He was silent.

On through Thomas Street towards Kilmainham; and then we could guess our temporary destination at least. We were turned in at Richmond Barracks and halted in the Square. It was a quiet orderly march except for noisy hostility evinced towards us by a few spectators. (These learned later and were different.)

In the Square we just looked around curiously and exchanged a few words. I saw at some distance from us, in a group, our plucky and devoted Cumann na mBan, now separated from our Garrison. No complaint could be made about the conduct of the British military from the time we left Bride Street. The officer at Marrowbone Lane was courteous.

But it was different in the Barracks. Suddenly we were split up into groups indiscriminately and roughly hustled by the barrack staff into rooms with space for about twenty persons in each. I can remember only one person in the room with me who was a member of our Garrison. Doors were locked and guards placed.

The following morning we were all brought to a large hall (the Gymnasium, I think) and put sitting on the floor. I saw Con Colbert at a distance from me among the crowd but I did not speak with him. We were under guard and not permitted to move or stand up. Shortly afterwards detectives (known as G-men) came in to scrutinise us and to pick out victims for their exacting masters. So far, no names taken nor searching done.

Ceannt was tried by Court Martial in Richmond Barracks, on 4 May, 1916, the same day as Heuston.

On that day he wrote two letters to his wife and made some notes on the court-martial charge sheet.

Letters to his Wife, 4 May, 1916

Richmond Barracks
4/5/16

My wife, at present at 5 Fitzwilliam Terrace, Dartry Road, Upper Rathmines.

The gold watch in my possession give to Mrs. Burgess.

The other things are yours to use as you think fit and this is to authorise the military authorities to hand all my things over to you. I have £2 in notes and about 12/- or 15/- in silver. Also a beads.

ÉAMONN CEANNT

Richmond Barracks

My wife at present at 5 Fitzwilliam Terrace, Dartry Road, Upper Rathmines.

Trial about to be resumed at 10 this (Thursday) 4th May '16.

I am cheerful and happy and hope Aine and little Rónán also are so. Whatever befals I shall try to accept my fate like a man and commend you and Rónán to the sympathy and support of our relatives and friends. Slán leat. Do not fret.

ÉAMONN CEANNT

These letters, written on printed message-blanks, are in the National Library.

Notes written on Court Martial charge sheet

Copy of Charge.

Did an act, to wit: Did take part in an armed rebellion and in waging war against His Majesty the King, such act being of such a nature as to be calculated to be prejudicial to the Defence of the Realm and being done with the intention of and for the purpose of assisting the enemy.

(1) My position—shall not deny anything proven or admit what is not proven.

Legal advice necessary. Deny latter portion of charge.

(2) Is Crown case closed?

(3) Rebut Major's evidence.

4. — 1. Republic duly established.

— English were the aggressors.

5. Communicate with my wife.

Witnesses :—

(This document is on exhibition in Kilmainham Gaol Museum.)

The following day, unaware as yet of the findings of the Court Martial, but "expecting the worst—which may be the best," he wrote to his wife.

Letter to his Wife, 5 May, 1916

Richmond Barracks
5 May, 1916.

To my wife at present at 5 Fitzwilliam Terrace, Dartry Road, Upper Rathmines, or c/o Mr. Richard Kent,[6] 71 Richmond Road, Drumcondra. Writing in English to say I am well but am expecting the worst—which may be the best. Everyone amazingly cheerful and resigned to their several fates.

Can see there is a "reign of terror" outside.

Everyone seems to be here in Richmond Barracks. Lily[7] probably in Kilmainham. I saw her.

Not much comfort here, but I sleep well and we get ample rations. Make Mrs. B's[8] mind easy. I'm sure she's worrying. Tell Rónán[9] to be a good boy and to remember Easter 1916

for ever. I'm in excellent form. I'm sure all relatives etc.,
will be looked after later on. Don't expect you'll see No. 2
as you left it. Probably looted by this. Adieu or au revoir
—I don't know which.

Mr. M. A. Corrigan, Solr., 3 St. Andrew St. (undertakers
also) might get you or Richard to see me.

ÉAMONN CEANNT.

(This document is on exhibition in Kilmainham Gaol Museum.)

It has not been possible therefore to establish the exact date
on which Ceannt was transferred from Richmond Barracks to
Kilmainham, but it is certain that he was in Kilmainham on
Sunday, 7 May, as the addressed statements, etc., which follow
confirm.

Letter to his wife, 4 p.m., 5 May, 1916

(This letter, like several of the others written by Ceannt, is
on a printed message-blank. It is numbered ' 2 ' apparently in
Ceannt's hand in the appropriate blank space. The letter is in
the National Library.)

5/5/1916 4 p.m. Richmond Barracks

Áine (my wife)

Trial closed. I expect the death sentence which better
men have already suffered. I only regret that I have now
no longer an opportunity of showing how I think of you
now that the chance of seeing you again is so remote.
I shall die like a man for Ireland's sake.

ÉAMONN CEANNT.

(The date, including the date-line, is written, as are other
letters in the series, in blue indelible pencil. The words " Richmond Barracks " have been scored out in lead pencil and the
word " Kilmainham " written in their stead. This would appear
to establish that Ceannt was moved to Kilmainham on the 5th,
although we cannot be sure how long the letter may have
remained in his possession before he succeeded in sending it out.)

Statement written in Kilmainham, 7 May, 1916

Cell 88,
Kilmainham Gaol,
7 May, 1916.

I leave for the guidance of other Irish Revolutionaries who may tread the path which I have trod this advice, never to treat with the enemy, never to surrender at *his* mercy, but to fight to a finish. I see nothing gained but grave disaster caused, by the surrender which has marked the end of the Irish Insurrection of 1916—so far at least as Dublin is concerned. The enemy has not cherished one generous thought for those who, with little hope, with poor equipment, and weak in numbers, withstood his forces for one glorious week. Ireland has shown she is a Nation. This generation can claim to have raised sons as brave as any that went before. And in the years to come Ireland will honour those who risked all for *her* honour at Easter in 1916. I bear no ill will towards those against whom I have fought. I have found the common soldiers and the higher officers human and companionable, even the English who were actually in the fight against us. Thank God soldiering for Ireland has opened my heart and made me see poor humanity where I expected to see only scorn and reproach. I have met the man who escaped from me by a ruse under the Red Cross. But I do not regret having withheld my fire. He gave me cakes!

I wish to record the magnificent gallantry and fearless, calm determination of the men who fought with me. All, all, were simply splendid. Even I knew no fear nor panic and shrunk from no risk even as I shrink not now from the death which faces me at daybreak. I hope to see God's face even for a moment in the morning. His will be done. All here are very kind. My poor wife saw me yesterday and bore up—so my warden told me—even after she left my presence. Poor Aine, poor Rónán. God is their only shield now that I am removed. And God is a better shield than I. I have just seen Áine, Nell, Richard and Mick and bade them a conditional good-bye. Even now they have hope!

ÉAMONN CEANNT.

It seems that this statement, except for the last few lines, had been written by Ceannt before he met his visitors on Sunday, 7 May; that he added the last two sentences after he had parted with them. The statement that on the previous day his wife "bore up . . . even after she left my presence" would seem to indicate that she knew, at that time, that her husband was to be executed; that the verdict of the Court Martial had, at that stage, already been conveyed to Ceannt; that he had been told on Saturday, 6 May, that he was to be executed on Monday, 8 May—though Heuston, who was also executed on 8 May, did not know of his fate until some time in the evening of Sunday, 7 May.

Ceannt certainly knew of the verdict of the Court Martial in his case before 4 p.m on Sunday, when he wrote a note to his wife.

Nóta dá Bhean chéile, 7 Bealtaine, 1916

Date 7/5/16
Time 4 p.m.
Place (Kilmainham)

To. Áine, mo bhean,

Coinnigh é seo i gcuimhne orm a Áine a mhíle ghradh.

Abair le Rónán go bhfuilim ag fágháil bháis ar son na hÉireann.

Nuair a thiocfas ciall agus tuigsint aige tuigfidh sé an méid sin.

Dulce et decorum est pro patria mori.

Seo é an 7adh lá de Mhí na Bealtaine 1916.

From ÉAMONN CEANNT.

This note, written on a printed message-form, is on exhibition in Kilmainham Gaol Museum. Roman script has been substituted for the Gaelic script used by Ceannt.

Nóta dá Mhac, 7 Bealtaine, 1916

i bPríosún Chille Maighnean,
An 7mhadh lá de Bhealtaine, 1916

Dom' Mhaicín bhocht Rónán,
Ó n-a athair atá ar tí bás d'fhagháil amáireach ar son
na h-Éireann.

Slán agus beannacht.

ÉAMONN CEANNT

I.S.—Tabhair aire mhaith dho do mháithrín. Go gcúidigh-
idh Dia an bheirt agaibh, agus go dtugaidh Sé saoghal
fada faoi shogh agus faoi mhaise dhaoibh araon.
Go saoraidh Dia Éire.

Again, Roman script has been substituted for the Gaelic script
used in the original.

Notes written in Kilmainham, 7 May, 1916

Cell No. 20
Kilmainham Jail
7th May, 1916.

Arrangements for Áine (proposed)

(1) To take my place re weekly collections as long as they
are remunerative.

(2) To have my two Insurances looked after. I leave all
my possessions to my wife.

(3) Perhaps the D.M.O.A. would make a grant.

(4) Richard to apply for assistance out of any Fund which
may be organised for the relief of dependants.

(5) For the above purpose—(4)—to communicate with
J. R. Reynolds, An Cumann Urudhais, College Street,
who may be able to give information or guidance.

(6) I leave my watch-chain to Rónán subject to his
mother's approval. Also, if she approves, I would like
Mick, Richard, Nell, Lily, Mrs. Brennan, John P.
and Bill to get each some small token of me with my
blessing.   ÉAMONN.

(This document is on exhibition in Kilmainham Gaol Museum.)

It will be observed that these notes were written in Cell No. 20, the statement of 7 May (see above) in Cell No. 88.

Ceannt was the only one of the condemned men who left evidence as to the cells he occupied.

Cell No. 88 is on the top landing of the Central Compound. It was occupied, for a time, by Joseph Mary Plunkett, for a pencil inscription on a wooden panel in the wall read: This is Joseph Plunkett's cell —— me —— execution —— out —— a.m. May ——[10] (Signed) Grace Plunkett.

Cell No. 20 is on the ground floor of the Central Compound, the fourth cell from the end on the left-hand side as one enters from the front of the Jail.

It is clear, therefore, that Ceannt was brought down to the ground floor some time on Sunday, presumably so that it would be more convenient for the military to take him to the execution yard on Monday at dawn.

It seems that the same procedure may have been adopted in the case of some, at least, of the other condemned men, as we know now that the last four cells on the left on the ground floor of the Central Compound were occupied on the night of 7 May by Ceannt (20), Heuston (19), Mallin (18) and Colbert (17).

Letter to Commandant, Kilmainham, 7 May, 1916

Cash 12–2½
1 silver, Waltham, watch
1 gold chain with seal
1 rosary beads
1 latch key

Please hand above to my wife, 13 Alphonsus Road, Drumcondra

and oblige,
Yours faithfully
ÉAMONN CEANNT
11.35 p.m.   7/5/16

To The Commandant
Kilmainham Gaol

(This letter is in the National Library)

Valedictory message to friends, 7 May, 1916

Fágaim mo bheannacht agus mo mhíle beannacht ag na
daoine seo thíos uile.

ÉAMONN CEANNT

Capt. Séamus Murphy, formerly 7 St. Mary's Terrace,
  Rathfarnham
John P. Kent my brother and Colr. Sergeant William Kent
Joe Crofts 82 Lr. Camden Street
Mrs Mellows 21 Mountshannon Road
Lily Brennan with best wishes for the future
Seán Mac Giobúin c/o Corporation
Miss Crissie Doyle; Mary Nolan Buttevant

(This letter is in the National Library.)

Last Will and Testament, 7 May, 1916

Kilmainham Gaol,
7th May, 1916.

I hereby leave all I have in the world to my wife to do with
same whatever she thinks fit. (Would she please give my
watch-chain to Rónán.)

ÉAMONN CEANNT

The Notes above and the Will were probably the writing
which Father Augustine saw when he called in to Ceannt's cell
in the early morning of Monday, 8 May, 1916. (See below.)

Letter to his Wife, 8 May, 1916

2.30 a.m.
8/5/16

My dearest wife Aine,

Not wife but widow before these lines reach you. I am
here without hope of this world and without fear, calmly
awaiting the end. I have had Holy Communion and Fr.

Augustine has been with me and will be back again. Dearest "silly little Fanny." My poor little sweetheart of— how many—years ago. Ever my comforter, God comfort you now. What can I say? I die a noble death, for Ireland's freedom. Men and women will vie with one another to shake your dear hand. Be proud of me as I am and ever was of you. My cold exterior was but a mask. It has saved me in these last days. You have a duty to me and to Rónán, that is to live. My dying wishes are that you shall remember your state of health, work only as much as may be necessary and freely accept the little attentions which in due time will be showered upon you. You will be— you are, the wife of one of the Leaders of the Revolution. Sweeter still you are my little child, my dearest pet, my sweetheart of the hawthorn hedges and Summer's eves. I remember all and I banish all that I may be strong and die bravely. I have one hour to live, then God's judgment and, through his infinite mercy, a place near your poor Grannie and my mother and father and Jem and all the fine old Irish Catholics who went through the scourge of similar misfortune from this Vale of Tears into the Promised Land. Bíodh misneach agat a stóirín mo chroidhe. Tóig do cheann agus bíodh foighde agat go bhfeicfimid a chéile arís i bhFlaithis Dé—tusa, mise agus Rónán beag beag bocht.

Adieu

EAMONN.

This letter, now in the National Library, was written within an hour or so of Ceannt's execution, between the time of Father Augustine's first call to see and minister to him and his return to accompany Ceannt to the execution yard. Father Augustine has left an account[11] of Ceannt's death.

"But let me take only one man and tell you his story. The only man whom I shall take from the number, and whose name strangely stirs me now, is the brave, the gallant, the glorious, the upright Éamonn Ceannt.

There was poor Willie Pearse; and poor MacDonagh had gone; and poor Thomas Clarke had gone; and Major MacBride had gone in the lonely morning. He had gone, and others, too, had gone, when the time of Éamonn Ceannt came, with three other devoted Irish Volunteers.

Going about all that lonely, sad Sunday of the surrender, going about from place to place with Thomas MacDonagh, I saw Ceannt several times, where he had commanded in the South Dublin Union. Thomas MacDonagh had consulted him and some other officers, and the whole matter of surrender was left with MacDonagh. I was passing along with MacDonagh from the South Dublin Union, and, coming near that point where Robert Emmet was hanged for his love of Ireland, poor MacDonagh said to me : 'There's where Robert Emmet was executed,' and, looking at me wistfully, he added : 'It is strange how history repeats itself. It is very, very strange.' All that he meant I shall perhaps never, never know, but he meant this much at all events—and each of the men who surrendered for love of Ireland knew, and I very much fear all the English knew it too—he meant that he, too, would be called upon to lay down his life for his country.

A few days afterwards I saw Éamonn Ceannt again. I did for him what any priest would have done under the circumstances. Then, on a certain morning, he sent for me. The very first moment I entered his cell I saw a sheet of beautiful white paper with some lines of ink upon it. We spoke for some little time, and did something else, and then he said to me : 'Father, you have to make other visits, haven't you?' 'Yes.' said I, 'I have.' 'Well, Father,' said he, 'I would like you to come back to me again.' And then, taking out his watch, he looked at it and said : 'Father, I have yet an hour, have I not?' And I turned to the wall before I said : 'Yes, Éamonn, just another hour.'

I went away across the hall to minister to poor Mallin and when I came back again we prayed together as long as we could. I remember the Irish saints we invoked. . . .We invoked them all. And then, as I was going out, I said to him, leaving him my own crucifix : 'Éamonn, keep that, and I will be with you to the last.'

And so, when with another priest, I had gone out to the verge of the outer courtyard outside, I left him quickly and shot back and I saw Éamonn coming towards me down the hall, and my soul leaped to him, and my heart embraced him, and we went out together, he to die for Ireland, and I to live for my country.

I had to stand a short distance away, and what I am going to say now I have never said and I will never say again. I have never said it even to his dear heroic wife, Mrs. Ceannt. I am going to say it now, though. I know that you have not the heart, just as I have never had the heart, to say it to her.

They brought out a soap-box there and they asked Éamonn to sit down on the soap-box, and an officer came forward, and, when Éamonn was sitting there, asked him to stretch his legs out and, bearing my cross in his tied hands, and with his eyes blind-folded, the poor, sweet, gentle soul, the dying saint, who died with forgiveness of his enemies on his lips, and telling of the kindness of a British officer, he put out his feet, and the firing squad took their aim, and shot. . . .

When poor Ceannt tumbled over from the soap-box I stooped to take the crucifix which he was bearing in his hands and I saw that it was spattered with blood. . . ."

[1]"Personal Recollections," *Capuchin Annual,* 1966.

[2]In the course of a statement, in response to inquiries by the Editor.

[3]Magnificent? Word missing from manuscript.

[4]Row? Word missing from manuscript.

[5]Words missing from manuscript. Nurse Elizabeth O'Farrell has recorded that the men laid down their arms at the junction of Bride Street and Ross Road.

[6]His brother.

[7]"Lily" was Lily Brennan, Ceannt's sister-in-law. She was, in fact, in Kilmainham. A member of Cumann na mBan, she had been in action in the South Dublin Union.

[8]"Mrs. B." was Mrs. Brennan, Ceannt's mother-in-law.

[9]His son.

[10]Words indecipherable. This inscription has unfortunately been defaced in recent years.

[11]What follows is an abridged version—compiled from a newsman's report which is with the Devoy papers in the National Library—of a speech delivered by Father Augustine in San Francisco in July, 1919, and reported in the *Gaelic American,* 2 August, 1919.

And see bibliographical note p. x.

Conchúir Ó Colbáird   Con Colbert
1888–1916

CONCHÚIR Ó COLBÁIRD   CON COLBERT

After MacDonagh had formally surrendered to Brigadier-General Lowe at 3.15 p.m. on Sunday, 30 April, 1916, he was allowed to return to the South Dublin Union, to Marrowbone Lane Distillery and to Jacob's Factory to arrange for the surrender of the Garrisons at these centres. He was accompanied by Fathers Aloysius and Augustine. "At Marrowbone Lane," says Father Aloysius,[1] "a great number of people, particularly women and children, had gathered while MacDonagh and Father Augustine were in the works with the Volunteers. I had remained outside with the chauffeur. After what seemed a long time they returned to the car. I understood they had had some difficulty in persuading the Volunteers there to surrender. They were well fortified and had provisions to last for some time . . ."

Questioned as to the reactions of the men in Marrowbone Lane Distillery to the news brought there by MacDonagh, Séamus Ó Murchadha, of that Garrison recalled:[2]

The reaction of the men was, first of all, surprise—surprise because no major attack had been mounted against our outpost, surprise, because rumours of great successes for Republican arms had been filtering through, rumours that the whole country had risen, and many other such stories. And, secondly, there was a sense of disappointment among the men—and the women —for we were ready and willing to fight on and had a good supply of arms and ammunition.

The matter has to be considered, however, in relation to the most unusual event experienced around Dublin in many, many years, and to the mental attitude wrought in men living for one exciting week outside their normal domestic ways. It was not a time that conduced to ordered thought or discussion or favoured opportunities to obtain individual views.

With the first official indication of the actual position there would, of course, be a lessening of the spirit which had been maintained all during the week. The spirit was still, however, high enough to ensure that if our Commandant, who had our affection and confidence, ordered further resistance, his order would, I am satisfied, have been obeyed.

As to Con Colbert's reaction I can, I am afraid, add nothing to what I have said in a general way. Con was not with the rest of us when MacDonagh came in.

Colbert surrendered with the Marrowbone Lane Garrison when the South Dublin Union Garrison, led by Ceannt, joined them at the Distillery, and the combined Garrisons, having laid down their arms in Bride Street, were marched, under escort, to Richmond Barracks. They arrived there some time around six o'clock on Sunday evening.

Colbert's court martial took place in Richmond Barracks, probably on the same day as Heuston's, 4 May, and he was, more than likely, transferred to Kilmainham, with Heuston, on the same day, and told on Sunday, 7 May, that he was to be shot the following morning. He did not send for any of his people to visit him. (In a letter to his sister, Lila,—see below— he said that he felt that a visit "would grieve us both too much.")

Instead he wrote no less than ten letters. Those to Lila, Mark, Jim and Gretta are in the National Museum. The others remain in the possession of the addressees or their families.

Letter to his Sister, Lila, 7 May, 1916

Kilmainham Gaol
7th May, 1916.

My dear Lila,

I did not like to call you to this Gaol to see me before I left this world because I felt it would grieve us both too much, so I am just dropping you a line to ask you to forgive me anything I do owe you and to say "Goodbye" to you and all my friends and to get you and them to say a prayer for my soul.

Perhaps I'd never get the chance of knowing when I was to die again and so I'll try and die well. I received this morning & hope to do so again before I die.

Pray for me, ask Fr. Devine & Fr. Healy & Fr. O'Brien to say a Mass for me also any priests you know.

May God help us—me to die well—you to bear your sorrow.

I am, your loving brother,
CONN.

I send you a prayerbook as token. Write to Nan, Jack & Willie[3] & ask them to pray for me.

Letter to his Brother, Mack, 7 May, 1916

7/5/'16.

My dear Mack,

Just a line to say "Goodbye" and to ask you to pray for me. God has given me the grace to know when I'm to die. May He grant that I die well. Forgive me anything I owe you.

Goodbye,
Your loving brother,
CONN.

Letter to his Sister, Nora, 7 May, 1916

Kilmainham Gaol
7th May, 1916.

My dear Nora,

Just a line to say "Goodbye" to you and yours and ask you to say a prayer for my soul. Don't blame me—perhaps God's way of saving my soul.

Goodbye and God bless you and yours,
I am,
Your loving Brother,
CONN.

Letter to his Brother, Jim, 7 May, 1916

7/5/'16.

My dear Jim,

Don't fret when you see this, believe me I have a good chance of dying well, which may God grant. I'll pray for you all, so also you pray for me.

Goodbye,
I am,
Your loving brother,
CONN.

Letter to his Sister, Gretta, 7 May, 1916

> Kilmainham Gaol
> 7th May, 1916.

My dear Gretta,

Forgive the writer for his negligence & want of affection for now he'll not see you again. Say a prayer for his soul, which I hope will soon see heaven where I'll see those who are gone before and where I'll be able to pray for you.

Don't fret for with God's help I'll die in His Grace.

> With much love,
> I am,
> Your loving brother,
> CONN.

Letter to his Sister, Katty, 7 May, 1916

> Kilmainham Gaol
> 7th May, 1916.

My dear Katty,

Goodbye & God bless you.

Forgive me the little I owe you—I would I could have repaid ere I died, but 'twas not to be.

Pray for me when I am gone and I hope we'll all meet in Heaven—Give my love to Dick[4] and the children and remember me.

> Ever your fond brother,
> CONN.

Letter to his Aunt, Mary O'Donnell,[5] 7 May, 1916

> Kilmainham Gaol
> 7/5/'16

My dear Aunt Mary,

Just a line to ask you to pray for my soul & to get all your family and friends to do so also.

I am to be shot tomorrow morning at 3.45 a.m. and then God have mercy on me. I'll remember you all in my prayers too and we'll all, with God's Grace, meet in Heaven.

> I am,
> Your loving nephew,
> CONN.

Letter to his Cousin, Máire O'Donnell,[6] 7 May, 1916

Kilmainham Gaol
7/5/'16.

My dear Máire,

Just a line to ask your prayers for the repose of my soul, which is to depart at 3.45 tomorrow morning.

Get the nuns & all to pray for me—for you know what a sinner I have been. May God bless you & all.

I am,
Your loving Cos,
CONN.

Letter to two friends, Annie and Lily Cooney,[7] 7 May, 1916

Kilmainham Gaol
7th May, 1916.

My dear Annie and Lily,

I am giving this to Mrs. Murphy[8] for you. She'll not mind to hear of what is happening and she'll get you all to pray for those of us who must die. Indeed you girls give us courage, and may God grant you Freedom soon in the fullest sense. You won't see me again, and I feel it better for you not to see me, as you'd only be lonely, but now my soul is gone and pray God it will be pardoned all its crimes. Tell Christy[9] and all what happened and ask them to pray for me.

Goodbye dear friends and remember me in your prayers.

Your fond friend,
C. Ó COLBÁIRD.

Miss Annie Cooney,
Kilmainham Prison
or 16A Up. Basin St.,
Dublin.

F

Letter to the Dalys[10] of Limerick, 7 May, 1916

Kilmainham Gaol
7th May, 1916.

My dear Friends,

Just a line to say Goodbye & ask your prayers for my poor soul. May God prosper you & yours. May He save Ireland.

Goodbye
I am
Your fond friend
CONN

This letter was forwarded to the Dalys with a covering note (undated) as follows:

—Daly,
Sir,

Please find enclosed letter from the late C. Colbert.

I am Sir
Your obedient servant
W. S. Lennon
Major
Commdt.

Colbert was visited in his cell in Kilmainham by Mrs. Séamus Ó Murchadha, wife of Séamus Ó Murchadha of the Marrowbone Lane Garrison. Describing the visit Mrs. Ó Murchadha said:[11]

My husband was Captain of "A" Company of the Fourth Battalion of the Irish Volunteers who used to drill at Larkfield, Kimmage. He was in Marrowbone Lane Distillery during the Rising and, on Easter Tuesday, when I learned where he was, I went to see him. I remained in the Distillery and cooked for the Volunteers. I met Con Colbert there. I did not know him before that, only by appearance. I was in the Distillery up to the surrender on Sunday the 30th April. The men were in splendid spirits throughout. They did not like the idea of surrendering, but when they got the order from their superior officers, they obeyed it without hesitation. After the surrender about eighty girls, including myself, were arrested and detained in Kilmainham. I saw Con Colbert at Mass on Sunday, 7th

May, with Éamonn Ceannt, Michael Mallin and J. J. Heuston and a number of others. I saw five of the men going to Holy Communion that morning, including Con Colbert, Heuston and Mallin. I did not know the other two. The Volunteers marched out from the building where Mass was celebrated, before the women. We were in the gallery and we saluted the men as they passed out. We were afterwards severely reprimanded for doing so.

On that Sunday night, when I was in my cell with another girl, the sentry came to the door with a wardress and said someone wanted to see me. When I got outside the wardress asked me did I know anyone of the name of Colbert. I said I could not tell until I would see him. I was taken before the Governor who ordered that I be brought to Con Colbert.

There was a soldier present during our interview.

When I entered the cell Con was lying on the floor with a blanket over him. There was no plank bed or mattress of any kind in the cell and the night was bitterly cold. There was a little table and stool in the cell and a candle lighting on the table as Con was expecting the priest.

He jumped up when he saw me and said: "How are you? I am one of the lucky ones." Of course I knew what was going to happen to him when he said that. "I am proud," he said, "to die for such a cause. I will be passing away at the dawning of the day." I said: "What about Éamonn Ceannt?" He was the only other one of the men I knew. He replied: "He has drawn the lucky lot as well."

Con had his prayer-book with him and said he would leave it to his sister, Lila. "Here," he said, "is what I am leaving you," and he took three buttons belonging to his Volunteer uniform out of his pocket. "They left me nothing else," he added. He appeared to be happy and said he was quite resigned to go before his Maker. He said he never felt happier as he never thought he would get the honour of dying for Ireland.

I said to him that he was setting an example for all soldiers of the way they should die. The soldier who was present was crying. He said: "If only we could die such deaths."

I asked Con why he did not send for his sister, Lila. He said that he did not like to cause trouble. I said: "Never mind the trouble; they are bound to send for her." He said that she might find it hard to bear the strain.

I knelt down and asked him for his blessing. He gave it to me and said in a simple earnest way: "We will all meet above under happier circumstances."

He asked me when I heard the volleys fired on the following morning at Ceannt, Mallin and himself[12] would I say a Hail Mary for their departing souls. I said: "Of course I will." "If you are let down to exercise tomorrow," he added, "and

if you meet all the girls ask them to say one Hail Mary each
for the three of us who will be gone." I promised to carry
out his request.

When leaving him I said to him that a martyr's death was a
noble one. He was smiling as I was going out and said: "The
priest will be here in a minute now, so I will not lie down again."

I heard the volleys fired the following morning at break of
day and myself and the girl who was sleeping in the cell with
me got up and we said the De Profundis three times for the
men who were passing into eternity.

A report[13] in the *Evening Herald* of 31 May, 1916, prompted
Father Augustine, O.F.M.Cap., to write the following day to
the Editor of that paper.

To the Editor,
Evening Herald,
Dublin.
June 1, 1916.

Dear Sir,

In last evening's issue of your paper, towards the end of the
second news column of the front page, under the heading " Last
Moments of Volunteer Leader," it is stated that Cornelius
Colbert "died joking the men who were preparing him for
death." It is also asserted that when one of the soldiers was
fixing the white cloth on his breast, to indicate his heart, he
told them "his heart was far away at the moment."

This version is quite inaccurate and fanciful and I owe it
to his memory to give the true one.

There was no joking, not even the semblance of it. Poor
Colbert was far too beautiful and too reverent a character to
joke with anyone in such a solemn hour. I know very well where
his heart was then. It was very near to God and to the friends
he loved. What really happened was this. While my left arm
linked the prisoner's right, and while I was whispering something
in his ear, a soldier approached to fit a bit of paper on his
breast. While this was being done, he looked down, and address-
ing the soldier in a perfectly cool and natural way said:
"Wouldn't it be better to pin it up higher—nearer the heart?"
The soldier said something in reply, and then added: " Give me
your hand now." The prisoner seemed confused and extended his
left hand. "Not that," said the soldier, "but the right." The right
was accordingly extended, and having shaken it warmly, the
kindly human-hearted soldier proceeded to bind gently the
prisoner's hands behind his back, and afterwards blindfolded him.

Some minutes later, my arm still linked in his, and accompanied by another priest, we entered the dark corridor leading to the yard and, his lips moving in prayer, the brave lad went forth to die.

F.A.

---

[1]In his "Personal Recollections," *Capuchin Annual*, 1966.

[2]In a statement to the Editor.

[3]Nan, Jack and Willie were a sister and brothers living in San Francisco.

[4]Dick was Katty's husband.

[5]Mary O'Donnell, of Tullycrine, Co. Clare, was a sister of Colbert's mother. His cousin, Mrs. O'Donnell Loughrey, has told the Editor that Colbert visited her mother every year; that they were very close friends as well as being aunt and nephew.

[6]Máire O'Donnell was a nun in France at the time of Colbert's execution.

[7]Annie and Lily Cooney, members of Cumann na mBan, were prisoners in Kilmainham having taken part in the Rising with the Marrowbone Lane Garrison.

[8]Mrs. Murphy, wife of Séamus Ó Murchadha, was also a prisoner. She had been with her husband in Marrowbone Lane Distillery.

[9]"Christy" was Christy Byrne, Lieutenant of F Company (of which Colbert was Captain), later Vice-Commandant of the Fourth Battalion, Dublin Brigade.

[10]John, veteran Fenian, and his married brother and family of whom one, Edward, had already been executed on 4 May.

[11]In a statement given by her to a journalist some years ago.

[12]Colbert, it seems, was unaware that Heuston, too, was to be executed the following morning.

[13]The report, headed "Last Moments of Volunteer Leader," was as follows: Mr. Cornelius Colbert, Gale View, Athea, shot by Court Martial in Dublin, died joking the men who were preparing him for death, writes an Abbeyfeale man. When one of the soldiers was fixing the white cloth on his breast to indicate his heart he told them "his heart was far away at the moment."

And see bibliographical note p. x.

Tomás Ceannt   Thomas Kent

1865–1916

TOMÁS CEANNT   THOMAS KENT

In the early morning of Tuesday, 2 May, 1916—a couple of days after the surrender in Dublin—Bawnard House, Castlelyons, Co. Cork, the home of the Kent family, was surrounded by a party of Royal Irish Constabulary led by Head Constable Rowe.

Inside were Thomas, David, Richard and William Kent and their eighty-four-year-old mother.

The police called on the occupants to surrender. They refused and a pitched battle ensued during which Head Constable Rowe was killed and one of the brothers, David Kent, severely wounded. Mrs. Kent loaded the guns and handed them to her sons during the fray.

Military reinforcements were brought from Fermoy, about four miles away, and, at about 7 a.m. the siege having lasted for three hours, the whole family, including the aged mother, were ordered out of the house, their hands above their heads, and placed under arrest. In attempting to escape Richard Kent was shot and badly wounded.

Mother and sons were removed to Fermoy—David and Richard to the military hospital, where Richard died from his wounds two days later, Thomas, William and their mother to the military barracks. Mrs. Kent having been released about noon, Thomas and William were taken next morning, under military escort, to Cork Detention Barracks, Thomas in his bare feet.

Séamus Fitzgerald, who occupied the cell next to him, has told[1] that Thomas Kent was very strictly isolated from the other prisoners and that none of them had any contact with him.

Tried by Court Martial on 4 May for "the murder of Head Constable Rowe," Thomas was sentenced to death, William acquitted.

David, when sufficiently recovered, was transferred to Cork Detention Barracks, thence to Richmond Barracks, Dublin, where he, too, was court-martialled—on 14/15 June—and sentenced to death, but, in his case, the death sentence was commuted to five years' penal servitude.

Thomas was executed in Cork Detention Barracks on 9 May, 1916. He was attended, before his execution, by Father John Sexton, C.C., St. Patrick's, who was chaplain to Cork Military Hospital, and it was Father Sexton, no doubt, who reported Kent's last words, as published in *The Catholic Bulletin* in August, 1916.

Kent had expressed a wish that, after his death, Father Sexton would take charge of his Temperance Badge and give it to Father Ahearne of Castlelyons—

> From him I got it and I wish it to be returned to him untarnished. He may like to get it. Good-bye.

There is a story, though it has not been possible to get confirmation of it, that Kent was offered a stimulant before walking to his death but refused it, saying :

> I have been a total abstainer all my life and a total abstainer I'll die. I have done my duty as a soldier of Ireland and in a few moments I hope to see the face of my God.

This story rings true and is more or less confirmed by Father Sexton's report concerning Kent's wish that his Temperance Badge be returned, untarnished, to Father Ahearne.

Kent held in his bound hands, while he faced the firing squad, a rosary loaned to him by Father Sexton. It was recovered, blood-stained, after the execution, and given by Father Sexton to Miss Mary Chambers of Newport, Co. Mayo, who was a nurse in Cork Military Hospital in 1916 and who returned the rosary, some years ago, to the Kent family, who still have it.

Sa bhliain 1925 casadh an tOllamh Liam Ó Briain leis an bhfear a bhí i gceannas ar an scuad lámhaigh a bhásaigh Tomás Ceannt.

Chaith an tOllamh tráthnóna, an bhliain sin, i mbaile beag Reigate i Surrey, ar cuairt ag seanchara leis—Hereward T. Price —a bhíodh ina léachtóir in Ollscoil Bonn le linn don Ollamh bheith ina mhac léinn ann i 1914. Bhí deartháir leis an Uasal Price—ní cuimhin leis an Ollamh cia'n t-ainm baiste a bhí air

—san teach an tráthnóna ar fad "é páirteach san chomhrá ach gan aon rud á rá aige ach ar éigin."

Thionlaic an deartháir an tOllamh chuig an stáisiún traenach agus é ag imeacht.

I gcuntas a scríobh sé[2] deir an tOllamh:

". . . Ar ar mbealach go dtí an stáisiún labhair an deartháir agus sílim gur fearr dom ár gcuid cainte a chur síos i mBéarla chomh maith is is cuimhin liom é.

'Do you know,' ar seisean, 'I was feeling uneasy all the evening, feeling that I was sitting there under false pretences like.'

'How was that, what do you mean?' arsa mise agus ionadh orm.

'Well,' ar seisean, 'I was thinking that if you knew a certain thing about me you might refuse to sit in the same room with me. You see, I served in the Navy during the War and in the year 1916 I was stationed in Queenstown.[3] Your business in Dublin, during Easter, caused a rare shake-up in the forces in Cork and, to make a long story short, I found myself in charge of a firing squad, the squad which executed one of your men.'

'Kent?' arsa mise.

'Aye, that was the name.'

'How did he die?' arsa mise.

'Oh, very bravely,' ar seisean, 'not a feather out of him.' "

Tá an cuntas seo spéisiúil ar an ábhar go dtaispeánann sé gur ó Chabhlach Shasana a roghnaíodh an scuad lámhaigh a bhásaigh Ceannt. Bréagnaíonn an cuntas go críochnúil an scéal a scaipeadh go forleathan—gan aon bhunús leis—gur fiafraíodh de Cheannt, agus é ar tí a bhásaithe, an raibh aon "achaní deiridh" aige len iarraidh; go ndúirt sé go raibh, nach n-airrfaí ar aon Éireannach é a lámhachadh; gur géilleadh dá iarratas; agus gur piocadh an scuad lámhaigh dá réir ó na Scottish Borderers.

Ba dheacair a chreidiúint gur tugadh deis do Cheannt "achaní deiridh" a dhéanamh 'chor ar bith. Ba dheacra fós glacadh leis go mbeadh na Sasanaigh sásta malairt scuad lámhaigh a roghnú ag an nóiméad deiridh.

Agus, ar chuma ar bith, ní raibh na Scottish Borderers ar stáisiún in Éirinn i 1916. Aistríodh an reisimint as an tír tar éis dóibh pobal Bhaile Átha Cliath a ionsaí tráthnóna lae Smugláila na nGunnaí ag Beann Éadair, 26 Iúil, 1914.

[1]In a statement to the late Major Florence O'Donoghue.
[2]Chuig an Eagarthóir. Féach freisin, *Comhar*, Márta, 1967.
[3]Cóbh.

And see bibliographical note p. x.

Seán Mac Diarmada
1884–1916

SEÁN MAC DIARMADA

Seán Mac Diarmada was present at the momentous meeting of the Military Council of the Irish Republican Brotherhood in Liberty Hall on Easter Sunday morning when the decision was taken to strike at noon on Monday.

On Monday he walked ahead, with Clarke, from Liberty Hall to O'Connell Street. (Probably because he walked with a limp —the result of a serious illness in 1911[1]—he was not asked to march with the Garrison.) With Clarke, he awaited the arrival of the contingent of Irish Volunteers and Irish Citizen Army, led by Pearse, Connolly and Plunkett, who were to occupy the General Post Office, and when, at noon, the building was occupied, he entered with the leaders and took his place beside his comrades.

He had already at that time, written, probably in Liberty Hall, a dispatch to Major John MacBride and a covering note to the man, Ignatius Callender, who he hoped would be able to contact the Major.

The text of the covering note is available, but the terms of the dispatch—which never reached MacBride—are not.

Note to Ignatius Callender, 24 April, 1916[2]

> Dear Mr. Callender,
>
> Please deliver the enclosed to Major MacBride at once. Most urgent.
>
> Yours faithfully,
> SEÁN MACDERMOTT.

Though he had no formal military rank Mac Diarmada, because he was a member of the Provisional Government and because he was one of the leaders of the Irish Republican Brotherhood, was recognised by the Garrison as among the commanders.

On Easter Monday night, following consultation with the O'Rahilly and Clarke, he gave instructions to Seán T. O'Kelly,

who was a Staff Officer attached to the Headquarters Staff, to
call to Cabra Park to release Bulmer Hobson who, because he
was opposed to the Rising, and believed to be influencing
MacNeill, had been held incommunicado since Good Friday.

Note given to Seán T. O'Kelly, 24 April, 1916

Head Quarters
Irish Repub-
lican Gov.
24/4/16

Maurice Collins

Report to Ned Daly and release Hobson. Everything
splendid.

SEÁNMACD.

Seán T. O'Kelly added the words "at Richmond Hospital"
after Daly's name.

Thagair Seán T. Ó Ceallaigh don nóta seo ina leabhair:

"....Timpeall a deich a chlog oíche Luan Cásca tháinig Ó
Rathaille isteach i seomra na n-oifigeach agus bhí comhrá fada
dúthrachtach aige le Seán Mac Diarmada. Bhí Tomás Ó Cléirigh
ag éisteacht leis an bheirt ach ní dúirt sé mórán ar bith é féin.
D'imigh Ó Rathaille i gcionn tamaill agus ansin phléigh Ó
Cléirigh agus Mac Diarmada eatarthu féin pé fadhb a bhí
curtha ina láthair aige. Níorbh fhada go raibh fhios againn go
léir cad a bhí ag déanamh tinnis dóibh.
    Ghlaoigh Mac Diarmada orm os ard agus bhí a ghlór le
cloisteáil ar fud an tseomra:
    'A Sheáin T., an rachfá suas go dtí teach Mháirtín Uí Chon-
láin i bPáirc na Cabraí chun Hobson a shaoradh?'
    Dúirt mé go rachainn cinnte agus d'iarr mé air ordú scríofa
a thabhairt dom ar eagla nach mbeadh aithne ag na gardaí
orm na nach mbeidís sásta glacadh le mo fhocal leis féin. Thóg
MacDiarmada dialann bheag as a phóca, scríobh ar leathanach de le peann luaidhe 'Seán T. Ó Ceallaigh chun Bulmer
Hobson a shaoradh'[3] agus chuir cinnlitreacha a ainm leis.
Stróc sé an leathanach amach as an dialann agus thug domsa
é. Tá an blúire páipéir sin ina cháipéis stairiúil anois in
iarsmalann Scoil Uí Chonaill na mBráithre Críostaí i Sráid
Risteamain Thuaidh, Baile Átha Cliath....
    Dúirt Mac Diarmada nach raibh sé cinnte cé bhí ina gharda
ar Hobson san am áirithe sin mar gur athraíodh cúpla uair

na fir a bhí ina bhun. Ach mheas sé gurbh é Muiris Ó Coileáin
a bhí freagrach as anois. . . .

Dúirt Mac Diarmada liom a rá leis dul chuig an North Dublin
Union, a bhí faoi cheannas an Ghinearáil Ned Daly, nuair a
bheadh na cúrsaí seo socraithe againn. D'imigh mé liom. . . ."

Seán McLoughlin, who had come to the General Post Office
on Monday and again on Wednesday with messages from the
Mendicity Institute came again on Thursday morning. (He had
found that the Mendicity Institute Garrison had surrendered
when he returned there on Wednesday.)

On his way to the Post Office he had met his mother in North
King Street and had heard from her that his sister, Mary, who
was only a school-girl, was in the G.P.O., acting as a messenger.
His mother had told him to send his sister home. "Mary is too
young for that sort of thing," she had said.

Julia Grenan recalls[4] seeing McLoughlin coming into the
G.P.O., and hearing him address his sister. "Mary McLoughlin,"
he said, "your mother will murder you! She says you're to go
home!" And Miss Grenan recalls the gentle rejoinder of Mac
Diarmada who had also heard McLoughlin speak to his sister.
"Her mother will not murder her," he said. "Indeed she won't.
Her mother will be proud of her later on."

When, towards the end of the week, Connolly lay wounded
and Plunkett lay seriously ill, much of the direction of the fight
devolved on Mac Diarmada. Diarmuid Lynch tells of his being
active "with his usual geniality, thoroughness and imperturb-
ability."

What has been described as the "Last Dispatch from the
G.P.O." is attributed to him.

Dispatch from the General Post Office, 28 April, 1916

Army of the Irish Republic
(Dublin Command)

Headquarters.   Date. 28 April, 1916.

To. Tomas O Dubghaill, Officer in Charge Ballybough
Area.

To Officer in Charge
    You will find great difficulty in returning to head-

quarters Harbour area in hands of Military also Drumcondra and NCR areas, Seosamh Mac Nearaigh came by Richmond St Schools Charles St and thence via Railway St. If you cannot force an entry join with Michael O Tuathaigh who is in control Archbishop's House and the adjacent grounds as far as DWD distillery

Capel St area open

Two houses at corner of NCR and Jones's Rd held by military. D.S.

If pressed, disperse in twos and threes. Spare your ammunitions as we are practically done

Le meas mór

Seaghan Mac Díarmuid

Do tainig Monteithe annso indhiu   Na bach leis go foil

April 28

Headquarters G.P.O.

It has not been possible to trace the whereabouts of the original of this document. There is doubt as to its authenticity, and the numerous spelling errors add to this. The handwriting is unlike Mac Diarmada's—though the dispatch could have been written at his dictation—and the signature does not seem to be his. His usual signature was "Seán Mac Diarmada." The addendum in Irish is obscure. Monteith did not come to the G.P.O., during Easter Week.

Soon after the issue of that dispatch the General Post Office, a mass of flame, smoke and falling debris, became untenable, and the Garrison, forced to evacuate, dashed through machine-gun and rifle fire across Henry Street, into Henry Place, past the end of Moore Lane into Moore Street. There, throughout Friday night, they tunnelled their way through the walls of the houses as far as No. 16 which became their new headquarters.

On Saturday morning Dr. James Ryan, who was the Medical Officer attached to the Garrison, being concerned about the wounded—of whom there were eighteen apart from Connolly—asked Mac Diarmada "if we could possibly have them removed to hospital. He seemed dubious. I then suggested that I should approach the nearest British post, bearing a Red Cross flag, to discuss the matter. He laughed at my innocent trust in the Red Cross but said if I waited he would see what could be done."[5]

Shortly afterwards Mac Diarmada was in the headquarters room in No. 16 discussing with Pearse, Clarke, Plunkett and the wounded Connolly the question of negotiating terms.

William Pearse was there too, and Winifred Carney, Julia Grenan and Elizabeth O'Farrell.

"The meeting began," says Desmond Ryan, "some time after noon, and was conducted in low tones around Connolly's bed. At 12.45 Seán MacDermott asked Miss O'Farrell to improvise some white flags. One of these MacDermott hung out of the window of the room. Miss Grenan wept when Miss O'Farrell was chosen to carry a message to the nearest British post; it seemed certain death to go into the street where men had been shot down before their eyes. But Connolly roused himself and spoke reassuringly. Miss O'Farrell stepped out into the street waving the white flag high above her head. . . . In the head-quarters room, Connolly stares in front of him. Plunkett is calm. There are tears in MacDermott's eyes. Winifred Carney is weep-ing, pale and white. . . ."

The negotiations, as we know, resulted in a decision to sur-render unconditionally.

"Sadly and without speaking," says Julia Grenan,[4] "Pearse shook hands, one by one, with all in No. 16 before leaving to go with Nurse O'Farrell to meet General Lowe. All there, except Mac Diarmada and Willie Pearse, were in tears."

Connolly was taken on a stretcher to Dublin Castle. Pearse, having formally surrendered to Brigadier-General Lowe, was taken to British Army Headquarters at Parkgate. There he wrote the surrender order and signed copies of it, typed in British H.Q. It was 3.45 p.m.

Later on Saturday evening Nurse O'Farrell brought a copy of the surrender order to Moore Street.

"At last the officers called the men together," continues Desmond Ryan, "and they marched through the ruined walls, company by company, to a warehouse. Seán MacDermott read Pearse's letter to them, sombre, with a hint of tears in his eyes although his look was calm, clear, intense. Then MacDermott spoke with a touch of pride and passion in his voice, as he looked at the weary and haggard ranks in front of him who had listened in silence to the unconditional surrender order. He spoke simply, directed that food should be served out to the men, telling them to take one good meal as they might not be too well fed for some time where they were going. Again he explained the position:

> 'The only terms the British military authorities would listen to were an unconditional surrender. We surrendered not to save you but to save the city and the people of this city from destruction. You would have fought on. No matter, I am proud of you. You made a great fight. It was not your fault that you have not won the Republic. You were outclassed, that is all. They had the men, the munitions, the force. But this week of Easter will be remembered, and your work will tell some day.'

Then out into Moore Street marched the Volunteers, less than 200 of them, sleepless, weary, hungry, defeated, yet with a curious pride and sense of freedom stirring in them all. . . ."

The Garrison marched up O'Connell Street and, having laid down arms opposite the Gresham Hotel, were taken to the forecourt of the Rotunda Hospital. There they spent the night in the open, Mac Diarmada, as has been recorded elsewhere, being singled out for special ill-treatment.

His walking-stick was taken from him by the British officer in charge, whose churlish comment, when Mac Diarmada said he could not walk without it, was: "So the Sinn Féiners take cripples in their army," to which, according to Julia Grenan,[7] Seán replied with that dignity which sat so well on him: "You have your place, sir, and I have mine. You had better mind your place."

Dr. Ryan, who was beside Mac Diarmada at the time and who protested, has recorded[6] that "the rejoinders from this young officer are better left unrecorded."

Next morning the prisoners were marched to Richmond Barracks. "Miss Carney and I," says Julia Grenan,[5] "waited back to help Seán Mac Diarmada. He had explained to the officer that he could not march and so he was given a special escort for himself. Myself and Miss Carney were behind the Volunteers as we marched to the Barracks. Seán didn't arrive there until about three quarters of an hour after the rest of us. He limped in, completely exhausted from being out all night at the Rotunda and from the effort to walk to the Barracks."

Mac Diarmada was with Tom Clarke when the latter wrote to his wife from Richmond Barracks. (See above.)

He wrote a note to Mrs. Tom Clarke on the back of Clarke's note.

Note to Mrs. Tom Clarke, 30 April, 1916

Dear Caty,
I never felt so proud of the boys. 'Tis worth a life of suffering to be with them for one hour.
God bless you all.
SEÁN.

(This document is in the possession of John Daly Clarke.)

Nuair a tugadh Liam Ó Briain ina phríosúnach isteach i mBeairic Risteamain tráthnóna Dhomhnach Mion-Chásca bhí Seán Mac Diarmada ansin roimhe i measc na bpríosúnach. Tagrann sé dó ina leabhar:

".... B'é an cara ba mhó a bhí agam ansin Seán Mac Diarmada —Seán bocht bacach, grámhar, gliondarach, dathúil, dea-chroíoch Mac Diarmada—a bhí lena chaitheamh ar son na hÉireann dhá lá dhéag ina dhiaidh sin. Bhí fhios ag Seán go rabhas-sa i bhFaiche Stiabhna, thug cailín éigin an scéal isteach chuige an chéad lá. B'é an chéad fhocal adúirt sé: 'Céard é sin faoi t-ascaill agat?' Bhí a shúil air, dúirt sé, ó chonaic sé ag teacht isteach mé. Is éard a bhí ann seanchuilt a thugas liom ó Choláiste na Máinlia. 'Tabhair don Phluincéadach é,' ar seiseann, 'tá sé go han-tinn.' .... Bhí Seán Mac Diarmada gléasta díreach mar scaras leis deich lá roimhe sin. Tar éis dó a bheith ag ullmhú i gcomhair na hócáide móire seo le dhá bhliain níor chaith sé nóiméad machnaimh leis an bhfearas a bheadh air nuair a thiocfadh sé! ...

.... Tháinig Seán Mac Diarmada ag déanamh siúlóidín liom. Tháinig saighdiúir óg de na Notts and Derbies anall chugainn; stumpa de Shasanach óg fionn—an-fhionn, mar is minic chítear i Sasana agus annamh in Éirinn—agus dath an úill deirg ar a

dhá leicin. 'I say,' ar seisean go fiosrach, múinte, gan aon mhas-laitheacht dá laghad ina ghlór, 'I say, have you any idea what's going to be done with you blokes?' Bhreathnaigh Seán air agus tháinig an fhéachaint dúr sin ina shúile a bhíodh ann corr-uair in ionad na meidhre a bhíodh de ghnáth iontu. 'Some of us will be let out,' ar seisean leis an saighdiúir, 'and others will be shot; I'll be shot.'[8] 'Aoh!' arsa an saighdiúir ag bagairt a chinn beagáinín: is éard a bhí le rá aige, dar leat: 'Sea, is dócha gur fíor dhuit.' Ach chuaigh mar a bheadh scian thríomsa. 'Don't say that, Seán,' adeirim leis. 'Ah, do you think I care?' d'fhreagair sé, agus thosnaigh ag caint ar rud éigin eile....
....Shocraíomar sinn féin i gcomhair na hoíche....Tomás Ó Cléirigh agus cúl a chinn leis an mballa; taobh leis go dlúth bhí Seán Mac Diarmada, agus bhíos féin sínte le hais Sheáin.... Bhí comhrá agam i gcogar le Seán agus comhrá fada aigesean le Tom—an comhrá deiridh a bhí ag an mbeirt charad mór sin le chéile ar an saol seo. Is cuimhin liom Seán ghá rá go rabhdar cinnte go mbeadh na Gearmánaigh ag teacht de chabhair orainn. Is cuimhin liom go beacht focal adúirt sé go han-láidir: 'After all, the only failure in Ireland is the failure to strike!'....
....Tar éis tamaill thit a chodladh ar Sheán agus a cheann in ucht Tom...."

Fred O'Rourke of Jacob's Garrison—later with the St. Stephen's Green Garrison—recalls[9] that, at one stage, while he was in a room in Richmond Barracks with some six dozen others, the door was opened and

"Mac Diarmada, George and Jack Plunkett were pushed in. In a corner of the room was a large tank which the prisoners had been using as 'toilet accommodation.' It was full to over-flowing and the stench in the room was unbearable. No sooner was Seán inside the door than, noticing the stench—and the cause of it—he went mad with rage and started to kick the door. He continued to kick it and bang it with his fists until, eventually, an orderly came and opened it. Seán told him in no uncertain terms what he thought of the conditions, of the British Army in general and of those in Richmond Barracks in particular. The result was that ten buckets were produced, and, in relays of ten, we were allowed to empty the tank, after which a quantity of chloride of lime was thrown into it."

Ag leanúint le cuntas Liaim Uí Bhriain:

"....Tháinig an lá fá dheireadh ar glaodh amach mé sa tráthnóna ar chlós na beairice i dteannta dhá chéad nó trí chéad fear eile. Bhíodh sé sin ar siúl gach tráthnóna. D'imíodh leo agus ní fhillidís. Thuigeamar go raibh sé i ndán dúinne anois imeacht ina ndiaidh siúd go Sasana nó pé áit a rabhdar imithe ....Ach bhí dráma beag—tragóid bheag—ar siúl inár measc.... Cé tugadh amach as ceann de na seomraí agus a cuireadh isteach sna ranganna linne le dul go Sasana ach Seán Mac Diarmada! Thuig roinnt bheag daoine go mbeadh seans ann go dtiocfadh sé slán ón mbás dá seoltaí go Sasana é. Bhíodar ag faire. Bhí Seán T. Ó Ceallaigh ag faire ó fhuinneog anuas,[10] Donnchadh Mac Colla, Uachtarán an I.R.B., ó fhuinneog eile anuas agus cairde eile leis anseo agus ansiúd. Bhíos féin i mo sheasamh in aice leis. Bheannaíomar dá chéile ach ní raibh aon deis chainte agam leis. Ní raibh aon aithne ag na saighdiúirí Sasanacha ar éinne againn, ach fairíor! Sheol an diabhal cuid de na bleachtairí úd inár measc: an fear úd a luaigh mé cheana, an Cigire Love,[11] tháinig sé ag breathnú ar na ranganna agus dúirt sé: 'Is that McDermott I see there?' Ba leor an méid sin. Tugadh Seán amach agus cuireadh ar leataobh é.

Do dhubhaigh ar a chontanós, facthas dom, agus é sco ar siúl agus dúirt sé os ard leo: 'You have a lot of changing about.' B'é sin an focal deiridh a chualas uaidh, an uair dheiridh a leagas súil air. . . .''

Séamus Layng, of Portumna, was in the room—Block L, Row 6—in Richmond Barracks to which Mac Diarmada was brought back. Séamus recalls the occasion:[12]

Mac Diarmada was by no means disconsolate. He seemed to accept as inevitable that he would be shot. We tried to tell him that his being brought back didn't necessarily mean that, but he wouldn't listen. He said, in a matter-of-fact kind of way: "Seán Heuston and Con Colbert were shot and they didn't sign. Only Connolly and myself of the signatories are left. We'll be shot." He didn't seem in the least worried.

That night a British officer came to the door and asked: "Is John MacDermott here?" Seán, who was lying on the floor, stood up, saying "Yes" and limped towards him—he had no stick. The officer handed him a slip of paper with the charge: "That you took part in an armed rebellion, waged war against His Majesty", and so on.

Again, though we feared the worst, we tried to persuade Seán that this was not the end, but he wouldn't even discuss the matter. "Let's have a concert," he said. We did. Seán himself gave a recitation—"Brian Boy Magee."[13]

Next morning—the Court Martial was to be at 11—he begged the loan of a razor from a British Tommy and, having shaved and returned the razor, said to us with a smile: "I have to make a nice corpse, you know."

Then, when the soldiers came to take him away, he shook hands with each of us in the room in turn saying: "Pray for me at dawn." He gave me a penny and a two-shilling piece as keepsakes and was led away under escort.

We did pray for him at dawn, but he was not shot until three days later. I heard the shots.

Mac Diarmada was tried by Court Martial in Richmond Barracks on Tuesday, 9 May, 1916.

"Nuair a cuireadh triail air, throid sé," dar le Liam Ó Briain. "Thug sé a ndúshlán a chruthú gur chuir sé a ainm agus a shloinne le Forógra na Poblachta."[14]

He was sentenced to death and, the sentence having been confirmed by the General Officer Commanding-in-Chief, Mac Diarmada was told on 11 May that he was to be shot the next morning.

He wrote a letter to his brothers and sisters.

Letter to his Brothers and Sisters, 11 May, 1916

> Kilmainham Prison
> Dublin
> May 11th 1916

My Dear Brothers and Sisters

I sincerely hope that this letter will not come as a surprise to any of you, and above all that none of you will worry over what I have to say. It is just a wee note to say that I have been tried by Courtmartial and sentenced to be shot—to die the death of a soldier. By the time this reaches you, I will, with God's mercy, have joined in heaven, my poor father and mother as well as my dear friends who have been shot during the week. They died like heroes & with God's help I will act throuout as heroic as they did. I only wish you could see me now. I am just as calm and collected as if I were talking to you all or taking a walk to see Mick Wrynn[15] or some of the old friends or neighbours around home. I have priests with me almost constantly for the past twenty four hours. One dear old friend of mine, Rev. Dr. Brown Maynooth, stayed with me up to a very late hour last night. I feel a happiness the like of which I never experienced in my life before, and a feeling that I could not describe. Surely when you know my state of mind none of you will worry or lament my fate. No you ought to envy me. The cause for which I die has been rebaptised during the past week by the blood of as good men as ever trod God's earth and should I not feel justly proud to be numbered amongst them. Before God let me again assure you of how proud and happy I feel. It is not alone for myself so much I feel happy but for the fact that Ireland has produced such men.

Enough of the personal note. I had hoped Pat,[16] to be able to help you in placing the children in positions to earn their livelihood, but God will help you to provide for them. Tell them how I struck out for myself and counsel them to always practice truth honesty straightforwardness in all things and soberiety. If they do this and remember their country they will be all right. Insist on their learning the language and history. I have a lot of books and I am making arrangements with one of the priests to have them turned in to a library, but I can arrange that you get some of them for the children. You might like to get these clothes that I am wearing to have them in memory of me, so I will arrange if possible to have them sent to my old lodgings[17] and you ought to come there and take them and any other little things belonging to me that you'd like to have— of course for Dan[18] & Maggie[19] also. There are a few copies of a recent photo which you can take, and you might order more copies for friends who may like to have one. Of course you got the letter I sent you a few days before Easter. By the way, when you are in Dublin find if I owe any money to my landlady, and if so pay her. I don't think I do but at the moment I'm not certain. One word more about the children. Put some of them to learn trades if you can at all. You will see if they show any promise of mechanical or technical skill, they were too small when I saw them to advise. Tell Maggie she ought to try & get Mary Anne[20] to go for teaching. I don't know what Caty Bee[21] ought to do. As for Dan, I suppose he will decide for himself. God direct him. He need not regret having stayed at home so long.

Make a copy of this and send it to the others as soon as you can. A lot of my friends will want to hear about me from James[22] Rose & Kate.[23] They can tell them all, that in my last hours I am the same Seán they always knew and that even now I can enjoy a laugh and a joke as good as ever. I don't know if you will require a pass to get to Dublin, but you better find out before you start. Perhaps martial law will have been withdrawn before you can come, it was passed for one month only and I don't think it will be renewed. If I think of any other things to say I will tell them to Miss Ryan,[24] she who in all probability, had I lived, would have been my wife. I will send instructions to my landlady, but she knows you all right.

Good Bye, Dear Brothers & Sisters make no lament for me. Pray for my soul and feel a lasting pride at my death. I die that the Irish nation may live. God bless and guard you all & may He have mercy on my soul. Yours as ever

SEÁN

P.S.   I find I have not mentioned Patrick[25] or his mother, but they know they are included for old very old times sake, yes, long before there was a thought of Maggie marrying Patk. also Mary[26] and Bessie.[27] I'd love to clasp the hand of each of you and many other dear friends but I will meet you all soon in a better place. Remember me to all friends and give some money to Fathers Foy & McLoughlin[28] for mass for me.

GooBye
SEÁN

Mac Diarmada also wrote a letter to John Daly, veteran Fenian.[29]

Letter to John Daly, 11 May, 1916

Kilmainham Prison
Dublin.
May 11th, 1916.

My dear Daly,

Just a wee note to bid you Good Bye. I expect in a few hours to join Tom[30] and the others in a better world. I have been sentenced to a soldier's death—to be shot tomorrow morning. I have nothing to say about this only that I look on it as a part of the day's work. We die that the Irish nation may live. Our blood will rebaptise and reinvigorate the old land. Knowing this it is superfluous to say how happy I feel. I know now what I have always felt—that the Irish nation can never die. Let present-day place-hunters condemn our action as they will, posterity will judge us aright from the effects of our action.

I know I will meet you soon; until then Good Bye. God guard and protect you and all in No. 15.[31] You have had a sore trial, but I know quite well that Mrs. Daly[32] and all the girls feel proud in spite of a little temporary and natural grief that her son and the girls their brother as well as Tom are included in the list of honours. Kindly remember me specially to Mrs. Clarke and tell her I am the same Seán she always knew.

God bless you all.

As ever.

Sincerely yours,

SEÁN MAC DIARMADA.

This letter is in the National Museum.

From midnight (11/12 May) the Misses Phyllis[33] and Mary Ryan[24] spent a few hours with Mac Diarmada in his cell in Kilmainham. Miss Mary Ryan has given the following account of the visit.[34]

We didn't know at all that Seán Mac Diarmada was going to die until we got word from the military that he wished to see me, and my sister if she wished to come. We had hoped, as the executions had stopped for a good while, that himself and Connolly would be spared. But then we knew definitely.

We saw him in his cell. It was a small cell. There was a board raised slightly at one side on towards the end of the cell and beside it there was a roughish table, with a chair, a rather roughish chair too, in front of it. On the table was a candle in a candlestick—I think it was a copper-looking candlestick—and the candle—a very yellow tallow-looking candle—was guttering down all the time onto the table. On the table there were a paper and a pencil, some writing on the paper.[35]

There was an army officer around the place and a soldier standing inside the door.

We sat down on the wooden bed, on the slightly raised board, and Seán sat between us and put one arm around each of us, and talked to us in a way that was in no way sad, I might say. We talked about everything. We kept off the evil moment of asking him anything about what was going to happen. We talked about the things that happened during the Week, and about people that were in it, and people that weren't in it, and we had a good laugh about some of them. It was ridiculous in a way because there was no sign of mourning. We had to hold up, of course, when he held up, and so we showed no sign of sorrow while we discussed things.

He asked us about the girls that used to come into our house and about other girls as well. He said he would like to send them some little thing. And so we collected any few pennies we had between us. With a certain amount of difficulty we got a penknife from the officer. Seán scratched his initials on the pennies, and then he cut the buttons off his coat—I can't remember, I don't think he was in uniform[36]—and gave them to us to give to different people.[37] (This we did, indeed, but we hadn't enough, of course, to go round.)

We were there at twelve o'clock and we didn't leave till three. We were three hours with him and talked about everything under the sun. We talked an awful lot about the week of the Rising and about how other places had fared, as much as we knew.

When the priest[38] appeared at three o'clock—Seán was executed at a quarter to four—we stood up promptly and felt a great jerk, I am sure all three of us, to say good-bye. I was the last to say good-bye to him and he kissed me and said, just said: "We never thought that it would end like this, that this would be the end." Yes, that's all he said, although he knew himself long before that what the end would be for him.

Statement written in Kilmainham, 12 May, 1916

Kilmainham Prison
12 May, 1916.
3.30 a.m.

I, Seán Mac Diarmada, before paying the penalty of death for my love of Ireland, and abhorrence of her slavery, desire to make known to all my fellow-countrymen that I die, as I have lived, bearing no malice to any man, and in perfect peace with Almighty God. The principles for which I give my life are so sacred that I now walk to my death in the most calm and collected manner. I meet death for Ireland's cause as I have worked for the same cause all my life. I have asked the Rev. E. McCarthy who has prepared me to meet my God and who has given me courage to face the ordeal I am about to undergo, to convey this message to my fellow-countrymen.

God save Ireland.

SEÁN MAC DIARMADA.

It has not been possible to confirm the authenticity of this document but it has the ring of truth.

The original in Mac Diarmada's handwriting—if it exists, or ever existed—cannot be traced, but copies, in handwriting other than his, found their way into circulation. One such is in the National Library.

It is unlikely that a spurious document mentioning the name of the Jail chaplain, Father McCarthy, would have been circulated.

*   *   *

As stated by Mac Diarmada in his letter to his brothers and sisters Rev. Dr. (later Monsignor) Patrick Browne of Maynooth spent some hours with him on the night of 10 May. Monsignor Browne left no account of the visit but, shortly afterwards, paid tribute to Mac Diarmada in verse.

TO SEÁN MACDERMOTT

Your pale dead face with sure insistent claim
Shall haunt my soul as long as thought endures,
Waking remembrance of your wasted frame
Afire with that all-conquering soul of yours

As last I saw you, captive in the net,
And heard you in Kilmainham's prison cell
Review the patient years with no regret
And say in sight of death that all was well.

I know you walked (O sad, lame steps!) to die
With high disdain of all who hold life dear
And sacrifice their honour like a pawn;

No dimness born of agony and fear
Was in those spirit eyes when carelessly
They faced the rifles at the grey of dawn.

(The original manuscript of this poem is in the possession of Mrs. Seán MacEntee.)

---

[1]Eámon Martin, who fought in the Church Street area in 1916—he was wounded, but, happily, survives—knew Mac Diarmada both before and after the illness. In a statement to the Editor he says: Seán had no limp before that. He had for a few years up till then been working hard—very hard—travelling all over the country as a full-time organiser for the I.R.B., and he was also managing "Irish Freedom," the I.R.B. organ. In 1911 he was involved in—indeed, he was the leader of—the campaign to counter the display of loyalty to the British King, George V, who was visiting Ireland. Seán gave all his time to it, speaking at meetings, organising counter-demonstrations, and so on. The biggest counter-demonstration was at Bodenstown in July, 1911. On the way home, at Usher's Island on the quays, as we marched in military formation from Kingsbridge (now Seán Heuston Bridge), we were involved in a fracas with the D.M.P. Seán, in the thick of the mêlée, was injured. Very soon after that he was struck down with what was believed to be poliomyelitis. Whatever the disease, it struck him suddenly; there had not been, as far as I can recall, any developing symptoms. He went into hospital—it was the Mater. Thereafter he walked with a limp (a short or crooked leg) and always carried a stick.

[2]In A Diary of Easter Week, *Dublin Brigade Review* (National Association of Old I.R.A., 1939), Mr. Callender gives a full account of his efforts—which proved futile—to deliver the dispatch to MacBride.

[3]Bhí Seán T. ag scríobhadh as a chuimhne, ar ndóigh.

[4]In a statement to the Editor.

[5]*Capuchin Annual,* 1966.

[6]*Capuchin Annual,* 1966.

[7]*Wolfe Tone Annual,* 1935.

[8]Mac Diarmada had expressed the same sentiment to Dr. Ryan in Moore Street after the surrender (*Capuchin Annual,* 1966), and Piaras Béaslai related (*Michael Collins,* Phoenix, 1926) that in Richmond Barracks Mac Diarmada said to him: "There will be executions; I suppose I will be shot; but the executions will create a reaction in the country which will wipe out the slavish pro-English spirit."

[9]In a statement to the Editor.

[10]Tá cuntas ar aon dul le cuntas Uí Bhriain ag Seán T. ina leabhar.

[11]Inspector Love of the Dublin Metropolitan Police.

[12]In a statement to the Editor.

[13]"Brian Boy Magee" was Mac Diarmada's favourite "piece." He invariably recited it when called on to "do a turn" at parties, etc., and, according to Éamonn Dore, who heard him recite it many times, Mac Diarmada would be so overcome with emotion at the last verse that he would tear his shirt collar open.

[14]Only a perusal of the Court-Martial documents, held with the papers of the British Judge-Advocate-General in the Public Records Office in London, will reveal what actually took place at the Court Martial.

[15]Mac Diarmada's godfather.

[16]Mac Diarmada's eldest brother.

[17]15 Russell Place, North Circular Road, Dublin.
[18]Brother, in the United States.
[19]Sister, married to a Patrick MacDermott.
[20]Sister, married in the United States.
[21]Niece.
[22]Brother, in the United States.
[23]Sisters.
[24]Now Mrs. Richard Mulcahy.
[25]Husband of sister Maggie.
[26]Sister, married to a William Dick.
[27]Second youngest sister.
[28]Curates in Mac Diarmada's native parish, Cloonclare, Manorhamilton.
[29]John Daly had taken part in the Rising of 1867; had spent twelve-and-a-half years in English convict prisons by the side of Thomas Clarke who became one of his closest friends, as did Seán Mac Diarmada during the years of preparation for the 1916 Rising when all three took counsel together. Edward Daly, executed 4 May, 1916, was a nephew of John Daly.
[30]Tom Clarke.
[31]No. 15 Barrington Street, Limerick, where John Daly lived.
[32]Mrs. Daly, John Daly's sister-in-law, was the mother of Edward Daly.
[33]Now Phillis Bean Uí Cheallaigh.
[34]This account is based on an interview given to *Radio Telefís Eireann* and shown on TV at Easter, 1966.
[35]Probably Mac Diarmada's letter to his brothers and sisters or that to John Daly.
[36]Mac Diarmada was in civilian clothes.
[37]He also gave them his cigarette case—inscribed inside "Seán MacD. 12/5/'16"—for their brother, James, now Dr. James Ryan, who had, of course, been with him in the G.P.O.
[38]Father Eugene McCarthy, James' Street, chaplain to Kilmainham.
And see bibliographical note p. x.

Séamus Ó Conghaile   James Connolly
                    1868–1916

SÉAMUS Ó CONGHAILE   JAMES CONNOLLY

Shortly before noon on Easter Monday, 24 April, 1916, James Connolly, having been nominated by the Military Council of the Irish Republican Brotherhood as Commandant General of the Dublin Division of the Army of the Irish Republic, led from Liberty Hall the composite group of Irish Volunteers and Irish Citizen Army which was soon to occupy the General Post Office.

At his right marched his Commander-in-Chief, P. H. Pearse; at his left Commandant Joseph Mary Plunkett.

(Two other members of the Military Council, Thomas Clarke and Seán Mac Diarmada, had already gone ahead to O'Connell Street, and two others, Thomas MacDonagh and Éamonn Ceannt, were already on their separate ways to occupy Jacob's Factory and the South Dublin Union. The seven were to become the Provisional Government of the Irish Republic when the Proclamation, of which they were also the signatories, was read.)

Connolly had earlier signed a warrant appointing Michael Kelly to the rank of Lieutenant in the Irish Citizen Army.

Order Appointing Michael Kelly Lieutenant

Irish Citizen Army
Headquarters, Liberty Hall, Dublin.
Commandant James Connolly.
Date, 24th April, 1916.

By warrant of the Army Council, I hereby appoint Michael Kelly to take the rank of Lieutenant, with full power to exercise all the rights and perform all the duties belonging to that rank.

(Signed) JAMES CONNOLLY
Commandant.

(This warrant was found, after the surrender, in the College of Surgeons where Lieutenant Kelly fought under Commandant Michael Mallin.)

And he had issued what was probably his first dispatch as Commandant General of the Dublin Division—a note to Seán Heuston:

Order issued to Seán Heuston, 24 April, 1916

April 24th

To Captain Houston (*sic*)

Take the Mendicity Institute today at 12 o'clock at all costs.

J. CONNOLLY.

At noon, the column having arrived, via Lower Abbey Street and the North side of O'Connell Street, in front of the Imperial Hotel (now Clery's), Connolly gave the order—"Left Wheel: the G.P.O.: Charge!"—and the General Post Office was occupied. Having supervised the building of defences, the fortification of windows, the barricading of doors, having seen the green banner with the words IRISH REPUBLIC hoisted on the roof at the Prince's Street corner and the tricolour at the Henry Street corner, Connolly stood outside to listen to Pearse reading the Proclamation of the Irish Republic, and when Pearse had concluded "clasped his hand and cried out: 'Thanks be to God, Pearse, that we have lived to see this day!'"[1]

Another dispatch, issued by Connolly on Tuesday, survives:

Dispatch issued from the General Post Office, 25 April, 1916

ARMY OF THE IRISH REPUBLIC
(Dublin Command)

Headquarters   Date—25th April, 1916.

To Officer in Charge,[2] Resis[3] & D.B.C.[4]

The main purpose of your post is to protect our wireless station. Its secondary purpose is to observe Lower Abbey Street and Lower O'Connell Street. Commandere in the D.B.C. whatever food abd utensils you require. Make sure of a plentiful supply of water wherever your men are. Break all glass in the windows of the rooms occupied by you for fighting purpose. Establish a connection between

your forces in the D.B.C. and in Reis's building. Be sure
that the stairways leading immediately to your rooms are
well barracaded. We have a post in the house at the
corner   Bachelor's Walk, in the Hotel Metropole, in the
Imperial Hotel, in   General Post Office. The directions
from which you are likely to be attacked are from the
Custom House or from the far side of the river, Dolier
Street or Westmoreland Street. We believe there is a sniper
in McBurney's on the far side of the river.

JAMES CONOLLY

Commandant General.

The misspellings here are not attributable to Connolly but to
the typist.

During the week Connolly, inside and outside the General
Post Office, was a source of inspiration to the Garrison.

Desmond Ryan refers to "his force, authority and determination to keep the morale of the defenders to the highest point in
spite of the terrific pressure on them." Even after he was
wounded Pearse described him as "still the guiding brain of our
resistance."

On Thursday afternoon Connolly was wounded twice by
British snipers.[5] Dr. James Ryan has recalled :[6]

".....After Thursday morning we were completely isolated
....Up to this the hospital staff was not very busy. Only three
or four wounded had been received. Then I saw James Connolly
come in. Walking quickly to where I was standing he asked
if there was any private place where he might speak to me. I
led him behind the folding screen. Here he took off his coat
and showed me a flesh wound in his arm. He asked me to dress
it and, when leaving, begged me not to tell anybody. He feared
a garbled report of the gravity of the wound might reach his
men and, perhaps, undermine their morale. He immediately
returned to his duties but, before long, he was carried back on
a stretcher, this time suffering from a severe wound in the ankle.
It was badly lacerated, probably from a rifle bullet[7] at com-
paratively short range. Having no choice of anaesthetic I gave
him chloroform while Dr. O'Mahony, R.A.M.C., one of our
prisoners of war, and Mr. McLoughlin[8] put the leg in splints.
Connolly suffered great pain and it was only with the help
of frequent injections of morphia that he got any rest. We had

a number of wounded now, some from the sniper's bullet, others from shrapnel but, with the exception of Connolly and one other wounded on Tuesday, none gave cause for anxiety.

We were kept busy on Thursday night. Connolly required a good deal of attention. He slept very little and in the intervals the pain was ever present and severe...."

On Friday morning Connolly sent for his secretary, Winifred Carney, and dictated a manifesto to the soldiers under his command.

Manifesto issued from the General Post Office, 28 April, 1916

Army of the Irish Republic
(Dublin Command)
Headquarters, April 28, 1916.

To Soldiers:

This is the fifth day of the establishment of the Irish Republic, and the flag of our country still floats from the most important buildings in Dublin, and is gallantly protected by the officers and Irish Soldiers in arms throughout the country. Not a day passes without seeing fresh postings of Irish soldiers eager to do battle for the old cause. Despite the utmost vigilance of the enemy we have been able to get information telling us how the manhood of Ireland, inspired by our splendid action, are gathering to offer up their lives if necessary in the same holy cause. We are here hemmed in because the enemy feels that in this building is to be found the heart and inspiration of our great movement.

Let us remind you what you have done. For the first time in 700 years the flag of a free Ireland floats triumphantly in Dublin City. The British Army, whose exploits we are for ever having dinned into our ears, which boasts of having stormed the Dardanelles and the German lines on the Marne, behind their artillery and machine-guns are afraid to advance to the attack or storm any positions held by our forces. The slaughter they suffered in the first few days has totally unnerved them and they dare not attempt again an infantry attack on our positions.

Our Commandants around us are holding their own.

Commandant Daly's splendid exploit in capturing Linenhall Barracks we all know. You must know also that the whole population, both clergy and laity, of this district are united in his praises.

Commandant MacDonagh is established in an impregnable position reaching from the walls of Dublin Castle to Redmond's Hill, and from Bishop Street to Stephen's Green.

(In Stephen's Green, Commandant Mallin holds the College of Surgeons, one side of the square, a portion of the other side, and dominates the whole Green, and all its entrances and exits.)

Commandant de Valera stretches in a position from the Gas Works to Westland Row, holding Boland's Bakery, Boland's Mills, Dublin South-Eastern Railway Works, and dominating Merrion Square.

Commandant Kent holds the South Dublin Union and Guinness's Buildings to Marrowbone Lane, and controls James's Street and district. On two occasions the enemy effected a lodgment and were driven out with great loss.

The men of North County Dublin are in the field, having occupied all the Police Barracks in the district, destroyed all the telegraph system on the Great Northern Railway up to Dundalk, and are operating against the trains of the Midland and Great Western.

Dundalk has sent 200 men to march upon Dublin, and in other parts of the North our forces are active and growing.

In Galway Captain Mellows, fresh after his escape from an Irish prison, is in the field with his men. Wexford and Wicklow are strong and Cork and Kerry are equally acquitting themselves creditably. (We have every confidence that our allies in Germany and kinsmen in America are straining every nerve to hasten matters on our behalf.)

As you know, I was wounded twice yesterday and am unable to move about, but have got my bed moved into the firing line, and, with the assistance of your officers, will be just as useful to you as ever.

Courage, boys, we are winning, and in the hour of our

G

victory let us not forget the splendid women who have
everywhere stood by us and cheered us on. Never had man
or woman a grander cause, never was a cause more grandly
served.

JAMES CONNOLLY
Commandant-General,
Dublin Division.

This manifesto, phrased as it was in the most defiant and
hopeful terms, was obviously aimed at maintaining the morale
of the men. As Desmond Ryan points out: "His summary of
the situation was at variance with even the known facts, and
with Pearse's more outspoken and candid dispatch of the same
day."

A typed copy of the manifesto was among the documents
presented to Senator Margaret Pearse in 1946. (See above.)
To the typed copy—taken, obviously, from an official file—was
appended a note as follows:

The above interesting orders which were typewritten, were
found on the body of the O'Rahilly, one of the rebel commandants, who was shot by the 216th Sherwood Foresters as he
was leading a charge on one of their barricades in Moor (sic)
Street near the Post Office. Upon him also was a letter written
to his wife after he was wounded, in which he said he was
shot leading a charge. He got into an entry on the side of the
street and later endeavoured to crawl into an opening on the
other side. He was wounded, and before he died he wrote in a
firm hand a pencilled note to his wife and children.

The copy found on the O'Rahilly's body is in the National
Museum.

Continuing Dr. Ryan's narrative: [6]

"....On Friday morning the wounded numbered about sixteen. While I was on my rounds Mac Diarmada came up and
told me to prepare all casualties for removal to Jervis Street
Hospital. We got busy on this but when we reached Connolly
he refused to go, saying he must remain with his men. The
other wounded, in charge of Mr. McLoughlin with stretcher-
bearers and Cumann na mBan, then set out and reached Jervis

Street Hospital in safety. I remained, but now my only patient
was Connolly. He asked to be put in a bed with wheels or
castors so that he could be moved to the front hall. This was
done and he resumed command of the garrison. Nothing could
conquer the will of this man....Now came hurried orders for
evacuation....

Pádraic Pearse with drawn sword stood at the side door leading
into Henry Street and each man in turn rushed across to Henry
Place directly opposite....

Connolly was carried across on a stretcher....

There was little time for rest on Friday night though the
men were tired out. Some of them worked hard boring through
the walls dividing the houses on the East side of Moore Street,
others kept watch and some, overcome by fatigue, slept at their
posts. None of the leaders slept....

On Saturday morning we moved from house to house through
bored walls. The openings were small and Connolly's stretcher
would not pass through. We had to put him in a sheet and so
carry him northwards. He must have suffered torture during
that journey but he never complained...."

Richard P. Gogan, T.D., of the G.P.O. Garrison, recalls:[9]

"We were in the last group to leave the Post Office. The
group included James Connolly and the other members of the
Provisional Government. I believe that Seán Price was one of
Connolly's stretcher-bearers and that possibly Paddy Meagher
(R.I.P.) was another. When we moved over Henry Street into
Henry Place an attempt was made by a Volunteer to break
into a stable and he shot himself in the attempt. At this stage
Connolly pulled my rifle from me and told me to help carry
him. We brought him into a stable in Henry Place (O'Brien's
Mineral Water Factory). The people in the houses there—
"shut in" all the week—were maddened by hunger and by the
fire which extended from Messrs. Drago's premises in Henry
Street as far as the stables. In no uncertain language Connolly
told us to get him out of that! Seán Price and I carried him
from there to Cogan's shop at the corner of Moore Street.
There Dr. Jim Ryan attended him as well as a Volunteer, P. J.
Murray, who had been wounded in the retreat. Connolly gave
orders that holes were to be knocked in the walls up to the end
of Moore Street with the idea of joining forces with Volunteers
reported to be in the premises of Messrs. Williams & Woods.
This was done...."

Julia Grenan was in Cogan's shop. "We were in a parlour at
the back of the shop," she recalls,[10] "when Miss O'Farrell came

in. She had fallen as she rushed along and was, in fact, carried
in by one of the Volunteers. James Connolly was on the stretcher
on the floor. Miss O'Farrell asked him how he was feeling and
he said: 'Bad. The soldier who wounded me did a good day's
work for the British Government.' "

On Saturday morning, as we have seen, temporary headquarters were set up in No. 16 Moore Street to which the men had
tunnelled their way. Connolly was put to bed in a back room
and, around his bed, in "council of war," "the members of the
Provisional Government present at Headquarters" decided finally on an unconditional surrender.

After a sad leave-taking Pearse went out, with Nurse
O'Farrell, to meet Brigadier-General Lowe.

"Winnie Carney was kneeling at Connolly's bedside," says
Julia Grenan, "crying bitterly. 'Was there no other way?' she
asked. Connolly said: 'No. No other way. We could not see our
brave men burned to death. No. No other way.' "

After Pearse's departure Dr. Ryan was called to Connolly
who told him of the surrender. "He told me he wanted to be
prepared for a journey to the Castle," recalled Dr. Ryan.
"When I asked him what terms he expected, he said that the
signatories would be shot but the rest of us set free. Connolly
was soon ready and was taken to the Castle on a stretcher borne
by four[11] Volunteers in full uniform."

Séamus Devoy, one of the stretcher-bearers, recalled[12] the
journey to the Castle:

"....On the Saturday afternoon of Easter Week, following the
surrender, I was instructed by Capt. M. W. O'Reilly of G.H.Q.,
to go to the barricade at the top of Moore Street under a white
flag.

I was to inform the British officer in charge that Commandant-
General James Connolly, Commandant of the Dublin Division,
was badly wounded and would be taken to the Military Hospital
at Dublin Castle.

I was to request this officer to have a passage made in the
barricade to help the stretcher-bearers. This his men did and I
reported back to G.H.Q.

The bearer party, having removed all arms and equipment,
formed up under Captain Diarmuid Lynch of G.H.Q. Their
names were Michael Staines, Joseph Fallon, P. J. Byrne, Michael
Nugent, Liam Tannam and myself.

The first stop was outside Tom Clarke's tobacco shop in Parnell Street (then Great Britain Street), where Commandant-General Connolly had a few words with the Brigadier-General commanding the British forces in the G.P.O. area.

We then started for Dublin Castle via Capel Street, escorted by an officer and sixteen men of the British Army.

We arrived at the Upper Yard of the Castle and there was a short talk between Commandant-General Connolly and the British General Staff officers, after which the British Red Cross men carried our wounded chief into the hospital. The officer in charge of our escort then told us we were prisoners of war and we were marched away to Ship Street Barracks. . . ."

A Voluntary Aid Detachment (V.A.D.) nurse, describing her "Experiences at Dublin Castle during the Rebellion,"[13] referred to the arrival of Connolly:

". . . .The arrival of James Connolly caused an unusual stir. From the window I could see him lying on the stretcher, his hands crossed, his head hidden from view by the archway. The stretcher was on the ground, and at either side stood three of his officers, dressed in the Volunteer uniform; a guard of about thirty soldiers stood around. The scene did not change for ten minutes or more; they were arranging where he should be brought, and a small ward in the Officers' Quarters, where he could be carefully guarded, was decided upon. The nurses in charge of him acknowledged, without exception, that no one could have been more considerate, or have given less trouble. About a week after his arrival he had an operation on the leg. All through, his behaviour was that of an idealist. . . ."

Major de Courcy Wheeler, Staff Captain to Brigadier-General Lowe, had accompanied Pearse from Parnell Street, where he surrendered, to British Army Headquarters where Pearse interviewed Maxwell, the British Commander-in-Chief, and, soon after, signed the formal surrender order. Major Wheeler was then given the task of keeping guard over Pearse but was on that duty for only fifteen minutes when he was sent for by Lowe.

". . . .I was ordered," he recalled,[14] "to go at once to the Castle, show the order of Commandant-General Pearse to Commandant Connolly, in command of the Irish Citizen Army, who had been brought in wounded and a prisoner, to get him to sign it, or issue a similar order to his own men. When I arrived at Dublin Castle, part of which had been turned into a Red Cross Hospital,

I was conducted to the ward where Commandant Connolly had
been carried. He was in bed. I waited beside him while his
wounds were being dressed. I told him my orders and asked
him did he feel well enough to comply.

Having said he was alright, he read the order which had just
been signed by his Commander-in-Chief.

Commandant Connolly then dictated his own orders which I
wrote down underneath General Pearse's typed orders and this
document was signed and dated April 29/16 by Commandant
Connolly....This document has been reproduced in facsimile
in several publications...."

Surrender Orders, 29 April, 1916

> I agree to these conditions for the men only under my
> own command in the Moore Street District and for the
> men in the Stephen's Green Command.
>
> JAMES CONNOLLY
> April 29 / 16

Early on the morning of Low Sunday, 30 April, 1916, Fathers
Augustine and Aloysius, from the Capuchin Friary, Church
Street, called to Dublin Castle.

Father Augustine wrote

....I, being anxious, spoke to Father Aloysius and we decided
to walk over to the Castle. There we soon met Brigadier-General
Lowe who received us in a very gentlemanly manner. I told him
we had heard of the two surrenders (G.P.O. and Four Courts),
that a truce had been granted in our area (Church Street), but
that we were in quest of Pearse's document as we felt that the
Volunteers in our area would never lay down arms until they
felt quite sure about it. He assured us that the document was
genuine, that typed copies of it had been made, but that, unfortunately, he could not lay his hands on one just then. "But,"
he added, "Connolly is here and would reassure you on the
matter, if you were to see him." "Of course," we replied, and
he at once led us to where the leader of the Citizen Army lay
in bed. General Lowe remained outside. We entered, passing the
armed sentry at the end of the room, near the door. I remember
well, just as if it were but yesterday, the feeling of admiration
in my heart as I laid eyes for the first time on this man of fine
head and noble brow. Approaching his bedside I asked him if
the document said to have been signed by Pearse was genuine.

He assured me in the affirmative. "Did you also sign it?" I then asked. "Yes," he replied at once. Then, as I turned to leave him, he said: "But only for the men under my own command." These words are indelibly imprinted on my memory....

On Wednesday, 3 May—it was the day on which Pearse, Clarke and MacDonagh were executed—Connolly's daughter, Ina,[15] went to Dublin Castle in an unsuccessful attempt to see her father.

"I went to Dublin Castle," she wrote,[16] "and it was difficult for me to get directed to the proper quarters. The policemen would send me on, first to one place and then to another. They did not like to turn me away immediately. As I was allowed inside the gates I felt I had some hope. There are several buildings inside Dublin Castle. As I was sent from one building to another I came to the conclusion that father must not be here. When I saw a nurse in the distance, I ran after her and inquired if she could tell me where to go and whom to ask for. She brought me along to that part of the Castle which had been turned into a Red Cross Hospital. She told me whom to ask for and before she left me she said that father was very weak from loss of blood and was not improving.

I saw the officer in charge of the Hospital and he said that he would send word to father that I had called, and that all the family was in Dublin. He took the address and said he would let us know when a visitor would be allowed."

"After that," recalls Connolly's eldest daughter, Nora[17] "any news we got of Papa was from the newspapers and these told us that he was growing steadily weaker and that it was doubtful if he would recover. Then, day by day, the news of the executions nearly drove us out of our minds. We had heard of the shooting of Pearse, Clarke, MacDonagh; then of Willie Pearse, Plunkett, Ned Daly and the rest. Every time we heard the newsboys call out 'One more execution,' 'More executions,' we dreaded to look in the paper for fear we might read my father's name. And yet we felt we must buy the paper.

On Sunday afternoon a note was left in the letter-box addressed to Mama. It read: 'If Mrs. Connolly will call at Dublin Castle Hospital on Monday or Tuesday at 11 o'clock she can see her husband.'

Mama was in terror that Papa's time had come but everyone had been telling her that the fact of his being wounded was a good thing for him; that as long as he was wounded he would not be executed; that by the time he was well again public feeling would be so strong that the authorities would hesitate to shoot him. 'They'll never execute a wounded man,' was the cry.

I quieted Mama's terror somewhat by pointing out to her that the note said 'Monday or Tuesday' so that the day of his execution could not be either of those days. Still she was in an agony of impatience for Monday morning. On Monday she went to the Castle. Before she was allowed in to see Papa she was subjected to a most rigorous search. And she had to give her word of honour that she would not tell him of anything that had happened outside; and she had to promise that she would not bring in anything he could take his life with.

My youngest sister went with Mama. She wasn't yet 8. She was searched too.

Mama came home in a more contented frame of mind. She felt sure that Papa would be spared to her for some time. . . ."

On Tuesday, 9 May, 1916, Connolly was tried by court martial.

Statement to Court Martial, 9 May, 1916

(Evidence mainly went to establish the fact that the accused, James Connolly, was in command at the General Post Office, and was also Commandant-General of the Dublin Division. Two of the witnesses, moreover, strove to bring in alleged instances of wantonly risking the lives of prisoners. The court held that these charges were irrelevant, and could not be placed against the prisoner.)

I do not wish to make any defence except against charges of wanton cruelty to prisoners. These trifling allegations that have been made, if they record facts that really happened, deal only with the almost unavoidable incidents of a hurried uprising against long established authority, and nowhere show evidence of set purpose to wantonly injure unarmed persons.

We went out to break the connection between this country and the British Empire, and to establish an Irish Republic. We believe that the call we then issued to the people of Ireland was a nobler call, in a holier cause, than any call issued to them during this war, having any connection with the war. We succeeded in proving that Irishmen are ready to die endeavouring to win for Ireland those national rights which the British Government has been asking them to die to win for Belgium. As long as that remains the case, the cause of Irish freedom is safe.

Believing that the British Government has no right in Ireland, never had any right in Ireland, and never can have any right in Ireland, the presence, in any one generation of Irishmen, of even a respectable minority, ready to die to affirm that truth, makes that Government forever a usurpation and a crime against human progress.

I personally thank God that I have lived to see the day when thousands of Irish men and boys, and hundreds of Irish women and girls, were ready to affirm that truth, and to attest it with their lives if need be.

JAMES CONNOLLY, Commandant-General
Dublin Division
Army of the Irish Republic.

A copy of this statement was given by Connolly to his daughter, Nora, while, with her mother, she visited her father for the last time in the early morning of 12 May. (See below.)

On Tuesday, 9 May, some time after his court martial, Connolly's wife, Lily, called to Dublin Castle again to visit him. This time her eldest daughter, Nora, accompanied her.

"There were soldiers on guard at the top of the stairs," continues Nora's statement, "and in the small passage-way leading to Papa's room. They were fully armed—rifles with fixed bayonets. All that armed force to guard a wounded man who could not raise himself in his bed!

We were warned to discuss only personal matters with Papa —not to talk of the Rising or anything that had taken place since. Of course we said 'Alright.'

An officer of the R.A.M.C., stayed in the room all the time we were there.

Papa's wounded leg was in a cage.

I asked him was he in great pain. He said: 'No; but I was courtmartialled today. They propped me up in the bed. The strain was very great.'

I was very depressed at this news. I had been thinking he was safe at least until his wounds would be healed, but now I knew that if they Courtmartialled him while he was unable to sit up in bed they would not hesitate to shoot him.

But Papa was very cheerful as he lay in his bed talking of plans for the future. I know now that he must have known what his fate was to be but he never gave us a word or a sign. I asked him how he had been wounded. He told us:

'It was while I had gone out to place some men. On my way back I was shot above the ankle. Both bones in my leg were shattered. I was too far away for the men I had placed to see me, and too far away from the G.P.O. to be seen from there. So I had to crawl back until I was seen. I lost a lot of blood. They couldn't get it staunched.'

Papa was mainly concerned with leaving us; what would happen to a family of mainly girls and Mother. He was thinking of the old days and all the misery we had been through and that it would be no life for us at all. So he was advising us to go to the States. And then he spoke of his writings. He wanted me to get in touch with Sheehy Skeffington[18] to get him to arrange publication of some of his (Papa's) songs and to give the proceeds to Mama. This was the last straw. I had tried to keep to the rules until then but then I said: 'Skeffington is gone.' He said: 'What?' and I said: 'In Portobello Barracks,' and just left it at that, because I didn't want to be put out of the room in case there was something else I might manage to tell him. I did tell him some things. I told him that the papers had it that Liam Mellows[19] was still out with his men in the Galway hills, and that Larry Ginnell[20] was fighting for the men in the House of Commons.

'Good man, Larry,' he said, 'he can always be depended on.' He was very proud of the men who fought under his command. 'It was a good clean fight,' he said. 'The cause can't die now. The fight will put an end to recruiting. Irishmen now realise the absurdity of fighting for another country when their own is enslaved.'

And he praised the brave women and girls who had helped in the fight.

'No one can ever say enough to honour or praise them,' he said.

I mentioned the number of young boys who had taken part and told him that Rory[21] had been in prison.

'So Rory was in prison,' he said. 'How long?'

'Eight days,' I said.

'He fought for his country, and has been in prison for his country,' said Papa, 'and he's not sixteen. He has had a great start in life, hasn't he, Nora?'

Then he asked what happened when myself and my sister, Ina, went up North with Pearse's order that the Rising should take place after all. I told him that MacNeill's countermand had caused the forces to disband; that we had walked all the way back from Dundalk; that our journey North was in vain; that, in fact, we had done nothing.

'I think my little woman did as much as any of us,' he said as he hugged me with one arm around my shoulder.

We were discussing many things, but I was thinking all the time of his Court Martial and what the sentence would be. And I said to Papa that there was great talk among the people that because he was wounded he wouldn't be executed but he said: 'No. No. There is no hope of that. I remember what happened to Scheepers[22] in South Africa. He was wounded and they executed him. That will have no effect on what they decide to do, and that's that.'

Mama was very upset—It isn't a thing one wants to look back on very much—but Papa was very calm and very cool. I asked him again was he suffering much pain. 'No,' he said, 'I'm not suffering much pain. It has eased a good bit.' "

Connolly was visited in Dublin Castle again by his wife and daughter, Nora, in the early hours of the morning of 12 May.

Continuing Nora's statement:

"We were wakened up at about one o'clock in the morning. There was an Army lorry at the door and a British officer told us that the prisoner James Connolly wished to see his wife and eldest daughter. Mama had an idea that he wasn't well, that he had taken a turn for the worse. But it jumped to my mind immediately. All the signatories of the Proclamation had been shot except Papa and Seán MacDermott. I immediately said to myself: 'Papa is going to be shot.' Anyway we got ready. We went down and were taken in the Army lorry right through town. (We were staying in William O'Brien's house.)[23] It was an awfully queer eerie trip. There was still a horrible smell of burning in O'Connell Street. There was curfew and not a soul to be seen, not even a soldier, until we came to the bridge. There were a number of them there. When we were shown in Papa said: 'Well, Lily, I suppose you know what this means?'

She said: 'Oh no, Jim. Oh no!' and he said: 'Yes, lovie,' and then Mama broke down, sobbing, with her head on the bed. Papa said: 'I fell asleep for the first time tonight and they wakened me up at eleven and told me I was to die at dawn.'

Mama said: 'Oh no!' again, and then crying bitterly, 'But your beautiful life, Jim, your beautiful life!' and he said: 'Wasn't it a full life, Lily, and isn't this a good end?' And she still cried and he said: 'Look, Lily, please don't cry. You will unman me.'

So she tried to control herself. I was trying to control myself too. Then Papa said to me: 'Put your hand down on the bed.' So I put it down on the bed and he said: 'That's a copy of my statement to the Court Martial. Try and get it out.' The piece

Kilmainham Jail: Ceapach an Bháis—The Execution Plot.

of paper was folded up very tightly—very small. So I took it anyway.

And we stayed there talking of little things. He was trying to plan a life for us after he'd be gone.

One thing he said to Mama I remember: 'The Socialists will never understand why I am here. They will all forget I am an Irishman.'

And then they told us the time was up and that we'd have to go. (He was to be shot at dawn.)

So Mama—we couldn't get Mama away from the bed and the nurse[24] had to come and help her away.

And I went to the door. And then I went back again to him. And that was the last I saw of him."

James Connolly was executed in Kilmainham Jail on 12 May, 1916. *The Catholic Bulletin*[25] quotes the surgeon who attended him as having asked Connolly if at the moment of his execution he would pray for him and for those about to shoot him; and Connolly as having replied: "Yes, Sir, I'll pray for all brave men who do their duty according to their lights."

In the British House of Commons on 30 May, 1916,[26] Mr. Laurence Ginnell asked the Under-Secretary of State for War

the number and nature of the wounds which James Connolly, when he surrendered, was found to have sustained; whether the military authorities first decided that he should not be tried until his wounds were healed; whether, on the surgeon reporting that Mr. Connolly was dying of his wounds, they tried him; whether, being too ill to walk to or stand for his execution, he had to be carried on a stretcher to the place of execution, propped up in a chair there, and shot in that condition; and if he will give the date and place of any precedent for the summary execution of a military prisoner dying of his wounds.

The Under-Secretary of State for War, the Right Hon. Harold John Tennant, replied:

The medical authorities were consulted before the trial of James Connolly took place, and they certified that he was in a fit state to undergo his trial.

He was wounded just above the instep, and although he was unable to walk there was no reason why in the interests of humanity the execution should have been delayed.

The House will see that the hon. Member's question is characterised by the inaccuracy and exaggeration to which the House is becoming accustomed.

Mr. Ginnell: Will the right hon. Gentleman answer two clauses of the question—was this man certified to be dying when put on his trial, and what is the precedent for the summary execution of a dying man?

Mr. Tennant: I have already said that the medical authorities certified he was in a fit state to undergo his trial; therefore the other question does not arise.

---

[1]Desmond Ryan, in *The Rising*.

[2]Captain Thomas Weafer, killed in action on Wednesday, 26 April.

[3]Charles L. Reis & Co., 10/11 Lower O'Connell Street.

[4]Dublin Bread Company Restaurant, 6/7 Lower O'Connell Street.

[5]Desmond Ryan in *The Rising*. Diarmuid Lynch in *The I.R.B. and the 1916 Insurrection* disputes this. It is, however, in conformity with Connolly's own statement (see above), with Joseph Mary Plunkett's Journal (see above) and with Dr. Ryan's account (above). Lynch refers to "reports of those who attended him, which were that he received his first wound (in the arm) on Wednesday and his second (in the leg) on Thursday." As to the leg wound received by Connolly on Thursday there is no conflict. The "Report of Operations, Easter Week, 1916" in *The I.R.B. and the 1916 Insurrection* tells of Connolly's surveying the situation on Thursday afternoon as "enemy activities became more in evidence on the rear flank of G.H.Q.," and of his superintending, in person, the establishment of outposts in Liffey Street and Middle Abbey Street. "On his way back to the G.P.O. he received a very serious leg wound which rendered him virtually *hors de combat*. From Abbey Street he succeeded in dragging himself through Williams' Lane (where he was out of the enemy line of fire) as far as Prince's Street, whence he was brought in on a stretcher."

[6]*Capuchin Annual*, 1966.

[7]Seán McLoughlin, who was close by at the time, said (*Camillian Post*, Spring, 1948) Connolly "was struck in the leg by a piece of flying shrapnel," but Connolly himself spoke of a bullet to his daughter.

[8]Dan McLoughlin, fellow medical student of Dr. Ryan, who was also assigned to hospital duties in the G.P.O.

[9]In a statement to the Editor.

[10]In a statement to the Editor.

[11]But see Devoy's account, below.

[12]In an interview published in the *Irish Independent 1916-'66 Supplement*.

[13]*Blackwood's Magazine*, December, 1916.

[14]*Irish Press*, 20 April, 1949.

[15]Now Mrs. Connolly Heron.

[16]*Liberty*. October, 1966.

[17]Dr. Nora Connolly O'Brien, in a statement to the Editor. Her account is based on earlier statements of hers in her books—*The Unbroken Tradition* (Boni and Liveright, 1918) and *Portrait of a Rebel Father* (Talbot Press, 1935)—and in an interview given by her to Radio Telefís Eireann and shown on TV at Easter, 1966.

[18]Francis Sheehy Skeffington was murdered in Portobello Barracks by Captain Bowen-Colthurst on 26 April, 1916.

[19]Mellows had escaped capture but the fight in Galway had been called off since 28 April.

[20]Laurence Ginnell, M.P. for Longford-Westmeath.

[21]Rory—Connolly's son—served under his father in the G.P.O.

[22]Commandant Scheepers was captured in the Ladysmith District, South Cape Colony, in October, 1901. Suffering from enteric fever and appendicitis, he was tried on 18 December, 1901, sentenced to death, and shot on 18 January, 1902.

[23]43 Belvedere Place.

[24]The same nurse, in response to a request from Mrs. Connolly, cut a lock from Connolly's hair and sent it to her with a note:

> The Castle,
> Dublin.
> 12th May, 1916.
>
> Dear Mrs. Connolly,
>
> Enclosed you will find that which you asked me to get for you last night. I offer you my sincere sympathy in your great trouble.
>
> Yours,
> (Signed) B. Sullivan
> Sister

The lock and note are now on display in the Kilmainham Museum, presented by Dr. Nora Connolly O'Brien.

[25]July, 1916.

[26]*Hansard*, Fifth Series, Vol. LXXXII.

And see bibliographical note p. x.

Ruairí Mac Easmainn   Roger Casement
              1864–1916

RUAIRÍ MAC EASMAINN   ROGER CASEMENT

Roger Casement was captured at McKenna's Fort, Ardfert, Co. Kerry, on Good Friday, 21 April, 1916, three days before the outbreak of the insurrection. He was taken next day to Arbour Hill Military Detention Barracks in Dublin and thence, via Holyhead to London, where he was held in Brixton Prison before being conveyed to the Tower. He was tried, not by court-martial as were his comrades in Ireland captured after the military operations, but in the High Court of Justice in London, on the 26-29 June, on a charge of high treason.

During the months of his detention, during his trial and the hearing of an appeal, Casement naturally engaged in more extensive communication with legal advisers and others than was possible for the leaders who suffered summary treatment under martial law in Ireland. It is therefore not possible to present here a full collection of his writings and other reported statements between the outbreak of the insurrection and his execution. Nor indeed is it necessary. Casement's life and death have been the subject of a dozen works. They are of varying quality and interest but the principal documents are readily available. There is given below a series of extracts from his speech in response to the court's question "why the court should not pass sentence and judgment upon you to die according to law?"

Speech from the Dock, 29 June, 1916

My Lord Chief Justice, as I wish to reach a much wider audience than I see before me here, I intend to read all that I propose to say. What I shall read now is something I wrote more than twenty days ago. I may say, my lord, at once, that I protest against the jurisdiction of this Court in my case on this charge, and the argument that I am now going to read is addressed not to this Court, but to my own countrymen. . .

With all respect I assert this Court is to me, an Irish-

197

man, not a jury of my peers to try me in this vital issue, for it is patent to every man of conscience that I have a right, an indefeasible right, if tried at all, under this statute of high treason, to be tried in Ireland, before an Irish Court and by an Irish jury. This Court, this jury, the public opinion of this country, England, cannot but be prejudiced in varying degree against me, most of all in time of war.

I did not land in England; I landed in Ireland. It was to Ireland I came; to Ireland I wanted to come; and the last place I desired to land in was England. But for the Attorney-General of England there is only "England"—there is no Ireland, there is only the law of England—no right of Ireland; the liberty of Ireland and of Irishmen is to be judged by the power of England. Yet for me, the Irish outlaw, there is a land of Ireland, a right of Ireland, and a charter for all Irishmen to appeal to, in the last resort, a charter that even the very statutes of England itself cannot deprive us of—nay, more, a charter that Englishmen themselves assert as the fundamental bond of law that connects the two kingdoms. This charge of high treason involves a moral responsibility, as the very terms of the indictment against myself recite, inasmuch as I committed the acts I am charged with, to the "evil example of others in the like case." What was this "evil example" I set to others in "the like case," and who were these others? The "evil example" charged is that I asserted the rights of my own country, and the "others" I appealed to to aid my endeavour were my own countrymen.

The example was given not to Englishmen but to Irishmen, and the "like case" can never arise in England, but only in Ireland. To Englishmen I set no evil example, for I made no appeal to them. I asked no Englishman to help me. I asked Irishmen to fight for their rights. The "evil example" was only to other Irishmen who might come after me, and in "like case" seek to do as I did. How, then, since neither my example nor my appeal was addressed to Englishmen, can I be rightfully tried by them?

If I did wrong in making that appeal to Irishmen to join with me in an effort to fight for Ireland, it is by Irishmen, and by them alone, I can be rightfully judged. From this

Court and its jurisdiction I appeal to those I am alleged
to have wronged, and to those I am alleged to have injured
by my "evil example," and claim that they alone are
competent to decide my guilt or my innocence. If they find
me guilty, the statute may affix the penalty, but the statute
does not override or annul my right to seek judgment at
their hands.

This is so fundamental a right, so natural a right, so
obvious a right, that it is clear the Crown were aware of it
when they brought me by force and by stealth from Ireland
to this country. It was not I who landed in England, but
the Crown who dragged me here, away from my own
country to which I had turned with a price upon my head,
away from my own countrymen whose loyalty is not in
doubt, and safe from the judgment of my peers whose
judgment I do not shrink from. I admit no other judgment
but theirs. I accept no verdict save at their hands. I assert
from this dock that I am being tried here, not because it
is just, but because it is unjust. Place me before a jury of
my own countrymen, be it Protestant or Catholic, Unionist
or Nationalist, Sinn Feineach or Orangemen, and I shall
accept the verdict and bow to the statute and all its penal-
ties. But I shall accept no meaner finding against me than
that of those whose loyalty I endanger by my example and
to whom alone I made appeal. If they adjudge me guilty,
then guilty I am. It is not I who am afraid of their verdict;
it is the Crown. If this be not so, why fear the test?
I fear it not. I demand it as my right.

That, my lord, is the condemnation of English rule, of
English-made law, of English Government in Ireland, that
it dare not rest on the will of the Irish people, but it exists
in defiance of their will—that it is a rule derived not from
right, but from conquest. Conquest, my lord, gives no title,
and if it exists over the body, it fails over the mind. It can
exert no empire over men's reason and judgment and
affections; and it is from this law of conquest without title
to the reason, judgment, and affection of my own countrymen that I appeal. . .

I would add that the generous expressions of sympathy
extended me from many quarters, particularly from America,

have touched me very much. In that country, as in my own, I am sure my motives are understood and not misjudged— for the achievement of their liberties has been an abiding inspiration to Irishmen and to all men elsewhere rightly struggling to be free in like cause.

My Lord Chief Justice, if I may continue, I am not called upon, I conceive, to say anything in answer to the inquiry your lordship has addressed to me why sentence should not be passed upon me. Since I do not admit any verdict in this Court, I cannot, my lord, admit the fitness of the sentence that of necessity must follow it from this Court. I hope I shall be acquitted of presumption if I say that the Court I see before me now is not this High Court of Justice of England, but a far greater, a far higher, a far older assemblage of justices—that of the people of Ireland. Since in the acts which have led to this trial it was the people of Ireland I sought to serve—and them alone—I leave my judgment and my sentence in their hands. . .

My counsel has referred to the Ulster Volunteer move-ment, and I will not touch at length upon that ground save only to say this, that neither I nor any of the leaders of the Irish Volunteers who were founded in Dublin in November, 1913, had quarrel with the Ulster Volunteers as such, who were born a year earlier. Our movement was not directed against them, but against the men who mis-used and misdirected the courage, the sincerity and the local patriotism of the men of the north of Ireland. On the contrary, we welcomed the coming of the Ulster Volun-teers, even while we deprecated the aims and intentions of those Englishmen who sought to pervert to an English party use—to the mean purposes of their own bid for place and power in England—the armed activities of simple Irishmen. We aimed at winning the Ulster Volunteers to the cause of a united Ireland. We aimed at uniting all Irishmen in a natural and national bond of cohesion based on mutual self-respect. Our hope was a natural one, and if left to ourselves, not hard to accomplish. If external in-fluences of disintegration would but leave us alone, we were sure that Nature itself must bring us together. . .

How did the Irish Volunteers meet the incitements of civil war that were uttered by the party of law and order in England when they saw the prospect of deriving political profit to themselves from bloodshed among Irishmen?

I can answer for my own acts and speeches. While one English party was responsible for preaching a doctrine of hatred designed to bring about civil war in Ireland, the other, and that the party in power, took no active steps to restrain a propaganda that found its advocates in the Army, Navy, and Privy Council—in the Houses of Parliament and in the State Church—a propaganda the methods of whose expression were so "grossly illegal and utterly unconstitutional" that even the Lord Chancellor of England could find only words and no repressive action to apply to them. Since lawlessness sat in high places in England and laughed at the law as at the custodians of the law, what wonder was it that Irishmen should refuse to accept the verbal protestations of an English Lord Chancellor as a sufficient safeguard for their lives and their liberties? I know not how all my colleagues on the Volunteer Committee in Dublin reviewed the growing menace, but those with whom I was in closest co-operation redoubled, in face of these threats from without, our efforts to unite all Irishmen from within. Our appeals were made to Protestant and Unionist as much almost as to Catholic and Nationalist Irishmen.

We hoped that by the exhibition of affection and goodwill on our part towards our political opponents in Ireland we should yet succeed in winning them from the side of an English party whose sole interest in our country lay in its oppression in the past, and in the present in its degradation to the mean and narrow needs of their political animosities. It is true that they based their actions, so they averred, on "fears for the Empire" and on a very diffuse loyalty that took in all the people of the Empire, save only the Irish. That blessed word "Empire" that bears so paradoxical a resemblance to charity! For if charity begins at home, "Empire" means in other men's homes and both may cover a multitude of sins. I for one was determined that Ireland was much more to me than "Empire," and that if charity begins at home so must loyalty. Since arms were so necessary to make our organisation a reality, and to give to the minds of Irishmen, menaced with the most outrageous threats, a sense of security, it was our bounden duty to get arms before all else. . .

We have been told, we have been asked to hope, that after this war Ireland will get Home Rule, as a reward for the life-blood shed in a cause which whoever else its success may benefit can surely not benefit Ireland. And what will Home Rule be in return for what its vague promise has taken and still hopes to take away from Ireland? It is not necessary to climb the painful stairs of Irish history—that treadmill of a nation whose labours are in vain for her own uplifting as the convict's exertions are for his redemption—to review the long list of British promises made only to be broken—of Irish hopes raised only to be dashed to the ground. Home Rule when it comes, if come it does, will find an Ireland drained of all that is vital to its very existence—unless it be that unquenchable hope we build on the graves of the dead. We are told that if Irishmen go by the thousand to die, not for Ireland, but for Flanders, for Belgium, for a patch of sand on the deserts of Mesopotamia, or a rocky trench on the heights of Gallipoli, they are winning self-government for Ireland. But if they dare to lay down their lives on their native soil, if they dare to dream even that freedom can be won only at home by men resolved to fight for it there, then they are traitors to their country, and their dream and their deaths alike are phases of a dishonourable phantasy.

But history is not so recorded in other lands. In Ireland alone in this twentieth century is loyalty held to be a crime. If loyalty be something less than love and more than law, then we have had enough of such loyalty for Ireland or Irishmen. If we are to be indicted as criminals, to be shot as murderers, to be imprisoned as convicts because our offence is that we love Ireland more than we value our lives, then I know not what virtue resides in any offer of self-government held out to brave men on such terms. Self-government is our right, a thing born in us at birth; a thing no more to be doled out to us or withheld from us by another people than the right to life itself—than the right to feel the sun or smell the flowers or to love our kind. It is only from the convict these things are withheld for crime committed and proven—and Ireland that has wronged no man, that has injured no land, that has sought no dominion, over others—Ireland is treated to-day among the nations of the world as if she were a convicted criminal.

If it be treason to fight against such an unnatural fate as this, then I am proud to be a rebel, and shall cling to my "rebellion" with the last drop of my blood. If there be no right of rebellion against a state of things that no savage tribe would endure without resistance, then I am sure that it is better for man to fight and die without right than to live in such a state of right as this. Where all your rights become only an accumulated wrong; where men must beg with bated breath for leave to subsist in their own land, to think their own thoughts, to sing their own songs, to garner the fruits of their own labours—and even while they beg, to see things inexorably withdrawn from them—then surely it is a braver, a saner and a truer thing, to be a rebel in act and deed against such circumstances as these than tamely to accept it as the natural lot of men.

My lord, I have done. Gentlemen of the jury, I wish to thank you for your verdict. I hope you will not take amiss what I said, or think that I made any imputation upon your truthfulness or your integrity when I spoke and said that this was not a trial by my peers. I maintain that I have a natural right to be tried in that natural jurisdiction, Ireland my own country, and I would put it to you, how would you feel in the converse case, or rather how would all men here feel in the converse case, if an Englishman had landed here in England and the Crown or the Government, for its own purposes, had conveyed him secretly from England to Ireland under a false name, committed him to prison under a false name, and brought him before a tribunal in Ireland under a statute which they knew involved a trial before an Irish jury? How would you feel yourselves as Englishmen if that man was to be submitted to trial by jury in a land inflamed against him and believing him to be a criminal, when his only crime was that he had cared for England more than for Ireland?

The Will of Roger Casement, made in Pentonville, 1 August, 1916

I ROGER DAVID CASEMENT declare this to be my last will
I hereby revoke all wills and testamentary instruments here-
tofore made by me I devise and bequeath to my cousin
Gertrude Bannister everything I possess or can dispose of
and I appoint her and my Solicitor George Gavan Duffy
to be EXECUTORS of this my will IN WITNESS whereof I have
hereto set my hand the first day of August one thousand
nine hundred and sixteen—ROGER DAVID CASEMENT Signed
by the Testator as and for his last will in the presence
of us both present at the same time who in his presence
and in the presence of each other have hereto subscribed
our names as witnesses—J MIDDLETON P W— W TURNER
Warder.

WITH CASEMENT IN PENTONVILLE[1]

After he had been sentenced to death on 29 June, 1916,
Casement was taken to Pentonville Prison. Though he was,
intellectually, a Protestant,[2] he registered as a Catholic because
he wished to spend the last days of his life among his own, and
thought that he was more likely to meet a countryman in the
priest than in the parson. In this hope he was not disappointed,
for the Rev. Thomas Carey, M.R., Rector of the Catholic Church,
Eden Grove, Holloway, London, and Catholic Chaplain to
Pentonville Prison, was a Limerick man, who, though ordained
for the diocese of Cashel, had joined the English Mission. Until
his execution on August 3rd Roger Casement was under the
spiritual care of Father Carey and his curate, Father McCarroll,
a Scotsman.

Father Carey was informed on June 29th that Casement was
lodged in Pentonville Prison and had registered as a Catholic.
He immediately visited him. Father Carey's greeting and accent
revealed his nationality. This was like a ray of sunshine to
Casement in the condemned cell a few hours after he had been
sentenced to death.

In the course of a day or two, Father Carey came to the main
point, the religious question. He explained to Casement that
if he desired to become a Catholic and to die one, it must be,
not because it was the religion of the Irish people, or from
any such motive, but because he had convinced himself that it
was the one true Church and religion, and that his duty to
God and to his own soul demanded the change of religion. He

readily saw this, and then intellectually fought every step of his way, until, in the end, he had convinced himself that there was no choice for him, as he put it, "between the Catholic Church and religious anarchy, between the infallibility of the Pope and religious chaos."

Father Carey had, by this time, of course, grown quite familiar and intimate with Casement. And, for many reasons, he felt that it was advisable that Casement's confession of his whole life should be heard by one who was more of a stranger to him and who, at the same time, would understand him. Father Carey's choice of a confessor fell on the Rev. T. J. Ring, M.R., Rector of SS. Mary and Michael's church, Commercial Road, London, one of the best known and most prominent Irish priests in London, a County Cork man, who, though ordained for the diocese of Kerry, had like Fr. Carey, joined the English Mission. On the eve of the execution Father Ring came with Father Carey to reconcile Casement to the Church and to hear his confession. When Casement came to the prison chapel for this purpose he took off his shoes, for he considered the place he stood on to be holy ground, and then divested himself of his prison jacket so that, in so far as he could, he might make his submission to the Catholic Church in the garb of a free man. After the confession, Father Ring began to assist him to put on his jacket. He gently protested against this until Father Ring asked to be allowed the privilege of assisting a true penitent and servant of God, when he yielded. Then he asked that some farewell messages should be conveyed to his friends, and particularly to his sister in America, coupled with his hope and prayer that she, too, would embrace the Catholic faith, which had been such a help to him in his last days, and into which his mother had done her best to place all her children before her death. The priests impressed upon him that Holy Communion would be given to him on the following morning as Viaticum, or spiritual food for the journey into eternity, and that, especially as the strain upon him would be severe, he was not obliged to receive fasting. But he answered that it was his desire not only to receive fasting, but to go to his death with the Holy Communion as his only food. However, next morning the priests induced him to modify somewhat this rigid decision.

On Thursday, August 3rd, 1916, Father McCarroll said Mass at the prison, gave Casement his first and last Communion, and assisted him to make his thanksgiving and to gain a plenary indulgence. Soon after eight, Fathers Carey and Ring came to the prison for the final scene. When they entered the condemned cell Casement asked when the execution was to take place. Father Carey answered: "Nine o'clock." Casement said: "Good." He then thanked Father Carey, whom he addressed as his "Prison Father," for having instructed him and brought him to the knowledge of the true Faith, assured him that he "wholly accepted, wholly believed, and wholly trusted in the Divine Plan—Christ's Catholic Church," that he wished for a few years of life for one reason only, that he might show what a loyal son of the Catholic Church he was, and that he had joined her from conviction and not from any other motive. He said that he did not fear death, that he freely returned to God the life and faculties God had given him, hoping that in some way it would benefit his country.

Father Carey then gave the Papal Blessing with the plenary indulgence attached. All three knelt down and, Father Carey leading, Casement followed him uninterruptedly in prayer for nearly three quarters of an hour.

The hour of execution struck at last, and, to the knock at the cell door, Father Carey answered: "Ready." Father McCarroll had by this time arrived and, all three priests leading, Casement followed, repeating the final ejaculations. There was little time, for only forty seconds elapsed from the moment the officers began to pinion him until he was a dead man. He marched firmly to the scaffold. He was six feet two inches, and as he stood, erect as an arrow on the scaffold, he looked even taller. His last words were: "Into Thy hands, O Lord, I commend my spirit. Lord Jesus, receive my soul."

He received the final absolution as the bolt was drawn. The prayers for the departed were said; and a few hours later, he was buried in the prison grounds,[3] Father McCarroll officiating.

Casement's Last Written Words

(Fr. McCarroll in 1946 sent to the late Dr. Herbert O. Mackey copies of extracts he had made from a manuscript he had found among Casement's personal effects in the condemned cell after the execution. Dr. Mackey reproduced them in *The crime against Europe: the writings and poetry of Roger Casement* (Fallon, 1958).)

My dominating thought was to keep Ireland out of the war. England has no claim on us, in Law or Morality or Right. Ireland should not sell her soul for any mess of Empire.

If I die tomorrow, bury me in Ireland, and I shall die in the Catholic Faith, for I accept it fully now. It tells me what my heart sought long—but I saw it in the faces of the Irish. Now I know what it was I loved in them—the chivalry of Christ speaking through human eyes. It is from that source all lovable things come, for Christ was the first Knight.

And now good-bye. I still write with hope—hope that God will be with me to the end. . . .

And if I die, as I think is fated, tomorrow morning, I shall die with my sins forgiven and God's pardon on my soul, and I shall be with many brave and good men. . . .

Think of the long succession of the dead who died for Ireland—and it is a great death. Oh! that I may support it bravely. If it be said I shed tears, remember they come not from cowardice but from sorrow—and brave men are not ashamed to weep sometimes. I hope I shall not weep, but if I do it shall be nature's tribute wrung from me—one who never hurt a human being—and whose heart was always compassionate and pitiful for the grief of others. . . . The long waiting has been a cruel thing, three months and 11 days now. . . .

It is a strange, strange fate, and now, as I stand face to face with death, I feel just as if they were going to kill a boy. For I feel like a boy—and my hands so free from blood and my heart always so compassionate and pitiful that I cannot comprehend how anyone wants to hang me. . . .

It is they—not I—who are the traitors, filled with a lust of blood—of hatred of their fellows. These artificial and unnatural wars, prompted by greed and power, are the source of all misery now destroying mankind. . . .

I shall still hope till the sheriff comes, and if he comes it is to prepare to go to God with calm and hope and leave all here with an infinite blessing breathed from a finite heart. . . .

No man in the world ever got so much undeserved friendship as I have found these last days. The great outpouring of love and goodness on me is the greatest proof of God's love for sinful men.

God gave me into this captivity and death, and I kiss the Divine Hand that leads me to the grave. . . .

Alas, so much of the story dies with me—the old, old story—yet in spite of all, the truth and right lives on in the hearts of the brave and lowly.

It is better that I die thus—on the scaffold.

It was a glorious death for Ireland's sake with Allen, Larkin, O'Brien and Robert Emmet—and the men of '98 and William Orr—all for the same cause—all in the same way. Surely it is the most glorious cause in history.

"Ever defeated—yet undefeated."

ROGER CASEMENT

---

[1]This account is an abridged version of one published in *The Catholic Bulletin*, September, 1916.

[2]Son of a Protestant father and a Catholic mother, Casement had been christened, as a baby, in a Protestant church in the Isle of Man, but, on August 5th, 1868, before he was four years old, his mother had taken him with her other children to the Catholic church in Rhyl and had them all baptised conditionally.

[3]In March, 1965, the British Government, in response to a request from the Irish Government, agreed to the repatriation of the remains, which were reinterred in Glasnevin Cemetery.

And see bibliographical note p. x.

NA CHÉAD CHÚIRTEANNA AIRM[1]

le Piaras Béaslai, nach maireann.

Ó triaileadh mise an lá céanna leis agus ó bhíos ina theannta tar éis na " cúirte " b'féidir nár mhiste dhom cuntas a thabhairt ar an méid is cuimhin liom dá bhaineann le scéal an Phiarsaigh agus na beirte eile a triaileadh san chúirt chéanna.

Maidin Dé Domhnaigh, 30 Aibreán, 1916, tugadh sinn go léir go dtí Beairic Risteamain agus cuireadh isteach sinn san "Gymnasium"—halla mór folamh gan aon bhall troscáin ann. Bhí bleachtairí ann agus chromadar ar phríosúnaigh áirithe a phiocadh amach agus a chur ar leathaobh. Bhíos féin ar dhuine acusan—an chéad duine. Bhí an obair sin ar siúl ar feadh an lae, agus príosúnaigh nua á dtabhairt isteach i gcónaí. Fá dheireadh tugadh na príosúnaigh eile amach as an "Gym" agus níor fágadh ach na daoine a bhí tofa ag na bleachtairí—timpeall céad go leith. Bhí Tomás Ó Cléirigh ann agus Seán Mac Diarmada agus Ióseph Ó Pluingcéad (a bhí an-bhreoite). Bhíos ag comhrá le Tomás Ó Cléirigh agus Seán Mac Diarmada. Dúirt Tomás go ndéanfadh an tÉirí Amach maitheas iontach san tír. Thug Seán cuntas dom ar chúrsaí an ghéillte. Ní chuimhin liom an raibh Tomás Mac Donnchadha ann, ach táim lándeimhnithe de ná raibh an Piarsach ann.

Bhí Tomás Ó Cléirigh in éineacht liomsa ó oíche Dé Sathairn go dtí maidin Dé Luain, agus arís maidin Dé Máirt. Ní fhaca an Piarsach go dtí Dé Mairt.

Do chaitheamar an oíche san Gymnasium, sinn sínte ar an urlár agus saighdiúirí timpeall orainn. Ar maidin deighleadh gasraí dínn óna chéile. Cuireadh timpeall dachad againn isteach i seomra fé leith. Ar na daoine úd bhí Éamonn Ó Dálaigh, Éamonn Ó Dubhagáin, Seosamh Mac Aonghusa agus Proinsias Ó Fathaigh.

Tamall níba dhéanaí tugadh cuid againn, ina nduine is ina nduine, os comhair cúirte míleata. An Réamh-Scrúdú ("Preliminary Investigation") a tugadh air sin. Oifigigh agus saighdiúirí Gallda a bhí tar éis bheith ina bpríosúnaigh againn le linn an troda, bhíodar ann chun a dhearbhú gur aithníodar sinn agus go raibh gunnaí againn. Is dóigh gur tugadh an Piarsach os comhair na cúirte céanna.

Dé Luain fuaireamar páipéirí gairme á chur in ár leith go rabhamar páirteach in Éirí Amach "d'fhonn cabhraithe leis an namhaid."

Maidin Dé Máirt tugadh Éamonn Ó Dubhagáin, Seosamh Mac Aonghusa agus mise amach ón seomra ina rabhamar. Coimeádadh sinn ag feitheamh ar feadh i bhfad ar an bhfaiche os comhair an tí ina raibh an chúirt le suí.

Fé dheireadh tháinig an Piarsach, Tomás Mac Donnchadha agus Tomás Ó Cléirigh i láthair agus tugadh an seisear againn isteach i halla an tí. Tugadh Éamonn, Seosamh agus mise isteach i seomra ar an taobh deas den halla. Tugadh an triúr eile isteach ar an taobh clé. Bhí an dá chúirt ar siúl ar an linn chéanna.

Seomra cuíosach beag a bhí ann. Ní raibh ann ach an triúr oifigeach a bhí ina mbreithiúna, oifigeach eile mar chúisitheoir —ní raibh aon trácht ar chosantóir—beirt fhinné, na saighdiúirí a bhí dár ngardadh agus roinnt bleachtairí. Ní raibh aon fhuíollach slí ann. Is dóigh gur mhar a chéile an nós trialach a fuair an triúr san seomra eile agus an nós trialach a fuaireamar, agus, mar sin, is fiú cuntas a thabhairt air.

Maidir le dlí nó ceart nó cothrom ní raibh san "triail" ach cúis mhagaidh.

Do réir dlí na gcúirteanna míleata i Sasana ceaptar oifigeach chun an príosúnach a chosaint, agus tugtar caoi dó finnéithe d'fháil—dhá rud nár deineadh ag na "trialacha" seo.

Mar a dúirt mé ní raibh aon trácht ar chosantóir. Ní dúradh riamh linn go raibh cead againn finnéithe d'fháil. Ní raibh aon trácht ná smaoineamh ar a leithéid.

Triaileadh gach duine againn fé leith—Éamonn ar dtús, mise ina dhiaidh-sin agus Seosamh ar deireadh. I ngach cás do labhair an cúisitheoir ar dtús, agus ansin do ghlaoigh sé ar bheirt oifigeach a bhí tar éis bheith ina bpríosúnaigh againn Seachtain na Cásca chun a dhearbhú go bhfacadar "an príosúnach" agus go raibh arm tine aige. Ansin glaodh ar bhleachtaire chun cuntas a thabhairt ar cháilíocht an phríosúnaigh maidir le "dílseacht."

Ní tugadh aon chaoi—an chaoi ba lú—do na príosúnaigh an fhianaise do bhréagnú.

Fiafraíodh den phríosúnach an raibh aon ní le rá aige chun a chosanta féin.

Ní daoradh éinne chun báis ag an dtriail. Ní tugadh aon bhreithiúnas. (Ní gnách breithiúnas a thabhairt ag cúirt mhíleata Shasanach. Triaileadh mise arís san bhliain 1919 agus b'é an scéal céanna é.) Caithfead a admháil go raibh na hoifigigh anbhéasach, an-mhánla chugainn. Do réir dealraimh Sasanaigh ba ea iad—fir aosta—gan aon eolas acu ar Éirinn. Ní coimeádadh cuntas ar imeachtaí na cúirte—ní raibh aon ghléas chuigesin —ach amháin na nótaí a dhein na hoifigigh. Do dheineadar nótaí d'fhormhór na cainte a thug na príosúnaigh uathu. Do thóg sin a lán ama mar ní raibh aon luathscríbhinn acu.[2]

Tugadh amach arís sinn ar an bhfaiche agus coimeádadh sinn ag fanúint leis an dtriúr eile.

Fé dheireadh tugadh an Piarsach, Tomás Ó Cléirigh agus Tomás Mac Donnchadha amach ón gcúirt agus cuireadh an seisear againn isteach san Gymnasium. Bhí saighdiúirí in éineacht linn, ach bhí caoi againn comhrá le chéile. Níor labhair an Piarsach linn. Do shuigh sé ar an urlár agus é ag machtnamh leis féin. Ba dhóigh leat air go raibh sé chomh lán dá smaointe féin nár thug sé éinne eile fé ndeara. Níor oscail sé a bhéal ach aon uair amháin nuair a dhein sé gearán le saighdiúir fé rud éigin d'iarr sé agus ná fuair sé—ní chuimhin liom cérbh é féin. Bhí dealramh suaimhneasach sásta ar Thomás Ó Cléirigh. Bhí ardáthas air go raibh Éirí Amach ann, bíodh is gur theip air.

Maidir le Tomás Mac Donnchadha, bhí sé go meidhreach aigeanta, agus a lán le rá aige. D'inis sé dúinn go raibh na Gearmánaigh tar éis teacht i dtír i Sasana agus gur ghearr go mbeadh deireadh le hImpireacht na Breataine.

(I bhfad ina dhiaidh-sin fuaireas amach cad ba bhun le scéal Tomáis. Dé Máirt, 25 Aibreán, agus an troid ar siúl i mBaile Átha Cliath, tháinig scuadrún de chabhlach na Gearmáine go dtí Lowestoft agus Yarmouth agus chaitheadar sliogáin leis an dá chalafort sin. Shamhlaigh na Sasanaigh go raibh baint ag an ionsaí sin leis an Éirí Amach in Éirinn. Do réir dealraimh chuala Tomás ráfla éigin mar gheall air.)

An lá úd níor rith sé riamh chun m'aigne go lámhachfaí éinne ar maidin. Mheasas go mbeadh moill seachtaine ann sar a dtabharfaí an breithiúnas. Is dóigh liom gur mhar sin a bhí an scéal ag Tomás Mac Donnchadha, leis, ach go raibh tuairim mhaith ag an bPiarsach de cad a bhí i ndán dó.

Um thráthnóna tugadh an seisear againn go Cill Maighneann de shiúl cos.

---

[1]As aiste a foilsíodh in *Inniu*, 22 Samhain, 1946.

[2]Dar le Mr. Tennant, ag freagairt ceisteanna dó i nDáil Shasana, 29 Bealtaine, 1916, "All the usual and necessary notes were taken . . . in shorthand . . ." (Féach *Hansard*, Fifth Series, Vol. LXXXII.)
And see bibliographical note p. x.

From the

PERSONAL RECOLLECTIONS[1]

of Father Aloysius, O.F.M.Cap.

MONDAY, MAY 1ST, 1916

Early in the morning the son of Superintendent Dunne (D.M.P.), a subdeacon, called to me and said that Father Murphy, the military chaplain, had sent him to ask if I could call to the Castle during the afternoon. James Connolly, who was a prisoner and a patient there, had expressed a wish to see me. I called, and saw Father Murphy. He told me he had arranged for the necessary permissions. With Captain Stanley, R.A.M.C., I went to the ward. At the door the sentry challenged Captain Stanley and informed him he had orders to allow no one to see the prisoner without special instructions. Captain Stanley was obliged to return for his permit. The sentry asked me if I were Father Aloysius and, on my replying in the affirmative, said: "You can go in." However, as the nurses were engaged with Connolly, I delayed outside until they had finished and Captain Stanley had returned.

I entered with Captain Stanley, but I remarked that two soldiers with rifles and bayonets were on guard and showed no intention of leaving. I pointed out this to Captain Stanley, but he said it was necessary that they should remain; that he had no power to remove them. Then I said: "If that is so I cannot do my work as a priest. I have never before, to my knowledge, spoken to James Connolly. I cannot say if he may not be hard of hearing. Confession is an important and sacred duty that demands privacy and I cannot go on with it in the presence of these men." I had given my word that I would not utilise the opportunity for carrying political information or as a cover for political designs, and if my word was not sufficient or reliable they had better get some other priest. But I felt quite confident I would have my way. I suggested that we go to seek Father Murphy. On the way we met General Lowe. He greeted us warmly and said he had spoken to the General (Sir John Maxwell) of the work we had done on the previous day for peace and the prevention of bloodshed, and that he had expressed a wish to see us and would be pleased if we could call to Headquarters the following day. Hoping it might afford

us an opportunity for speaking a word on behalf of the
prisoners and securing fair and lenient treatment for them, I
consented. Then General Lowe, after some discussion acceded to
my demand for privacy for the purpose of attending the prisoner
Connolly.

I returned to the ward or room where Connolly lay. The
soldiers left and I was alone with Connolly. I told him I had
given my word I would act only as a priest and not in any
political capacity. "I know that, Father," he said. "You would
not get this privilege otherwise, and it is as a priest I want
to see you. I have seen and heard of the brave conduct of the
priests and nuns during the week and I believe they are the
best friends of the workers." I then heard Connolly's confession.

Captain Stanley met me again after I had left the ward, and
said it would be a consolation if one of the priests would drop
into the "Sinn Féin" ward in which the other prisoner-patients
were, and say a word to those in it, and let their friends know
they were alive. I said I would do so with pleasure and I was
permitted to go round to each bed and speak to the patients.
Some of them said they would be grateful if I would send them
prayer-books. Captain Stanley said he would distribute them
with pleasure if I sent them; and he did very kindly distribute
the books which were sent. I cannot refrain from saying here
that Captain Stanley showed himself, all through, a Christian
and a humane man, and James Connolly spoke to me of his
very great kindness to him, although Stanley was politically
and in religion at variance with the prisoners. . . .

Called to the Castle for permit to visit prisoners and others
needing my services. The permit "to pass through the streets
of Dublin by day or night" was signed by Lord Powerscourt.
Referring in my presence to the events of the preceding days,
Lord Powerscourt and some officers paid a tribute to the bravery
of the Volunteers, one of the officers remarking that "they were
the cleanest and bravest lot of boys he had ever met.". . . .

TUESDAY/WEDNESDAY, MAY 2ND/3RD, 1916

In the morning I gave Holy Communion to James Connolly.
Later in the day I went with Father Augustine to Headquarters,
Infirmary Road, and met General (Sir John) Maxwell.

Between 10.30 and 11 p.m. a note was handed in at the
Franciscan Friary, Church Street:

> Kilmainham Detention Barracks,
> 2.5.16
>
> Sir,
>
> The prisoner, H. T. Pearse, desires to see you, and you have

H

permission to visit him. Failing you, he would be glad to see any of the Capucines.

I am, Sir,
Your obedient servant,
[Signature illegible]
Major
Commandant.

Revd. Father Aloysius.

There is, of course, an error, as H. T. Pearse should be P. H. Pearse; then Capucines should be Capuchins. The signature on the original reads W. S. Lennon, but could possibly be W. T. Linnon.[2]

A military car was waiting at the Friary gate and, accompanied by another Father, I went with the soldiers. They told us they had a couple of calls to make and we were driven through the city in the direction of Charlemont Bridge. Sniping from the roofs of the houses was so bad that when we got as far as Charlemont Bridge the soldiers thought it advisable to abandon their plan and return. Later I heard that the calls the military proposed making were to Mrs. MacDonagh and Mrs. Pearse with the object of bringing one to see her husband, the other to see her son, before the executions.

When I reached Kilmainham I was informed that Thomas MacDonagh also wished for my ministrations. I was taken to the prisoners' cells and spent some hours between the two.

"You will be glad to know that I gave Holy Communion to James Connolly this morning," I said to Pearse when I met him. "Thank God," he replied. "It is one thing I was anxious about."

Pearse assured me that he was not in the least worried or afraid; and that he did not know he deserved the privilege of dying for his country. He was anxious that his mother should get some papers and a letter which he had just written. He knew that I could not take anything out, and he would not wish it, but he would be glad if I would speak to the officer in charge and make the request to him. The officer assured me that the papers would be given to Mrs. Pearse,

I told Pearse that I would go to Rathfarnham at the earliest possible moment to break the news myself to his mother. Then he made his confession. After that I gave Holy Communion to him. I can never forget the devotion with which he received the Most Blessed Sacrament. I could not help picturing to myself a scene in the Catacombs in the days of the persecutions in Rome. The bare cell was lighted from a candle at a small opening in the cell wall, and I had barely light to read the ritual. But the face of the man, as he lifted it up to receive his God, seemed to beam with light. And then the earnestness with which he recited the words of thanksgiving after Holy Communion! The same description would apply to Thomas MacDonagh. Both assured me that they were happy; and that their one thought was to utilise every moment left to them to prepare for death. I told them that I should be near them at the end, although they would most probably be blindfolded and would not see me, and I asked them to make little aspirations and acts of contrition and love of God. I left them in the most edifying disposition sometime between 2 a.m. and 3 a.m.

To my astonishment I heard that orders were given that all friends should leave the prison and that the orders referred to me, too. I protested that I was present not merely as a friend but in the capacity of a priest, and held that I should be permitted to remain with the prisoners to the end. The officer in charge said that he had to carry out his instructions. I asked him to communicate with the Provost-Marshal and put my views before him. He phoned and then told me he was instructed I could not remain. I had no option. Leaving the Jail I saw a little company of soldiers approach. Afterwards I was told they were bringing Willie Pearse. I returned to Church Street and said Holy Mass for their souls.

In the morning about 9.30 I called back to Kilmainham to ask the officer for a rosary beads which Sister M. Francesca had left with her brother (Thomas MacDonagh) the previous night. I availed myself of the occasion to make a protest. I said that in every civilised community the clergy were permitted to remain with the prisoner and administer the last rites of the Church. I had not been permitted to remain to administer Extreme Unction, as I was not permitted to be present at the execution. I requested him to convey my protest officially to the authorities. I am glad to say that at the later executions the priest was allowed to remain to the end and that when I attended James Connolly in the Castle a week later, I was taken with him in the ambulance to Kilmainham and was present at the execution.

I went to Mrs. MacDonagh and Mrs. Pearse to break the sad news to them. I told Mrs. Pearse that I believed Willie would be spared; that I could not conceive of them executing her second son. "No," she said. "I believe they will put him to death too. I can't imagine Willie living without Pat. They were inseparable. It was lovely to see the way they bade good-night to each other every night. Willie would never be happy to live without Pat." Indeed she had a strong conviction from the day when they said good-bye and walked out of St. Enda's that she would never see them alive again. . . .

Father Sebastian, O.F.M.Cap.

Father Aloysius, O.F.M.Cap.

Father Augustine, O.F.M.Cap.

Father Albert, O.F.M.Cap.

WEDNESDAY/THURSDAY, MAY 3RD/4TH, 1916

Wednesday night—Message to say that some of the Fathers were wanted to attend executions—Plunkett, Daly, O'Hanrahan, and Willie Pearse executed in the early hours of Thursday— Fathers Albert, Augustine, and, I think, Sebastian attended.

FRIDAY, MAY 5TH, 1916

John MacBride executed, attended by one of the Fathers.

SUNDAY, MAY 7TH, 1916

Message that four or five executions were to take place and that the services of some of the Fathers would be required. . . .

THURSDAY/FRIDAY, MAY 11TH/12TH, 1916

Called to Castle to see Connolly. Connolly had not slept and seemed feverish. I said that I would let him rest and would call in morning to give him Holy Communion. Uneasy about him I tried to get contact with Captain Stanley, but he could not be found. Reached Castle gates, and, still uneasy, decided to return and make another attempt to see Stanley. Saw him and was assured that there was no danger of any steps being taken : he reminded me that Asquith had given to understand that no executions would take place pending debate which was on that night. Got back to Church Street some time near 7 p.m. About 9 p.m. Captain Stanley called and told me that my services would be required about 2 a.m. He was not at liberty to say more but I could understand.

About 1 a.m. car called and Father Sebastian accompanied me to Castle. Heard Connolly's confession and gave him Holy Communion. Waited in Castle Yard while he was being given a meal. He was brought down and laid on stretcher in ambulance. Father Sebastian and myself drove with him to Kilmainham. Stood behind firing party during the execution. Father Eugene McCarthy, who had attended Seán MacDermott before we arrived remained and anointed Connolly immediately after the shooting.

---

[1]As published (in part) in *La Vie de Pearse* (Louis N. Le Roux) translated by Desmond Ryan, and in the *Capuchin Annual*, 1966.

[2]Major W. S. Lennon is correct. He was later seconded to the Egyptian Army. And see bibliographical note p. x.